WRITING PARTNERSHIPS

Writing Partnerships

Service-Learning in Composition

Thomas Deans
Kansas State University

National Council of Teachers of English
1111 W. Kenyon Road, Urbana, Illinois 61801-1096

Staff Editor: Tom Tiller
Interior Design: Jenny Jensen Greenleaf
Cover Design: Pat Mayer

NCTE Stock Number: 59184-3050

Library of Congress Cataloging-in-Publication Data

Deans, Thomas, 1967–
   Writing partnerships: service-learning in composition/Thomas Deans.
      p. cm.
   Includes bibliographical references and index.
   ISBN 0-8141-5918-4 (pbk.)
      1. English language—Rhetoric—Study and teaching. 2. English
   language—Rhetoric—Study and teaching—Social aspects. 3.
   Interdisciplinary approach in education. 4. Education, Cooperative.
   5. Community and college. 6. Student service. I. Title.
   PE1404.D387 2000
   808'.042'071—dc21

                                                            00-041138

For Jill and Griffin

Contents

Acknowledgments

This book is about partnerships between universities and communities, but it would not have been possible without the many partnerships which I have been fortunate enough to form during its writing. Foremost, I wish to thank three innovative teachers—Laurie Gullion, Bruce Herzberg, and Linda Flower—who invited me into their classrooms and shared their approaches to writing, literacy, and social action.

From the outset, Anne Herrington has supported the project and shaped it through careful readings of early drafts, as has Peter Elbow. Zan Goncalves was my first collaborator in experimenting with service-learning and has enriched my teaching and research ever since.

Sarah Miller compiled the appendices, and her able assistance was supported by a grant from the Graduate School at Kansas State University. Tom Tiller at NCTE shepherded the text through editing and production, improving it along the way.

My students have propelled this research through their receptiveness to practicing writing as community action. Moreover, I extend my thanks to the many community organizations with which I have collaborated in Amherst, Massachusetts, and Manhattan, Kansas, for sharing their expertise.

My sisters, Kate, Dianne, Sue, and Ginny, and my mother, Barbara, have been steadfast in their support from the start. And I am ever grateful to my most enduring partner, Jill, for sharing the journey.

English Studies and Public Service

The pairing of college writing instruction with community action marks a relatively new (and growing) movement in rhetoric and composition. Increasingly, novice college writers are working in teams to compose research reports, newsletter articles, and manuals for local nonprofit agencies; tutoring children and bringing that experience back to the classroom as a text to be analyzed alongside other texts; and collaborating with urban youth to craft documents in intercultural, hybrid rhetorics. As one who sees promise in such community-based pedagogies, I have entered the fray, integrating community outreach into my teaching as well as developing university–community partnerships hinging on writing instruction. In this study I step back from the range of existing service-learning courses and projects in order to explore how the movement relates—in theory and in practice— to composition studies. My approach balances discussions of composition theory, critical pedagogy, and rhetoric with three case studies of particular service-learning initiatives.

The Commission on National and Community Service defines service-learning as a method of teaching that: (a) provides educational experiences under which students learn and develop through active participation in thoughtfully organized service experiences that meet community needs and that are coordinated in collaboration with school and community; (b) is integrated into the students' academic curriculum or provides structured time for a student to think, talk, or write about what the student did and saw during the service; (c) provides a student with opportunities to use newly acquired skills and knowledge in real-life situations in their own communities; and (d) enhances what is taught in school by extending student learning beyond the classroom and into the community, thus helping students to develop a sense of caring for others (*National Community Service Trust*

Act of 1993). Thus, service-learning is not volunteerism or community service; nor is it simply an academic internship or field placement. While service-learning may draw on these practices, it is at heart a pedagogy of action and reflection, one that centers on a dialectic between community outreach and academic inquiry. I use the terms *service-learning, community-based learning,* and *community writing* to refer to programs covered under this definition and, more generally, to initiatives that move the context for writing instruction beyond the bounds of the traditional college classroom in the interest of actively and concretely addressing community needs.

Reports of service-learning from the field are largely encouraging. Practitioners have opened new contexts for teaching and learning that simultaneously address disciplinary learning goals and pressing community needs. Teachers and students speak of reenergized classrooms and a boost in motivation. Moreover, pedagogical values now universally lauded in composition—active learning, student-centered learning, cooperative learning, lifelong learning, cross-cultural understanding, critical thinking, authentic evaluation—are built into the very blood and bone of most community-based academic projects. Until recently, much of the evidence in support of service-learning has been anecdotal—teaching narratives of renewed student engagement, improved writing competency, and expanded social awareness and ethical development. Because part of this study is about trusting experience, we should not dismiss out of hand the teaching lore in support of service-learning. But there is also a growing body of empirical research that analyzes how community-based pedagogies relate to particular learning and development outcomes, and much of that research, like the teaching narratives, points to promising possibilities for service-learning.

For example, in a comprehensive study of college-level service-learning, Janet Eyler, Dwight E. Giles Jr., and John Braxton gathered data from fifteen hundred students at twenty colleges and universities in an attempt to answer some key questions about the value added to student learning by combining community service and academic study. The study measured students' self-assessments of citizenship skills (including listening and verbal skills, leadership skills, and capacity for tolerance), confidence that they can and should make a difference in their communities, community-related values, and perceptions of social problems and social justice. As might be expected, the data revealed that students who opt for a service-learning component in a course differ significantly from those who opt out. Students who selected the service-learning option scored higher on virtually every outcome measured (10).

More important, the study finds that participation in service-learning has a discernible effect on student learning. The authors conclude that service-learning programs appear to have an impact on students' attitudes, values, and skills, as well as on the way they think about social issues, even over the relatively brief period of a semester (13). However, the authors qualify that conclusion: "While the effect is significant, it is small; few interventions of a semester's length have a dramatic impact on outcomes. What is impressive is the consistent pattern of impact across a large number of different outcomes; service-learning is a consistent predictor and often the only significant or best predictor beyond the pre-test measure of the variable" (13). As might be expected, positive interaction with faculty, one of the other factors measured in the study, also contributed independently to many outcomes; still, according to the researchers, "these interactions did not wash out the effect of service on students" (11). Furthermore, service-learning was "the only significant or best predictor" of two student outcomes that are of particular interest to composition teachers: the capacity of students *to see problems as systemic,* and the ability *to see things from multiple perspectives.* The study suggests that service-learning makes a unique impact on college students with respect to these two factors, improving student outcomes with greater predictability than even the level of faculty–student interaction.[1] In turn, if one assumes that an important goal of composition courses is to encourage critical consciousness, then one needs to attend to service-learning, insofar as it is a pedagogy that helps students see problems as systemic and helps them acknowledge multiple perspectives.

In a different study, using data collected from 3,450 students (2,309 service participants and 1,141 nonparticipants) attending forty-two institutions, the Higher Education Research Institute

— 3 —

at the University of California at Los Angeles analyzed the impact of community outreach work on students. After accounting for the influence of the characteristics that predispose students to engage in community service (not service-learning, but community service more generally), researchers discovered significant positive correlations between service and student outcomes in all three areas they measured: civic responsibility, academic attainment, and life skills (Sax and Astin). For example, with respect to civic responsibility, undergraduates who engaged in service were more likely than nonparticipants to strengthen their commitment to promoting racial understanding, to participating in community action programs, and to influencing social values. With respect to academic development, those who engaged in service saw their grades rise slightly, were nearly 50 percent more likely to spend at least one hour a week interacting with faculty, and spent more time studying than did nonparticipants. With respect to life skills, service participants showed greater positive change in all outcomes analyzed, with the largest differences occurring in understanding of community problems, knowledge and acceptance of various races and cultures, and interpersonal skills. Moreover, a separate longitudinal study of more than twelve thousand students over a nine-year period confirmed long-term benefits, particularly greater commitments to racial understanding and to civic involvement in the years after college.[2]

While these results of the UCLA studies pertain to community service in general, researchers found additional benefits for students in course-based service-learning. Students who have participated in academic service-learning report a deeper commitment to their communities, better preparation for careers, improved conflict management, and greater understanding of community problems.[3] Likewise, a cluster of other empirical studies of service-learning suggests discernible learning and development outcomes (see Osborne, Hammerich, and Hensley; Mabry; Reeb, Katsuyama, Sammon, and Yoder; Miller; Markus, Howard, and King; Kendrick).

The results of such research are important because they confirm and sharpen the anecdotal support for service-learning, even as they temper the sometimes overenthusiastic claims made in its name. Still, quantitative studies never tell the whole story; they often overlook significant contextual concerns and they always have limitations (the research discussed above, for example, is based almost exclusively on self-reported data). Moreover, and of particular note for my focus on college composition, these studies tell us precious little about situated student writing or rhetorical competency. Because of this oversight, composition researchers themselves need to take up the charge and investigate community writing projects in context, as I do in the three case studies of community–university partnerships that form the core of this book.

While I focus on English studies, and more specifically on college writing instruction, we should note that service-learning is afoot across the disciplines. In the sciences, social sciences, arts, humanities, and preprofessional disciplines, one can find active, even if relatively small, pockets of community-based learning at a range of colleges and universities. Some early adopters of service-learning are working in isolation; some are connecting with others on their campuses; some are networking within their disciplinary and professional organizations; and some are collaborating across disciplines and campuses through national organizations that promote service-learning. Those opting for community-based pedagogies are a diverse lot who hail from a range of institutions and who practice varied approaches to teaching and social action, but they all share a commitment to improving the quality of undergraduate education by combining classroom learning with community outreach. They believe that they have discovered an innovation that encourages curricular synergies and student learning in ways that traditional pedagogies often do not.

Such claims might sound familiar, since in years past we have experienced cross-disciplinary swells of enthusiasm for such movements as writing across the curriculum and instructional technology. These movements are akin to service-learning not simply because they are cross-disciplinary and focus on improving pedagogy, but also because, when done well, all encourage active, rigorous, and reflective learning. These approaches invite students to assume agency in their own education and to draw on that education when venturing beyond campus. Moreover, just as composition specialists have played leading roles in cross-curricular movements such as writing across the curriculum, it is important that they assert themselves as leaders in the service-learning movement. Not only do most service-learning projects—no matter the discipline—involve significant writing components, but also they advance teaching values—student-centered learning, collaborative inquiry, critical reflection—that compositionists have long championed.

There is, of course, a salient irony in inviting writing teachers to embrace the term "service," which has been a problematic word for composition studies for so long (see Crowley; Mahala and Swilky). However, service-learning practitioners do not associate service with *sub*service or with academic housekeeping. Instead, they redirect the meaning of the word toward its more vital associations with democracy, outreach, and social action. Furthermore, far from composition field's experience of "service" dragging it into institutional limbo, the affirming sense of civic service in service-learning might even have the potential, as suggested recently by Ellen Cushman, to play a significant role in the ongoing efforts of English studies to characterize its teacher-scholars as "public intellectuals" ("Public").

Why Now?

Some forms of what is now being called service-learning have been practiced for decades under other banners—experiential learning, field work, literacy outreach, action research, and certain kinds of critical pedagogy. However, as the number of courses and programs continues to grow, as formal service-learning administrative units are added to colleges and universities, and as a corpus of scholarly work on service-learning begins to take shape, one can discern something genuinely new under way in the current movement. With respect to composition, the editors of a recent collection of essays on service-learning and composition have gone so far as to name it a "microrevolution"—small enough to go unnoticed by large segments of the profession but significant enough to prompt a rethinking of how we conceive of the teaching of writing and, more specifically, its connection to social action (Adler-Kassner, Crooks, and Watters).

All this raises the question, *Why now?* And, in particular, *Why now for rhetoric and composition?* Most service-learning practitioners who experiment with community-based pedagogies do so because they see them as a way to improve their teaching, to motivate students, to advance disciplinary learning, to facilitate student agency, or to enact values they hold dear, such as expanding public consciousness of social injustice or connecting cognitive learning to grounded social action. Yet some have tagged service-learning an educational fad, the latest in a long line of pedagogical quick fixes that will recede once the next big thing comes along. Still others have dismissed service-learning outright on the assumption that it represents a dressed-up version of paternalistic charity or noblesse oblige that will inevitably reproduce the injustices it purports to address.

Such dismissals of service-learning tend not only to prejudge the movement before examining its actual practices and outcomes but also to ignore the seismic shifts now under way in higher education. Such shifts are highlighted by some of our most perceptive observers of university life—people like Ernest Boyer, Clark Kerr, and Derek Bok. All suggest that we have entered a critical period in which colleges and universities need to reimagine not only how they go about teaching and doing research but also how they relate both to their host communities and to society more generally. Bok, former president of Harvard, questions whether "our universities are doing all that they can and should to help America surmount the obstacles that threaten to sap our economic strength and blight the lives of millions of our people" (6). Boyer, a longtime observer of higher education, urges colleges and universities to "respond to the challenges that confront our schools, and our cities" ("Creating" 48). Kerr, once president of the University of California system, predicts that "better integration of education with work and public service is clearly forthcoming" (223). In concert with such institutional changes, higher education in the United States is also in the process of reimagining the very definition and purpose of liberal learning, with many voices arguing the need for a Deweyan pragmatist orientation that avoids the extremes of both "ivory tower" and utilitarian conceptions of education in favor of an integrative perspective that puts liberal education in service to democracy (see Orrill). The service-learning movement does not pretend to have the only fitting response to such sweeping concerns, but it does claim, and rightly so, to take them seriously and to respond at the level of teaching and learning.

Major theoretical shifts in the disciplines have also set the stage for service-learning—changes that make this movement more than simply an innovative teaching approach. In particular, the disciplinary discourse of rhetoric and composition, as it has unfolded over the past decade, posits a sound theoretical footing for community-oriented pedagogies. As a discipline, rhetoric and composition has adopted the broadly defined "social perspective" on writing. The discipline prefers to see itself as having evolved from studies of the lone writer to more contextual understandings of composing; from a narrow, functional definition of literacy, focused on correctness, to a broader definition; from an exclusive focus on academic discourse to the study of both school and nonacademic contexts for writing; from presuming white middle-class culture as normative to analyzing and inviting cultural difference; and from gatekeeping at the university to facilitating the advancement of all students.

Many scholars have suggested that in order for compositionists to align our practice with theoretical stances more social in orientation, we should adopt a critical pedagogy or cultural studies approach. I find such advocacy for having students read and analyze culture and ideology extremely promising; students should indeed learn habits of cultural critique and critical reading (which we usually ask them to express in academic essays). Yet I also recognize the theoretical and pedagogical corollary that students should learn to *write* themselves into the world through producing rhetorical documents that intervene materially in contexts beyond the academy. Just as some feminist scholars contend that critiques of patriarchal structures need to push beyond the language and genres dictated by the dominant culture, so too is there a need for writing teachers who imagine composition as a site for social justice work to push beyond the traditional genres dictated by the academy. In other words, we must persist in more coherently and more creatively matching our writing strategies to the claims we make for our reading strategies.

Most service-learning writing teachers, like composition instructors who are committed to critical literacy or cultural studies approaches, underscore the imperative to *read* the complex social forces that constitute one's cultural context—what Freire calls "reading the word and the world" (Freire and Macedo). But service-learning instructors also ask students to *write* purpose-driven documents for audiences beyond the classroom. Thus, in addition to inviting abstract critical *interpretation* of cultural phenomena, service-learning initiatives demand the logical corollary, that is, grounded, active *intervention* in the very cultural context we inhabit.

If the general inclination of members of the discipline is to theorize about writing as a social act, then service-learning is one means by which to underscore and extend this commitment. Take, for example, some of the most widely held theoretical stances in composition studies and how service-learning affirms and potentially extends each one:

- ◆ While the social turn in composition has resulted in widening the audience for student writing from the lone teacher to peer groups, service-learning does the same and takes *the next logical step of widening the audience for student writing to include those beyond the classroom.*

- ◆ While the social turn in composition encourages teachers and students to see their writing not as skills and drills but as participation in a disciplinary discourse community, service-learning writing takes *the next logical step of asking students and teachers to situate their work in both disciplinary and wider nonacademic communities.*

- ◆ While the social turn in composition has led researchers to study sites of writing and literacy beyond the academy, community-based writing takes *the next logical step of asking students themselves to write within nonacademic discourse communities.*

- ◆ While the social turn in composition underscores the need to encourage multicultural awareness and understanding in our classrooms, community-based writing takes *the next logical step of asking students to cross cultural and class boundaries by collaborating with community partners who often inhabit subject positions different from those of the students.*

- While the social turn in composition (particularly as it takes the form of critical pedagogy) speaks to the ethical, democratizing, and consciousness-raising potential of the writing classroom, many forms of service-learning confirm such critical intellectual habits and go *the next logical step of marrying them with pragmatic civic action.*

Therefore service-learning—and, within that broad umbrella, what others alternately call community service writing, community-based learning, literate social action, activist research, or academic outreach—can be viewed as the fruition of some of the most important contemporary theoretical claims of rhetoric and composition studies. Given such theoretical footings—in addition to the promising cognitive and motivational outcomes suggested by the first wave of programs—it is no wonder that interest in service-learning is on the ascent at institutions ranging from community colleges to liberal arts colleges to research universities.

Furthermore, if we take the long view, in the history of Greek and Roman rhetoric we find compelling warrants for service-learning. Aristotle's *Rhetoric* was intended, after all, not to help students succeed in school settings but rather to equip rhetors to intervene in the public sphere. Isocrates, Cicero, Quintilian, and a host of others speak of the need to connect rhetorical practice to civic responsibility, which is, certainly, a central concern of contemporary service-learning theory and practice. Likewise, in the sweep of U.S. history—from Thomas Jefferson and Benjamin Franklin to Jane Addams and John Dewey—one finds examples of experiential learning combined with democratic aspirations that support a service-learning approach to teaching and learning.

Emerging Conversations about Service-Learning

Throughout the history of U.S. higher education, service to the community—be it the local, national, or global community—has been integral to the missions of a wide range of colleges and universities, whether motivated by an ethic of public service, a mandate to extend research to the general public, or a commitment to particular religious beliefs. The current service-learning movement builds on this past and on several strands of educational history that emphasize the integration of higher learning with grounded social action, especially the extension programs spawned by the land grant movement of the 1860s, the progressive education reforms of the first half of the twentieth century, and the civil rights and activist movements of the 1960s (Stanton, Giles, and Cruz).

Likewise, English studies has a long-standing tradition of concern for social justice. Much of our theory is propelled by commitments to democracy, equality, critical literacy, and multiculturalism. Moreover, much of our classroom practice is motivated by a commitment to prepare all students for reflective and critical participation in their personal, cultural, working, and civic lives. Yet as English teachers, we focus nearly all our energies on the textual realm and limit our teaching of reading and writing to the classroom space, trusting that the critical and imaginative habits of mind we encourage in the classroom will carry over into the world beyond. I believe that many such habits *do* carry over; but I also recognize the need for connecting the work of English studies directly to action in local communities. Just as critical theory and cultural studies have demanded that we widen our reading beyond the traditional literary canon, service-learning demands that we widen the sites for writing and learning beyond campus gates. Some disciplines that have long-standing traditions of integrating fieldwork with academic study, such as education or anthropology, find this move quite natural. However, for teachers of composition and for others in the humanities, moving beyond the bounds of campus may feel unfamiliar, even risky.

Recent enthusiasm for service-learning across the disciplines and at all levels of schooling should hearten us, as should the first wave of community-based college writing courses. Across the country, service-learning is being heralded as a promising pedagogical approach by scores of school and community partners. It also finds allies in university administrators, foundations, local community leaders, government agencies, professional associations, and the general public. Thus, those new to service-learning can benefit from growing networks of service-learning educators and learn from their collective experiences—the successes as well as the failures.

Community-based learning is new to nearly all quarters of English studies, except for some small pockets of technical writing and journalism. And even though the past ten years have seen a surge in rhetoric and composition scholarship focused on sites of writing beyond the classroom, our teaching practices, for the most part, lag behind this research trend, particularly with respect to writing in nonprofit and community settings. However, important experiments in service-learning, as well as research into the theoretical dimensions of this pedagogy, are now under way—and with increasing range and vigor. Some teachers are dipping a toe in the water, adding a small or optional service-learning component to an existing composition course. Some are wading in waist deep by more fully integrating community writing into new and existing courses. Some are diving in headfirst, setting up comprehensive programs, collaborating with other administrative units on campus, and cultivating long-term relationships with community partners.

Service-learning is also working its way into the professional forums and disciplinary discourses of English. At the 1997 Conference on College Composition and Communication (CCCC), thirty-three papers headlined service-learning; two workshops advised participants on how to start a program; two special interest groups convened; and one keynote speaker lauded service-learning as a particularly apt response to major institutional changes in higher education. The 1998 CCCC featured many service-learning papers and added a symposium and a number of local community site visits during the conference. The 1999 CCCC continued this upswing in interest with a range of diverse papers, workshops, and presentations on service-learning.

Networks formed by and for teachers and scholars in rhetoric and composition have emerged and continue to develop—for example, the CCCC Service-Learning and Community Literacy Special Interest Group. National organizations working to support service-learning now include such groups as Campus Compact, the American Association for Higher Education, the National Society for Experiential Education, the National Information Center for Service Learning, the American Association of

Community Colleges, and the National Council of Teachers of English. The Invisible College, a cross-disciplinary faculty association focused specifically on service-learning in the disciplines, is now active. Furthermore, service-learning is supported by various administrative units at particular universities, such as Edward Ginsberg Center for Service and Learning at the University of Michigan, the Feinstein Institute for Public Service at Providence College, the Bentley College Service-Learning Project, and the Haas Center for Public Service at Stanford University, among others.

Scholarly publication, perhaps the most powerful legitimizing force in the academy, is also making a place for service-learning. Publications offering broad overviews and bibliographies of service-learning are now available (e.g., Barber and Battistoni; Delve, Mintz, and Stewart; Jacoby and Associates; Julier; Kendall and Associates; Kraft and Swadener; Leder and McGuinness; Lempert; Lisman; Parsons and Lisman; Rhoads; Rhoads and Howard; Schine; Waterman, *Service-Learning;* Zlotkowski, *Successful*). The first peer-reviewed journal devoted to service-learning, *The Michigan Journal of Community Service Learning,* was launched in 1995. In rhetoric and composition, the first collection of essays explicitly connecting service-learning and composition studies, *Writing the Community: Concepts and Models for Service-Learning in Composition,* was published in 1997. Articles are starting to surface in *College Composition and Communication, College English, Composition Studies,* and *The Writing Instructor.* More and more composition graduate students are writing dissertations that center on service-learning. Without doubt, further research and reflection on community writing is in the pipeline.

Community-based learning in composition may still be a largely experimental and marginal activity, but it seems to have secured at least a beachhead in the disciplinary discourse. Thus this book contributes to an emerging body of research investigating the intersections of service-learning, college writing pedagogy, and composition studies. In addition, particularly through my discussion of John Dewey and Paulo Freire in Chapter 2, the book develops a coherent and substantial theoretical framework to guide the development of community writing initiatives.

Guiding Purposes

While service-learning practices are gaining steam, and some particular programs are well-researched, the movement as a whole remains largely unstudied. Among the available research on courses and projects, there is little sense of how one initiative relates to others or to the broader landscape of composition studies, rhetoric, and critical theory. Therefore, this study adopts a comparative and contextualizing approach, even as it examines three particular service-learning projects in action. It is guided by five purposes:

◆ To examine the theoretical assumptions of a diverse range of university/community partnerships that hinge on college-level writing instruction and rhetoric.

◆ To sort those community writing practices into coherent categories, so as to understand more clearly their literacy aims, ideological assumptions, and curricular goals.

◆ To relate the aims, assumptions and practices of service-learning writing initiatives to current scholarly discourses in composition studies, rhetorical theory, and critical theory—and in particular to the writings of John Dewey and Paulo Freire.

◆ To balance deliberations on theory with discussions of lived experience by presenting empirical case studies of three exemplary service-learning writing projects.

◆ To assert that service-learning writing initiatives deserve a place in the college English curriculum, and to suggest how teachers and administrators might thoughtfully design and support such courses and programs.

As a first step in analyzing service-learning, I propose a taxonomy for this relatively new but already quite diverse movement in writing pedagogy and research. Yet even as I do this, I examine root theoretical and curricular concerns in English studies. I take my cue, in part, from James Britton's early work. Describing the contributions of Britton and Albert Kitzhaber to the Dartmouth Conference of 1966, Joseph Harris sees them as speaking out of two fundamentally different theoretical frames—

Kitzhaber wanting to define the field of English, and Britton questioning the assumptions and aims of the field. Harris remarks: "While Kitzhaber looked to theory for a map of the subject to be studied, for a set of principles that would organize what we need to know about how texts are composed and interpreted, Britton took a more rhetorical or performative view of it as a means to an end, a form of reflection on action whose aim is to change teaching in direct and immediate ways" (142).

I do some mapping by dividing community writing programs into three categories: writing *for* the community; writing *about* the community; and writing *with* the community. However, I also critically examine my categories, putting each in dialogue with scholarship in composition and critical theory. Ultimately, my findings function, in Harris's words, as "a form of reflection on action whose aim is to change teaching in direct and immediate ways."

Sorting Courses and Programs: Three Paradigms for Community Writing

A dizzying range of courses and programs march under the banner of service-learning. Just as approaches to teaching composition vary widely, so too do the ways that teachers combine writing instruction and community action through service-learning. The variety of initiatives currently under way is at once encouraging and overwhelming. Some courses look like standard composition courses with a service-learning add-on (whether required or optional). Some are (or resemble) technical writing courses or internship programs with a nonprofit rather than a corporate focus. Some foreground critical pedagogy and cultural critique. Some center on intercultural inquiry or problem-solving. Some devote nearly all of their energies to personal narratives of and reflections on student outreach experiences. Some gather a mixed bag of service-learning strategies into one course. Some are comprehensive literacy projects or cross-disciplinary efforts rather than revamped composition courses. Given this range—and in order to discuss community writing with any degree of clarity—we must first sort through the variety of courses and programs.

One method of sorting composition initiatives that has surfaced in service-learning research is a division between "writing *about* service" and "writing *as* service" (Bacon, "Instruction"). Making such a division is helpful. But to my mind, the most fruitful way to sort service-learning initiatives is to discern their distinct literacy goals and then group courses according to their assumptions and aims. In other words, one needs to ask, "What is this service-learning course supposed to *do*?" As Laura Julier suggests, a thoughtful investigation of service-learning in composition throws us back upon a basic question of purpose with which all teachers of writing must wrestle, what Erika Lindemann has called a "prior question."

The taxonomy I propose emerges from putting questions of purpose to a range of service-learning courses and programs. From "What is this service-learning course supposed to *do*?" follow other more specific questions, such as: Which literacy outcomes does each service-learning initiative privilege? What kind(s) of texts does each initiative generate? How does each define "social action"? What are the ideological assumptions embedded in each course or curriculum? How are relationships arranged among student, teacher, and community partner? Which audiences are being addressed? How is student writing assessed?

Putting such questions to current service-learning initiatives leaves us with three distinct groupings of community writing programs: those that write *for* the community; those that write *about* the community; and those that write *with* the community. Figure 1 illustrates these differences. Note that the chart is intended as a hypothesis, a schema that outlines how different types of service-learning initiatives foreground discernibly different literacies and learning outcomes. The three categories are, of course, simplifications that will betray the lived complexities of actual programs—that is, all the lines I've drawn will leak. Much like James Britton's creation of the "poetic," "expressive," and "transactional" categories to describe the range of student writing, the taxonomy is intended as a heuristic for unpacking the aims and assumptions of a diverse range of literacy practices.

The categories will become clearer in later chapters as I examine the three paradigms and present a case study of each. In short, writing-*for*-the-community courses are those through which

FIGURE 1. *Three paradigms for community writing.*

	Writing *for* the Community	Writing *about* the Community	Writing *with* the Community
Primary Site for Learning	Nonprofit agency	Classroom	Community center
Privileged Literacies	Academic and workplace literacies	Academic and critical literacies	Academic, community, and hybrid literacies
Most Highly Valued Discourse	Workplace discourse	Academic discourse	Hybrid discourses
Primary Learning Relationship	Student–agency contact (instructor as facilitator)	Student–instructor (service as facilitator)	Student–community member (instructor as facilitator)
Institutional Relationship	Instructor–agency contact person	Instructor–community site contact	Instructor/department–community center
Goals	(1) Students learn nonacademic writing practices and reflect on differences between academic and workplace rhetorics. (2) Students reflect on service experience to attain critical awareness of community needs. (3) Students provide needed writing products for agencies.	(1) Students serve at schools or community sites and reflect on their experiences. (2) Students develop critical consciousness and habits of intellectual inquiry and societal critique. (3) Students write journals and compose academic-style essays on community issues and/or pressing social concerns.	(1) Students, faculty, and community use writing as part of a social action effort to collaboratively identify and address local problems. (2) Students and community members negotiate cultural differences and forge shared discourses. (3) University and community share inquiry and research.
Assessment	Can the students move ably between academic and workplace discourses? Have students critically reflected on the writing and service processes? Did students produce documents that will be of real use to the agencies?	Have students provided adequate service to the community site? How sophisticated a critique of social concerns can students demonstrate in academic discussion and writing? Has student academic writing improved?	Have local and academic community members engaged in collaborative writing or research? Can students reflect critically on issues such as cultural difference? Has the local problem been effectively solved, addressed, or researched?

college students collaborate with understaffed nonprofit agencies to provide workplace documents (grant research, newsletter articles, news releases, manuals, brochures) for the given agency. The student or team of students enters into a client relationship with the nonprofit, and the writing that the student or team generates constitutes both a service for the nonprofit client and a medium for student learning in a "real-world" rhetorical situation. This approach to community writing changes the traditional composition classroom in three major ways: it adds workplace and public genres to traditional essay genres; it shifts the exigency and motivation for writing from meeting teacher and grading expectations to meeting the standards articulated by the community partner; and it changes the teacher–student relationship because the classroom instructor is no longer the sole authority in creating or assessing assignments. Writing-*for* courses, with their instrumental bent, value workplace literacies and thus differ significantly from most courses that abide in the writing-*about*-the-community paradigm.

In writing-*about*-the-community courses, students engage in traditional community service (often tutoring youth or working at a homeless shelter) and then draw on that lived experience in their writing of essays. Gaining lived experience through working with people in need can open new perspectives for students, particularly as they write about complex social issues. Here the emphasis is generally on personal reflection, social analysis, and/or cultural critique. How these are weighted depends on the instructor. Even though the source materials (including the student outreach experiences) and the topic choices (which often emerge from those outreach experiences) for student writing differ from those of most composition classrooms, students express their reflection, analysis, or critique in familiar academic discourses (the journal, the reflective essay, the research paper), and are evaluated according to largely traditional methods of academic assessment. Thus, writing-*about* courses tend to advance academic and critical literacy goals.

Writing-*with*-the-community initiatives take a different approach, often adopting a grassroots sensibility. These programs elude easy categorization but generally follow a pattern in which university faculty and students collaborate directly with community members (rather than through established nonprofit or governmental agencies) to research and address pressing local problems. Writing-*with* initiatives take many forms, including activist research, literacy work, proposal writing, and collaborative problem solving. They tend to value many different literacies (academic, community, and even hybrid literacies) and often devote significant attention to intercultural communication. In later chapters, I draw on the example of the Community Literacy Center of Pittsburgh.

With the chart of service-learning categories I do not mean to imply that programs do not cross fences. In fact, they do. For example, at Michigan State University, first-year writing is usually taught within a curriculum focusing on U.S. civic history. Since 1994, the writing program has been introducing service-learning in some sections, including projects through which students work with nonprofit agencies, writing *for* agency needs (newsletters, brochures, research, and so on). Yet they also read, discuss, and write *about* service, ethics, democracy, and social action in U.S. history and culture.[4] As I discuss in Chapter 6, courses I teach are often similarly divided (in terms of the class time, amount of student writing, and methods of assessment) between reading and writing *about* the community and producing needed written documents *for* nonprofit agencies. Still, I maintain that the writing-*about*-the-community and writing-*for*-the-community strands of such courses, while complementary, value distinctly different literacies, engage distinctly different learning processes, require distinctly different rhetorical practices, and result in distinctly different kinds of texts.

I do not argue that any one of the three paradigms is morally superior or inherently more ethical than the others. Each is built on its own assumptions, evinces its own internal logic, and works toward different goals. Any one of the paradigms might work best within a particular local community or college context. Understanding the fitness, the *kairos*, of a particular approach to its particular context is the most pressing imperative. Thus, rather than attempt to construct a hierarchy that argues for a "best" kind of service-learning, I prefer to analyze the key differences among programs, as well as the implications of those differences. As Keith Morton points out, some service-learning theorists and practitioners measure their efforts using a "continuum" which places charity as the lowest form and advocacy as the highest form of service. Articulating an alternative to such hierarchical thinking and ranking, Morton argues instead that "there exist a series of related but distinct community service paradigms, each containing a world view, a problem statement and an agenda for change" ("Irony" 24). Morton's three community service paradigms are charity, project, and social change, and his method for sorting them seems to me both generous-minded and analytically sound. He emphasizes that we should feel free to evaluate the *quality* of particular initiatives as they aspire to the goals of particular paradigms (their "thinness" or "thickness"). However, to judge but one paradigm truly worthy would unnecessarily limit the diversity of approaches right from the start and, in turn, create the misleading impression that only one kind of service—advocacy—really matters.

I borrow Morton's method, but not his particular categories, in proposing three paradigms for service-learning in rhetoric and composition. Writing *for* the community, writing *about* the community, and writing *with* the community constitute three related but distinct paradigms, and each, done well, has its own integrity (and its own limitations) based on its own assumptions and goals. A particular course fitting any one of the paradigms could be conducted either coherently or haphazardly, thoughtfully or uncritically. Much depends on the foresight, planning, and follow-through of the particular instructor. Thus, every service-learning course and teacher should heed the ancient Greek dictum: know thyself. This demands that service-learning teachers interrogate the assumptions and aims embedded in their own practices and proceed in the light of critical self-awareness.

The Ethics of Service: Questions of Power, Representation, and Reciprocity

Before moving on to articulate a theoretical foundation for service-learning and discuss case studies, it is vital that we step back and consider key ethical concerns attendant to any form of community outreach. Many teachers are wary, and rightly so, of the dangers of community service, and in particular the habit of casting individuals and communities in the uneven roles of "server" and "served." Take, for example, John McKnight's searing indictment of how professionalized service systems tend to define need. McKnight alerts not only professional servers (like social or health care workers) but also service-learning practitioners to the potentially counterproductive and disabling consequences of their efforts.

> Professionalized definitions of need produce a logical and necessary set of remedial assumptions, each with its own intrinsically disabling effects.
>
> The first of these assumptions is the mirror image of the individualized definition of need. As *you* are the problem, the assumption is that *I*, the professionalized server, *am the answer. You* are not the answer. *Your peers* are not the answer. *The political, social and economic environment* is not the answer. Nor is it possible that there is no answer. *I*, the professional, am the answer. The central assumption is that service is a unilateral process. *I*, the professional, produce. You, the client, consume. . . .
>
> We will have reached the apogee of the modernized service society when the professionals can say to the citizen:
> We are the solution to your problem.
> We know what problem you have.
> You can't understand the problem or the solution.
> Only we can decide whether the solution has dealt with your problem.
> ("Disabling" 239–41; see also McKnight, *Careless*)

McKnight's critique of deficit model approaches to professionalized service resonates with similar arguments in composition studies against deficit models of basic writing. His skepticism about the role of the server raises important issues that need to be on the minds of service-learning teachers and students. Community-based learning faces the complex ethical issues inherent in the service professions (including social work, medicine, and teaching), the ethical quandaries attendant upon research conducted by ethnographers and anthropologists, and the questions of power that accompany collaboration across disparities of wealth and privilege. Among the most formidable challenges for service-learning are broaching such ethical matters with critical rigor, designing programs for mutuality with community constituencies, and problematizing the "do-gooder" mentality entrenched in our culture and our students (see Rhoads). Abiding ethical questions for service-learning include:

- How can service-learning avoid the precarious server/served relationship critiqued by McKnight? Who is serving whom, and why?

- When is service-learning in danger of lapsing into habits of paternalistic charity or noblesse oblige?

- When and how do service-learning pedagogies reproduce rather than disrupt dominant ideologies?

- How do service-learning advocates fruitfully confront the differences in power, class, race, ethnicity, identity, and culture that often separate universities and their members from local communities and their members? When are these issues avoided, and at what cost?

- How do the often problematic histories of universities intervening in surrounding communities relate to current practices?

- How does service-learning structure a reciprocal and dialectical relationship between "serving" and "learning"? In other words, how does one avoid "using" community constituencies for the benefit of student education and at the same time maintain academic rigor?

- When are community partners really benefiting from service-learning? And when are they not?

- What happens when students enter local communities for only brief encounters, usually a semester or shorter, despite the preferences of many community partners for long-term commitments?

- How should instructors deal with unmotivated or resistant students? Also, how should they deal with well-intentioned but relatively immature or underskilled students?

Simply posing these questions is almost enough to send one running from service-learning. But while such inquiries are demanding, they are not defeating. Some (but not all) of the issues have been anticipated and addressed in the several iterations of the "Principles of Good Practice" in the service-learning literature (Honnet and Poulsen; Lisman 127–47; Mintz and Hesser). Certainly, we must continually raise these key ethical questions in our research on service-learning. Even more important, we have a responsibility to bring them squarely into the classroom and to our community partners for reflection and dialogue—which, fortunately, is something that many service-learning teachers already do.

Lorie J. Goodman recommends sustained inquiry into the ethical dimensions of service and furthermore reminds us that service-learning advocates should reexamine their most commonplace terms, including *community* and *service. As* Goodman explains, *community* has become a contested term in composition studies. Scholars have questioned how certain uses of community (which often assumes an emphasis on consensus) can function to gloss over important matters of difference and squelch dissent. The same process characterizes service-learning programs which fail to account for the voices and perspectives of community members, which can be steamrolled in the rush to meet student and academic demands. Use of the word *service* evokes not only the specter of unequal server–served relations (recall McKnight above) but also a gendered history in which women, both within and outside the academy, have been enculturated to submerge their selves in service to others (see JoAnn Campbell, "Vexation").

Ethical questions persist for service-learning, and they need to be addressed in a critical but hopeful spirit. One could fill a semester (and more) with theoretical and philosophical deliberations on the ethical concerns and dilemmas attendant to community outreach. However, a service-learning pedagogy demands not only contemplation but also action. Devoting all of one's teaching energies to abstract reflection forecloses any opportunity for grounded action and can ultimately lead to intellectual detachment, fatalism, or paralysis. In contrast, service-learning strives for an equitable balance between serving and learning, an equitable dialectic between pragmatic action and critical reflection, and an equitable consideration of university and community perspectives. Perfect balance, perfect dialectic, perfect consideration will ever be elusive. Thus, service-learning courses always entail risk. (But doesn't everything worthwhile?) Shying from that risk by insisting on perfection or some form of ideological purity is bound not only to sabotage student agency but also to trap both teachers and students in a loop of abstract deliberation, ever avoiding the test of experience.

Fruitful inquiry into the abiding ethical complexities of service is central to responsible service-learning courses and to what Robert Rhoads terms "critical community service" (204). Open dialogue on key social justice issues, exacting self-awareness, and reciprocal relationships with community partners need to be fundamental components of community-based pedagogies. This hopeful but critical stance—demanding an active, engaged ethics—is evident in the pragmatist philosophy of John Dewey and the liberatory pedagogy of Paulo Freire. Their work provides context and depth to current discussions on the relationship of community writing practices to composition studies. They also offer service-learning practitioners compelling theoretical foundations that support experiential learning, community involvement, and a dialectic of critical reflection and grounded action.

Service-Learning Writing Initiatives in Context

We need to know the social situations with reference to which the individual will have the ability to observe, recollect, imagine, and reason before we get any intelligent and concrete basis for telling what a training of mental powers actually means either in its general principles or in its working details.
JOHN DEWEY, *"Ethical Principles Underlying Education"*

I think that it is not so important to ask ourselves, Could education at the university level be like this? but rather, Is it possible that we, in a political perspective of transformation, will be able to use to our advantage the university space created by society?
PAULO FREIRE, *Paulo Freire on Higher Education*

James Berlin wrote that "a college curriculum is a device for encouraging the production of a certain kind of graduate, in effect, a certain kind of person" (*Rhetorics* 17). While not an entirely new idea—one can find traces of it as far back as Quintilian—Berlin's comment on the power of a curriculum to shape a student raises important questions for educators in English. What kind of person do we hope that our curricula will encourage? Put another way, what kind of literacy (or kinds of literacies) should we value most highly in English courses? With respect to composition, the most widely offered and required course in U.S. higher education, teachers and scholars need to ask: *What particular kind of writer do we hope to encourage?*

tonomous text and in place of a crafted personal statement, rhetorical literacy places a writer—a rhetor, if you will—as an agent within a social and rhetorical context" (249). For Flower, rhetorical literacy centers on "literate action," which includes the practice of not only established academic and public discourses but also innovative hybrid and intercultural discourses. Consonant with (even if distinct from) Elbow's earlier call for a "larger view of human discourse" in the composition classroom, Flower's stance posits community-based writing instruction (although she prefers the term "literate social action") as a fitting site for the practice of contemporary rhetorical theories that claim both to account for social context and to intervene in the world.

Complementing such justifications from within English studies, Shirley Brice Heath reminds us that forces *beyond* the walls of the academy are already acting to prompt significant changes in the structures of college composition. Heath suggests that the essayistic tradition which serves as the mainstay of first-year composition is growing ever more disconnected from the personal and workplace writing demands that our diverse students face off campus ("Rethinking").[2] She also points to alternate sites of writing and literacy instruction—an inner-city theater group, a community literacy course, a workplace-based writing course—and notes that "a variety of institutions [other than colleges and their composition courses] are responding to personal, spiritual, and civic needs, as well as business changes, to develop opportunities and add courses or build programs to meet these needs. . . . In the new settings, these groups enable writers to merge formal and informal writing across genres, audiences, and institutional and personal contexts" ("Work" 231). Anticipating a growing mismatch between college writing instruction and the needs of the wider community, Heath predicts reform, and suggests that the "first and likely changes will be interlinking institutions. Just as we have seen ourselves cross disciplines, we will watch more and more of us move across institutions" ("Work" 240). The kinds of institutions due for "interlinking" with schools, according to Heath, include workplaces, nonprofits, community service organizations, youth groups, churches, social service providers, public health agencies, cultural centers, arts organizations of all kinds—any site where the multiple literacies of most interest to our students are practiced. Her call for "interlinking" contexts for teaching writing and literacy resonates with the aims of service-learning.

John Dewey's Pragmatic Experimentalism as a Foundation for Service-Learning

Behind these contemporary voices in composition theory, one can hear the echoes of earlier educational movements, with none more important for service-learning than progressive education. The chief philosopher of progressivism, John Dewey, is fast becoming *the* touchstone for service-learning practitioners and theorists, and with good reason (see Saltmarsh; Giles and Eyler, "Theoretical"; Jacoby; Morton and Saltmarsh; Hatcher; Peck, Flower, and Higgins). Dewey's writings on pragmatic philosophy mark one of the most important and characteristically American movements in nineteenth- and twentieth-century philosophy. Dewey's pragmatism, articulated in a large body of work from the 1890s to the 1950s, extends the work of William James and C. S. Peirce. It critiques essentialist notions of truth in favor of a social constructivist approach and argues for a socially engaged philosophy that deals with the "problems of man" rather than the "problems of philosophy."[3]

Dewey's writings on progressive education have long been invoked to undergird the theory and practice of active, experiential, and student-centered education (ranging from elementary school to college, and from project-based learning to internship programs).[4] Dewey is an apt thinker to call on to contextualize service-learning not only because of his deliberations on experiential learning but also because he connects these matters, through his social philosophy, to the issues of reflective activity, citizenship, community, and democracy. In other words, Dewey comprehensively thinks through not only *learning* but also *service* and the nature of their dialectical relationship.

Another reason Dewey's voice resonates with service-learning advocates may have something to do with the nature of the social context out of which he spoke. Alan Ryan draws telling parallels between Dewey's time and our own.

The 1990s are turning out to be astonishingly like the 1890s. Not in the sense that exactly the same anxieties strike us on exactly the same occasions. But Dewey was moved to write about individual unease and social and political failures in a context that resembles our own in crucial ways. Dewey's America was one in which the problems of the inner city were appalling. In the early 1890s homelessness in Chicago sometimes reached 20 percent; unemployment frequently hit one in four of the working population. . . . Social conflict was everywhere: Strikes were physically fought out with a violence we have not seen for sixty years. The upper classes were apparently indifferent to the fate of the poor and even to the fate of the working near poor. In the cities the response of the better-offs was to remove themselves to the suburbs . . . and in the courts it was to make it impossible for unions to strike. . . . Nor was it clear what any individual person should or could do about all this. (24)

While Dewey's writings "breathe an air of crisis," Ryan underscores that it is "important to see how insistent he [Dewey] was that the crisis was also an opportunity or, if you like, how insistent he was that opportunity was there if we were prepared to take it and that an activist philosophy was implicit in the American mind and desperately needed" (24). Ryan's remarks suggest one reason why Deweyan pragmatism resonates with service-learning practitioners.[5]

I gather my commentary on Dewey around his exploration of two basic relationships: knowledge to action, and the individual to society. Much of Dewey's pragmatic philosophy is devoted to bridging such dualisms, to revealing the vital "continuities" and interactions between such terms.[6] He reconciles the knowledge/action dualism by articulating a theory of *experimentalism*, and he reconciles the individual/society dualism by ever returning to principles of *civic participation* and *democracy*. These two strains of thought, each pivotal to community-based writing instruction, provide scaffolding for theory building in service-learning.

Action/Reflection in Deweyan Thought

At the level of the individual, Dewey puts experience and experimentalism, as well as the recursive relation of knowledge to action, at the center of his theory of learning. Unpacking the relationship of reflection to action, he writes:

> The nature of experience can be understood only by noting that it includes an active and a passive element particularly combined. On the active hand, experience is *trying*—a meaning which is made explicit in the connected term experiment. On the passive, it is *undergoing*. When we experience something we act upon it, we do something with it; then we suffer or undergo the consequences. . . . The connection of these two phases of experience measures the fruitfulness or value of the experience. . . . Two conclusions important for education follow. (1) Experience is primarily an active-passive affair; it is not primarily cognitive. But (2) the measure of value of an experience lies in the perception of relationships or continuities to which it leads up. (*MW* 9: 147)*

Active element and passive element. Trying and undergoing. Doing and reflecting. Education, for Dewey, is a form of growth through *active experimentation* and *reflective thought*.

Throughout his writings in both philosophy and education, Dewey also insists that the means can never be divorced from the ends. How one learns is intimately connected to what one learns. Since Dewey wants learners to become active participants in the world, he forwards an active and participatory theory of learning and pedagogy. He articulates the process of sound, experiential "reflective inquiry" as having five phases: (1) perplexity, confusion, doubt in response to a situation whose character is yet to be determined; (2) a conjectural anticipation, a tentative interpretation of the given elements; (3) a careful survey of all attainable considerations which will define and clarify the problem at hand; (4) a consequent elaboration of the tentative hypothesis to make it more precise and more consistent; and (5) the development of a firmer hypothesis upon which to act—one which

---

* John Dewey's writings are often cited from the multivolume collections published by the Southern Illinois University Press, edited by Jo Ann Boydston: *The Early Works, 1882–1898; The Middle Works, 1899–1924;* and *The Later Works, 1925–1953.* Here, the abbreviation *MW* is used for the *Middle Works* series, and *LW* for the *Later Works* series, followed by the volume number, a colon, and page numbers.

itself remains open to further testing and revision (*MW* 9: 157; qtd. in Saltmarsh 18).

For Dewey, knowing emerges from palpable experience, from the "forked road of doubt," and is realized through action. Knowledge is born of *inquiry*, a recursive relation to experience through which thought is intertwined with action—reflection in and on action—and proceeds from doubt, to the resolution of doubt, to the generation of new doubt. According to Dewey, "[Subject matter] becomes an object of study—that is, of inquiry and reflection—when it figures as a factor to be reckoned with in the completion of a course of events in which one is engaged and by whose outcome one is affected" (*MW* 9: 141). Yet he sharpens this general theory by insisting that although learning emerges from experience, "the belief that all genuine education comes about through experience does not mean that all experiences are genuinely or equally educative" (*Experience* 25). Dewey's primary requisite for a *quality* experience is that it "live fruitfully and creatively in future experiences" (28).[7]

Consequently, Dewey believes that "educational institutions should be equipped so as to give students an opportunity for acquiring and testing ideas and information in active pursuits typifying social situations" (*MW* 9: 169). For Dewey, this means developing a problem-posing and problem-solving curriculum (terms he used several generations before we encounter them in composition studies). Moreover, whereas many classrooms emphasize competition among students to learn the same material, Dewey emphasizes the diversity of knowledge and interests that individuals bring to the classroom (although he is relatively quiet on cultural or ethnic diversity) and how such a range of student capabilities and interests can be celebrated and utilized rather than downplayed and homogenized. He suggests that the student wants to "work out something specifically his own, which he may contribute to the common stock, while he, in turn, participates in the productions of others. . . . The child is born with a natural desire to give out, to do, and that means to serve" ("Ethical Principles" 118–20; see also Fishman and McCarthy, "Teaching" 345). Certainly, service-learning writing projects present the potential for providing such active, cooperative, and experiential contexts for education. In fact, they not only draw on the desire of students to "to give out, to do, to serve" but also take Dewey's call for student learning through "active pursuits typifying social situations" one logical step further by presenting *genuine* social situations—service in the community—as contexts for doing and learning.

The Individual/Society Relation in Deweyan Thought

Like most contemporary teachers and researchers in rhetoric and composition studies, Dewey's writings affirm and explore the radical interconnectedness of individual cognition and social context. His writings are preoccupied with this relation and with collapsing the dualisms that separate the self from society.[8] He is a philosopher of social action rather than of detached knowledge and, therefore, never fails to connect his theories of individual learning to the larger context of how individuals should relate to society. For Dewey, education is ultimately social in its aims. He writes: "Unless education has some frame of reference it is bound to be aimless, lacking a unified objective. . . . There exists in this country such a unified frame. It is called democracy" (*LW* 11: 415).

Dewey insists that "the conception of education as a social process and function has no definite meaning until we define the kind of society we have in mind" (*MW* 9:103). When he writes of society, Dewey assumes a democratic society, and his conception of a democracy is elemental to understanding how he thinks individuals and educational institutions should ideally function within it. While most definitions of democracy hinge on political factors—government structures, individual civil rights, or a social contract—Dewey's definition emphasizes cultural factors—civic participation, open communication, and social interaction. As Dewey explains in *The Public and Its Problems*, democracy for him is "not an alternative to other principles of associated life. It is the very idea of community itself" (148). Later, in *Democracy and Education,* he reinforces this concept:

> A democracy is more than a form of government, it is primarily a mode of associated living, a conjoint communicated experience. The extension in space of the number of individuals who participate in an interest so that each has to refer his own

action to that of others, and to consider the action of others to give point and direction to his own, is equivalent to the breaking down of those barriers of class, race, and national territory which kept men from perceiving the full import of their activity. (*MW* 9: 93)[9]

Therefore the Deweyan conception of democracy is communitarian in character, emphasizing the possibilities of cooperative life rather than the dangers of unchecked power or conflicting interests. As Alan Ryan remarks, "The ideal [for Dewey] was to transform the great society into the great community" (219). Cornel West extends this line of thinking by noting that "the pragmatist tradition has been the distinctive philosophical tradition to make democracy not just a mode of governance but a way of being in the world" (*Prophetic* 117).[10]

Since Dewey's conception of democracy rests on social interaction, it makes sense for his theory of education to follow. Making an explicit connection between knowledge and democracy, Dewey notes that "since democracy stands in principle for free exchange, for social continuity, it must develop a theory of knowledge which sees in knowledge the method by which one experience is made available in giving direction and meaning to another" (*MW* 9: 355). Democratic education for him is to be seen "as a freeing of individual capacity in a progressive growth directed to social aims" (*MW* 9: 58). Toward this end, he proposes to teachers that "the introduction of every method which appeals to the child's active powers, to his capacities for construction, production, and creation, marks an opportunity to shift the center of ethical gravity from an absorption which is selfish to a service which is social" ("Ethical Principles" 120). In other words, Dewey favors any opportunity through which we can redirect curriculum from lessons that quiz individual accumulation of knowledge to projects that draw on individual talents within collaborative efforts that intervene in social settings, whether classrooms or local communities.

Dewey also concludes that "the only way to prepare for social life is to engage in social life" ("Ethical Principles" 116). Likewise, the radical interaction and "continuity" between the individual and society is a cornerstone of Dewey's social, political, and ultimately educational philosophy. He writes:

More important than choosing sides in this debate is recognizing that in Dewey's stance on multiculturalism, his characteristic preference for dialectical thinking is evident: he emphasizes the need to shape a vital common national experience and couples this with an affirmation of the importance of diversity. As we recognize the richness and usefulness of Dewey's thinking for service-learning, we need attend to alternate readings of pragmatism, and to compare the Deweyan approach to those of theorists who are more attentive to matters of power and oppression (as I do below with Paulo Freire).

Throughout his work, Dewey states that a primary aim of schools should be to help students become good citizens in the broadest sense ("Ethical" 112). The individual and the school must be continuous with society even as they are agents of service and transformation. Dewey argues for the value of vocational and "practical" education but insists that instruction not be subservient to business interests any more than it should be beholden to the "traditional education" which the progressive education movement so vigorously opposed. He reflects: "The problem is not that of making the schools an adjunct to manufacture and commerce, but of utilizing the factors of industry to make school life more active, more full of immediate meaning, more connected with out-of-school experience" (*MW* 9:326). As this remark suggests, Dewey was a supporter of vocational education. (He wrote several essays on the value of vocational elements in the curriculum.) However, Dewey was not an uncritical advocate for turning schools into adjuncts for industry. Even while explicitly anti-Marxist throughout his life, Dewey was wary of unbridled capitalism and he repeatedly stressed the ethical obligation of education to prepare students for citizenship rather to train them as instruments of corporate profit. For example, he writes in *Democracy and Education*:

There is a standing danger that education will perpetuate the older traditions of a select few, and effect its adjustment to

newer economic conditions more or less on the basis of acqui-
escence in the untransformed, unrationalized, and unsocialized
phases of our defective industrial regime. . . . Education would
then become an instrument of perpetuating unchanged the existing order of society, instead of operating as a means of its
transformation. . . . The desired transformation . . . signifies a
society in which every person shall be occupied in something
which makes the lives of others better worth living, and which
accordingly makes the ties which bind persons together more
perceptible. (*MW* 9: 326)

Such critique resonates with neo-Marxist analyses of cultural
institutions reproducing themselves and the inequitable power
relations of society. Yet Dewey is more invested in reform—in
"strengthening the ties that bind people together" and in social
reconstruction—than in revolutionary change. As Stanley Fish
notes, "Pragmatism is the philosophy not of grand ambitions but
of little steps" (432).[11] Likewise, Dewey's socialist and
communitarian approach to political action is defined by "mediation" and "gradualism" (Saltmarsh 20). He trusts individuals
to act and reflect critically and incrementally within a moderate
capitalist system (through education, dialogue, and service) toward the end of a more participatory democratic community.

Teachers and administrators, Dewey suggests, are the most
appropriate agents of change for democratic education because
progressive educators facilitate schools more connected to civic
life, students more active and reflective, and a society closer to
the ideal of democracy as "a mode of associated living, a con-
joint communicated experience" (*MW* 9: 93). In this process,
service becomes a key term for Dewey: "The growth of the child
in the direction of social capacity and service, his larger and more
vital union with life, becomes the unifying aim [of education];
and discipline, culture, and information fall into place as phases
of this growth" (*School* 92). Dewey insists that educators should
play a central role in "saturating" the student with the "spirit of
service" (*MW* 1: 20). Furthermore, "Interest in community wel-
fare, an interest which is intellectual and practical, as well as
emotional—an interest, that is to say, in perceiving whatever
makes for social order and progress, and for carrying these principles into execution—is the ultimate ethical habit to which all

the special school habits must be related if they are to be animated by the breath of moral life" ("Ethical Principles" 118). Students must have the ability "to take their own active part in aggressive participation in bringing about a new social order" (*LW* 9: 128). Ideally, Dewey would have schools function as "genuine community centres," so that their influence would ramify "to take in the main interests of the community in such things as nutrition, health, recreation, etc." (*LW* 9: 185). And taking seriously "the main interests of the community" is, in fact, something that service-learning initiatives already do.

Paulo Freire's Praxis in Service-Learning Practice

Along with John Dewey, Paulo Freire serves as a theoretical anchor for many service-learning advocates. Community-based academic projects speak to Freire's belief that, as he writes, "the distance between the university (or what is done in it) and the popular classes should be shortened without losing rigor and seriousness, without neglecting the duty of teaching and researching" (*Christina* 133). As a self-described radical, Freire's goals are ambitious—no less than the political transformation of individuals and society through literacy education, critical reflection, and collective social action.

Dewey and Freire, who both label themselves progressives, share a scorn for philosophies of education that rely on mechanistic, static, industrial, or elitist metaphors. Instead they build their philosophies around core concepts of experience, growth, inquiry, communication, mediation, problem posing/solving, consciousness-raising, ethical social action, and transformation. Stanley Aronowitz links Dewey and Freire by describing them as groundbreaking philosophers of education and as among our few public, engaged intellectuals. He even remarks that "there are enough resemblances . . . to validate the reduction of Freire to the Latin John Dewey" ("Humanism" 10). However, Aronowitz also fears that in academic disciplines and classroom practice both Dewey and Freire are too often watered down and cast as promoters of depoliticized teaching methods (such as valuing student experience as a starting point for learning, or including more dialogue in the classroom). He reminds us that Dewey was a leader in the teacher union movement and that Freire's ideas were developed within the context of grassroots literacy work. Like Dewey, Freire discusses how individuals learn through the active, collaborative tackling of complex and experiential problems, and how individuals and schools should function in society to promote a more participatory, curious, and critically aware citizenry. However, Freire's hopes for radical structural change are more politically oppositional and more attuned to both class conflict and cultural diversity than are Dewey's.

My reading of Freire confirms his many parallels with Dewey, but it also discerns critical differences between the two educators and the implications of those differences for service-learning. Both Dewey and Freire are humanists who see the educational process as bringing action and reflection, theory and practice, means and ends, self and society, into intimate, and ultimately transformative, dialectical relationship. Dewey describes the ideal dialectic in terms of *continuity*, Freire in terms of *dialogue*. Both imagine the educational process as a key mechanism in fostering an increasingly critical and active citizenry, with Dewey hanging his hopes on ever more interconnected civic participation and Freire focusing his on radical critique, "critical consciousness," and "praxis."

There are, certainly, important differences in the educational philosophies of Dewey and Freire. Among the most significant is Freire's emphasis on accounting for the particular culture, class, and race of each learner, anthropological factors which Dewey largely sidesteps when speaking of students. In addition, Freire, true to his Marxist influences, focuses on radical socioeconomic change, which problematizes (and politicizes) the educational system and its place in a dominant (and to his mind oppressive) social order, while Dewey focuses on communication and problem solving, assuming a largely benevolent social order in need of revitalization rather than revolutionary restructuring. For Dewey, "philosophy was aimed at the enhancement of democratic education, and his conception of democracy was cultural, not political" (Saltmarsh 19). In contrast, Freire's conception of democracy, while attentive to culture, foregrounds matters of political power. Whereas for Dewey education prepares and motivates participation in the polis, for Freire education *is* politics (deepened by the belief that most formal education serves dominant political interests).

This difference in ideological orientation is due in large part to the dramatically different cultural contexts out of which the two philosophers emerged. Dewey cultivated his philosophy from within the U.S. academy and his own middle-class sensibility. And while Freire also worked within a university setting for most of his life, his philosophy was influenced profoundly by his Third World context and his work in grassroots adult literacy circles with marginalized and dispossessed persons. Thus Freire views nearly everything, especially education, through the lens of political power. While both Dewey and Freire are progressive in their theories and practices, then, only Freire can be considered radical.[12]

Action-Reflection in Freirean Thought

Freire defines his key term *praxis* as "action-reflection." As he explains, "Within the word we find two dimensions, reflection and action, in such radical interconnection that if one is sacrificed—even in part—the other immediately suffers" (*Oppressed* 75). The sacrifice of action leads to verbalism, vacant words; the sacrifice of reflection leads to activism, uncritical behavior. He elucidates, "Either dichotomy, by creating unauthentic forms of existence, creates also unauthentic forms of thought, which reinforce the original dichotomy" (*Oppressed* 76). Like Dewey, Freire rails against entrenched dualisms and insists on a dynamic and holistic conception of learning. His praxis implies a concurrent, recursive, ongoing process of action-reflection: "authentic reflection clarifies future action, which in its given time will have to be open to renewed reflection" (*Politics* 156). As with Dewey, the truly educative experience motivates further inquiry and action. In fact, when he revisits *Pedagogy of the Oppressed* thirty years later in *Pedagogy of Hope*, Freire further underscores the recursivity of "action-reflection" by introducing the term "action-reflection-action" (53). In doing so, he reiterates both the cyclical character of the ideal learning process and the impera- tive to apply abstract intellectual work to grounded social action.

When it comes to individual cognition, Freire sees knowing as a constructive, experiential process and posits learning as emerging from "the situation." He writes: "Liberating education consists in acts of cognition, not transferals of information. It is a learning situation in which the cognizable object (far from be- ing the end of the cognitive act) intermediates the cognitive ac- tors—teacher on the one hand and students on the other" (*Oppressed* 67). This "intermediation" (or one of its Freirean corollaries—dialogue, dialectic, true communication, commun- ion, action-reflection, praxis) serves as a centerpiece for Freire's learning theory. As with Dewey and his experiential "split road of doubt" as the starting place for learning, Freire locates learn- ing in one's creative response to a situation, that is, in the rela- tion of the individual to the material problem. Freire writes, "To be an act of knowing . . . the adult literacy process must engage the learners in the constant problematizing of their existential situations" (*Politics* 56). However, while Dewey and Freire both emphasize the value of starting from the "existential situations" of students, their understanding of what constitutes that "exis- tential situation" differs with respect to how they understand culture. As Moacir Gadotti explains, "For Dewey, culture is sim- plified as it doesn't involve the social, racial and ethnic elements while for Paulo Freire it has an anthropological connotation as the educational action always takes place in the culture of the pupil" (117).

A Freirean "an act of knowing" hinges on "inquiry" (a term also central to Dewey, and used in much the same sense). Freire explains: "For apart from inquiry, apart from praxis, men can- not be truly human. Knowledge emerges only through invention and reinvention, through the restless, impatient, continuing, hope- ful inquiry men pursue in the world, with the world, and with each other" (*Oppressed* 58). As an alternative to traditional edu- cation, which he critiqued in his famous analogy of the banking approach (in which teachers and students treat knowledge like a static commodity to be accumulated like capital), Freire imag- ines learning as involving "action, critical reflection, curiosity, demanding inquiry, uneasiness, uncertainty." He asserts that "all these virtues are indispensable to the cognitive subject, the person who learns!" (Shor and Freire 8).

In a work focusing on higher education, Freire insists: "We must expect [college] curricula to stimulate curiosity, a critical spirit and democratic participation" (Freire et al. 69). Freire's understanding of the relation of knowledge to action, like Dewey's, recommends learning situations that are experiential, collaborative, active, and community-oriented—all of which are, we should note, hallmarks of service-learning writing projects.

As has been demonstrated by critical teachers like Ira Shor, however, a Freirean approach to teaching and learning can be enacted in composition courses without a service-learning component (see *Critical; Empowering*). Such a classroom can, by introducing themes relevant to the experiences of students, animate the "dynamic movement" between "reading the word" and "reading the world" that is central to Freire's conception of the literacy process (Freire and Macedo 35). Shor and many American composition teachers have designed instruction to encourage the problematization of and critical reflection on such generative themes as dominance, oppression, work, politics, and schooling. Moreover, the reading, writing, and analytical strategies that students learn in such courses can help them develop the facility with academic discourse and higher-order thinking that they will need in order to succeed in college-level courses across the curriculum (Bizzell).

Such liberatory teachers are particularly adept at unveiling the ideologies that support oppression, and, indeed, sharing strategies for ideological analysis with students can be an important kind of empowerment. But the neo-Marxist approach of liberatory pedagogy also assumes a certain kind of faith—a faith that critical intellectual habits will translate into effective social action, that an attitude displayed in class will lead to action in the wider community. While most courses that espouse a liberatory pedagogy encourage student dialogue and student/teacher parity (and thus make for a more democratic dynamic *within* the classroom), they are generally not integrated with active participation in social justice movements or organizations outside the classroom—something important to Freire but rarely mentioned by academic

Freirean educators. Good critical dialogue in the classroom can, certainly, be viewed as a significant form of social action in its own right; but Freire, particularly later in his career, recognized the limits of critical dialogue on its own. He asserts, "Let me make it clear, then, that, in the domain of socioeconomic structures, the most critical knowledge of reality, which we acquire through the unveiling of that reality, does not of itself alone effect a change in reality" (*Hope* 30; see also *Freedom* 72–79). Therefore, while the inclination of American compositionists who subscribe to Freirean theory is to help students develop a disposition of and language for radical critique through classroom instruction and dialogue, we cannot assume that such hoped-for shifts in student consciousness, however commendable, will result in any social transformation or traceable material intervention in reality beyond the classroom.[13]

Most U.S. versions of Freirean pedagogy ask students to "read the word and the world" but are less prone to structure opportunities for students to *write* themselves into the world beyond the academy. As Nora Bacon has suggested, service-learning's contribution to liberatory pedagogy may not hinge on helping students develop an abstract critical consciousness that mirrors that of their teachers; instead, what makes service-learning radical is the way that it can reconstruct the role, even the identity, of the student ("Critical"). For example, even as Freire rails against "banking" modes of education and liberatory teachers heed him by making their classrooms more dialogic, institutional practices in the academy and in composition still tend to infantilize students by casting them as learners whose writing matters to few beyond the classroom. Even the most eloquent student essays will rarely find an audience beyond the teacher, an exigency other than the teacher-defined assignment and due date, or an institutional acknowledgment other than a grade. Service-learning disrupts this process. It positions students not as deficient or passive novices who need to learn to perform critical consciousness for teachers and for grades, but rather as agents in the world beyond campus who pair outreach work with critical reflection (writing *about* the community), who use writing to aid social service organizations (writing *for* the community), and/or who help craft collaborative documents that instigate social change (writing *with* the community). While most advocates of critical pedagogy hope that teaching critical consciousness will lead to future social action, service-learning more immediately casts students as writers and social agents, thus ushering into practice the "action-reflection-action" dynamic celebrated by Freire.

The Individual/Society Relation in Freirean Thought

Freire wishes for no less than a revolution, and, for him, the "revolutionary process is eminently educational in character" (*Oppressed* 133).[14] While some may take this, especially given his early works, to imply that Freire believes that systematic education is "the lever for revolutionary transformation," his more recent writings revise this claim. Echoing (albeit unknowingly) Dewey's speculation that "I do not suppose that education alone can solve it [socioeconomic inequity]" (*LW* 17: 316), Freire remarks that "We should never take literacy as the triggering of social transformation. Literacy as a global concept is only part of the transformative triggering mechanism" (Freire and Macedo 107). Formal education alone is not the lever for transformation because Freire believes that systematic schooling is almost always a conservative enterprise. He writes:

> My optimistic position is nowadays more clearly defined as the following: I am absolutely convinced that the main task of systematic education is the reproduction of the ideology of the dominant class, that of reproducing the conditions for the preservation of their power, precisely because the relationship between systematic education, as a subsystem, and the social system is one of opposition and mutual contradiction. Therefore, when talking about reproduction as the task of the dominant class, there is the possibility of counter-acting the task of reproducing the dominant ideology. . . . [W]e clearly perceive a permanent movement, very dynamic and contradictory, between the task of reproduction and that of counteracting the reproduction. These two tasks are dialectic: one is the task of the system, the other is ours; therefore, it is determined by the system but not requested by it. (Freire et al. 31)

This "dynamic and contradictory" situation leaves the critical educator "swimming against the tide." Freire believes that "the university cannot be the vanguard of any revolution; it is not in the nature of the institution" (Freire et al. 62). Still, ever hopeful, he does leave open the hope that schools can become both more democratic in their practices and more inviting of community involvement ("Education and Community Involvement"). Furthermore, he offers hope to individual teachers by emphasizing "a space, however small, in the practice of education, in the educative system as a subsystem," that can be used for liberatory purposes; and, he contends, it is this "minimum space that we must use to our advantage" (Freire et al. 34). It is this counterreproductive "minimum space" that both critical pedagogies and service-learning projects infused with a Freirean spirit can inhabit.

Ira Shor lists the basic descriptors of Freirean pedagogy as *participatory, situated* (in student thought and language), *critical, democratic, dialogic, desocializing, multicultural, research-oriented, activist,* and *affective* ("Education" 33–34). Mainstream composition scholarship and practice already take for granted some of these characteristics by emphasizing a process-oriented pedagogy, participatory peer groups, classroom dialogue, and respect for student language. But critical pedagogy in the Freirean tradition goes further by incorporating all of Shor's descriptors and adopting such a politically and pedagogically ambitious agenda.

For Freire, social action begins through one's understanding of consciousness. He defines consciousness as "constituted in the dialectic of man's objectification of and action upon the world" (*Politics* 69)—that is, in the individual's understanding of his or her relation to society. Freire articulates three progressive levels of consciousness: *semi-intransitive, naive transitive,* and *critically transitive consciousness.* These range from immersion in the dominant mass consciousness of society (semi-transitive), through an emerging awareness of oneself and societal structures (naive transitive), to a critical, historical, dialectical problematization of society and one's relation to it (critical consciousness) (*Politics* 71–81). Thus *conscientization* is marked by "depth in the interpretation of problems; by the substitution of causal principles for magical explanations; by the testing of one's own findings and openness to revision . . . ; by refusing to transfer responsibility; by rejecting passive positions; by soundness of argumentation; by the practice of dialogue rather than polemics . . . ; by accepting what is valid in both old and new" (*Education* 18). Clearly, this formulation implies a literacy that demands more than functional reading and writing. Freire shuns the "functional literacy" often posited as the goal of literacy projects and composition programs because it encourages students to progress no further than a naive transitive consciousness and serves dominant rather than liberatory interests (see Lanskshear; Knoblauch and Brannon; and Bizzell). According to Freire, critical literacy geared toward the goal of critical consciousness should be the practice of the liberatory educator.

Shor describes the four main qualities of critical consciousness as *power awareness* (understanding social history), *critical literacy* (analytically reading, writing, and discussing social matters), *desocialization* (examining the internalized myths and values of mass culture), and *self-organization/self-education* (taking initiative in ongoing social change) ("Education" 32). Although since 1987 Freire had largely given up using the term "critical consciousness" because he found it so loosely appropriated as to lose its meaning, most still associate the term with him. And while Freire may have surrendered the term (replacing it with others like "critical awareness," "the unveiling of reality," and "the moment of revelation of social reality"), he has not discarded the import of the concept to his educational philosophy.

In his early work, Freire puts critical consciousness at the center of his educational philosophy. Moving from naive transitive consciousness to critical consciousness implies an increasingly reflective, abstract, and critical grasp of one's social, historical, and class situatedness. It means coming into consciousness and ultimately metaconsciousness of ones relationship to the cultural and economic order. *Conscientization* is, as with Freire's understanding of individual cognition, a dialectical and dialogical process that grasps the dynamic relationship between objectivity and subjectivity, between material conditions and individual consciousness. Freire's notion of critical consciousness goes beyond most understandings of "critical thinking" as discussed by American educators, who primarily focus on independent thinking and analytical reasoning. Freire demands more—a willingness to enter into dialogue with the dispossessed in society, to unpack dominant myths embedded in our socialization, and to comprehend power and class relations.

Still, Freire's philosophy is not aimed only at changing minds; it is also intended to change material conditions. And Freire wanted to change not only schools but also larger cultural and economic structures of oppression. In his political thinking are evident the influences of both liberation theology and Marxist social theory (even though Freire corrects for the Marxist neglect of individual subjectivity, personal agency, and local culture). His early works suggest that critical consciousness can lead to social transformation. Reflecting on that work later in life, Freire regrets that he had "spoken as if the unveiling of reality automatically made for its transformation" (*Hope* 103). In more recent works Freire asserts that while "unveiling of reality" remains the central act of the critical literacy process, concrete and collective action must follow in order to fully realize his vision. Thus, community-based projects which pair critical consciousness aims with grounded action are a fitting manifestation of Freire's theory in practice. As Freire observes in a conversation with Ira Shor, "For me, the best thing possible is to work in both places simultaneously, in the school and in the social movements outside the classroom" (Shor and Freire 39). Thus, in reading Freire one discovers a compelling invitation to service-learning.

Like Dewey, Freire writes very little in particular about writing, and virtually nothing about college writing instruction—and yet he remains important to composition studies in the United States, as evidenced by the many applications of Freirean theory to U.S. college writing classrooms (see Berlin, "Freirean"; Bizzell; Knoblauch and Brannon; Shor, *Critical*; Shor and Freire, Chapter 5; Villanueva). Freire is relevant to compositionists because he is a comprehensive thinker about learning, teaching, curriculum, ideology, and social action—all of which are indivisible from understanding the context, practice, and implications of college writing instruction. But unlike Dewey, who was a philosopher of the U.S. middle class, Freire's writings are rooted in and acutely aware of the social context of Brazil, where disparities of class, wealth, and power are more dramatic; where the material and psychological consequences of imperialism are ever present; where universal schooling is not taken for granted; where technology lags behind that of the United States; where the tradition of Marxist social theory plays a significant role on the political stage; and where the dissemination of and standards for literacy differ markedly from the literacy practices of the United States.[15] Sociopolitically and geopolitically, then, Freire is far removed from U.S. education—and yet his theory and example still matter here, especially in relation to service-learning projects.

However, Henry Giroux fears that "what has been increasingly lost in the North American and Western appropriation of Freire's work is the profound and radical nature of its theory and practice as an anti-colonial and postcolonial discourse" ("Politics of Postcolonialism" 193). Giroux reminds us to keep in mind not only the Third World as the crucible for Freire's thought but also his personal circumstances:

> For Freire, the task of being an intellectual has always been forged within the trope of homelessness: between different zones of theoretical and cultural difference; between the borders of non-European and European cultures. In effect, Freire is a border intellectual, whose allegiances have not been to a specific class and culture as in Gramsci's notion of the organic intellectual; instead, Freire's writings embody a mode of discursive struggle and opposition that not only challenges the oppressive machinery of the State but is also sympathetic to the formation of new cultural subjects and movements engaged in the struggle over the modernist values of freedom, equality, and justice. (195)

Therefore Freire's work cannot be simply appropriated by educators in more industrialized nations as a recipe; such advocates of radical pedagogy can better grasp Freire within a postcolonial discourse that acknowledges his historical context and radical ambitions. As Freire himself notes, "My educational experiments in the Third World should not be transplanted; they should be created anew" (*Politics* 190). Freire's theories do still resonate in context of the United States, with its class stratifications, poverty, inequities of schooling, and racial polarization, even though the United States is far from Freire's cultural home. The need to "create anew" projects for critical literacy and social transformation remains pressing. While most North American appropriations of Freire are framed in terms of critical pedagogy, service-learning college writing initiatives can constitute another vital form of Freirean cultural action for liberation.

Although a supporter of revolutionary change and class struggle, Freire is not a doctrinaire Marxist, as he puts much faith in individual agency and incremental change. Still, unlike Dewey, his explicit goals include a revolutionary restructuring of the political and economic status quo. While Dewey wanted to significantly reform and democratize the dominant culture and its institutions (particularly schools), his political ideology often recommended that those in the margins surrender to the mainstream, to a common "democratic faith." Such a stance runs counter to Freire's insistence that dominant cultures are by definition oppressive, and that their traditional institutions (particularly schools) are almost always instruments of oppression, even though critical teachers can create counteroppressive spaces for genuine learning and dialogue within such institutions.

In concert with the skepticism demanded by desocialization and critical analysis, there is an idealistic, even utopian, strain in critical pedagogy. Peter McLaren and Tomaz Tadeu da Silva remark that "critical pedagogy must serve as a form of critique and also a referent of hope" and they suggest that it can be likened to a kind of "social dreaming" (69). Henry Giroux refers to "a pedagogy of possibility" ("Introduction"). Freire is not afraid to use words rarely uttered in academic circles, such as *hope, love, utopia,* and *dream.* For example, he writes: "Transformation of the world implies a dialectic between . . . two actions: denouncing the process of dehumanization and announcing the dream of a new society" (*Freedom* 74). Freire also speaks of utopias—but not naive utopias. He clarifies by returning again to the trope of dialectic: "This is a utopianism as a dialectical relationship between denouncing the present and announcing the future. To anticipate tomorrow by dreaming today" (Shor and Freire 187).

Freire's announcement of utopian possibilities facilitates a critique of the present and underwrites an oppositional political agenda. His emphasis on political democracy and revolutionary socioeconomic transformation stands in contrast to Dewey's emphasis on cultural democracy and incremental social reconstruction. Dewey prefers working hypotheses and reform to revolutionary visions of future utopias. Both Freire and Dewey are visionaries, but while Freire often looks to a city on a hill, Dewey, according to Alan Ryan, "was a curious visionary, because he did not speak of a distant goal or a city not built with hands. He was a visionary about the here and now, about the potentiality of the modern world, modern society, modern man" (368). Dewey writes of working not toward "ends that are alleged to be general or ultimate" but toward "ends in view" that emerge from existing conditions, involve purposeful activity, and remain flexible (*MW* 9: 107–17). Freire's utopian faith in revolutionary outcomes marks an alternative to Dewey's pragmatist faith in provisional outcomes—each a powerful version of hope.

I began this chapter by asking, What kinds of writers do we hope that our composition courses will encourage? Many service-learning practitioners answer this question with Dewey's pragmatic experimentalism or Freire's critical pedagogy in mind. Yet Dewey and Freire are certainly not the only theoretical exemplars available for service-learning. For example, since neither is attentive to gender, a feminist perspective (some have suggested Carol Gilligan's "ethic of care") could also function fruitfully as a lens through which to examine service-learning initiatives (see Foos; Novek; Rhoads). Still, Dewey and Freire are enduring figures in educational theory and are valuable as frames of reference for examining particular service-learning composition courses and programs. Thus, I often return to their work as I discuss case studies in the following chapters.

In these chapters I describe service-learning initiatives that encourage the development of particular kinds—often quite different kinds—of socially engaged writers. I then move on to discuss my own applications of service-learning. In my courses, I want to encourage versatile and reflective writers who not only learn strategies for negotiating the writing challenges of college but also venture beyond the classroom (and beyond academic discourse) to serve their communities by applying their still-emerging literacy skills to pressing social problems. Service-learning courses are, in my experience, one way—perhaps the best way—to encourage the development of capable and socially engaged writers. The teachers whose classrooms I study express similar aspirations.

Each of the next three chapters presents research on an exemplary service-learning initiative. In these case studies, I account for student experiences of service-learning to some degree, but perhaps not as much as I should. Rather, my focus deliberately remains trained on the curricular aims and assumptions of the particular community-based projects. Thus the approach is more analytic and comparative than ethnographic, and most attention is devoted to curricular and pedagogical arrangements as they relate to rhetorical, critical, and composition theory.[16]

Writing for the Community: "Real-World" Writing, Nonacademic Literacies, and Writing in Sport Management

"The biggest goal that I have is that students have an exposure to a real client relationship where they're tailoring their writing to an exceedingly clear audience."
LAURIE GULLION, personal interview

One of the most popular forms of service-learning brings college students into partnership with nonprofit agencies, where the students undertake what are essentially mini-internships and compose purpose-driven documents like grant proposals, research reports, newsletter articles, and brochures. Some instructors have followed the lead of Stanford University, which integrated agency projects into selected first-year composition courses starting in 1989 and has since disseminated its program in textbook form (Watters and Ford, *Writing* and *Guide*). And most are motivated by the prospect of inserting students into real-world rhetorical situations beyond the bounds of the classroom. Wade and Susan Dorman of Louisiana State University remark on their motivation: "We wanted students writing *to* and *in* the community, rather than merely *about* the community" (126).

Most writing-for-the-community initiatives (or what some also call "writing *as* service" [Bacon, "Instruction"]) are conducted largely in accord with a Deweyan approach to learning. They tend to focus on the same synergistic relations of knowledge to action and the individual to society discussed in the Dewey

the social perspective on nonacademic writing, and (3) research on audience.

Moving between Academic and Workplace Literacies

The service-learning assignments for Gullion's class demanded that student teams venture off-campus to meet with community agency contacts (generally several times) and compose texts in unfamiliar formats (e.g., manuals, brochures, grant applications). The community-based portion of the class accounted for 65 percent of the course grade. Each student kept a writing log, while the teams collaboratively wrote a project proposal, a progress report memorandum, and the project itself. After the projects were completed, each group gave an in-class oral presentation. The audience for the proposal, memo, and writing log was Gullion; the audience for the final project was the agency (and often the constituency served by the agency as well); and the audience for the oral presentation consisted of the instructor and fellow students. Of course, Writing in Sport Management remained within an academic context—a required course that would ultimately be graded according to fairly traditional academic measures. As with many service-learning initiatives, the movement between academic and nonacademic contexts, codes, literacies, and assessment measures caused a significant degree of dissonance in students accustomed to conventional college patterns. One student commented in our interview:

> At first I didn't like it at all. . . . I guess I have conflicting opinions on it. . . . Some things were good and some things were bad. . . . To do my own and do the editing part was fine; but to involve my partners' work and their workload—I had to spend four or five hours a day on the computer to get the images and formats correct. . . . And if they didn't know [how to use the computer], I had to assist them . . . and that part was frustrating.

Others complained of "difficult" first meetings with contacts, a "lack of direction" from supervisors, and, in particular, problems with communication and division of work within student groups.

While Gullion's students most often located their problems in peer-group dynamics or interaction with agency contact persons, they also experienced struggles with the cognitive and rhetorical challenges of their agency projects. This should come as no surprise, given available research on the movement between nonacademic and academic literacies. Anne J. Herrington, for example, studied students in chemical engineering courses designed to simulate professional contexts within academic structures and concluded that "learning the conventions of a school community may be all the more difficult if one is shifting from a context where social conventions of a school community are dominant to a context where those of a professional community are dominant" ("Academic Settings" 355). Stephen Doheney-Farina documents a similar phenomenon in the case of Anna, a student who moved from an academic context (an undergraduate English curriculum) to a nonacademic context (a public health agency internship). Doheney-Farina unpacks the conflicting values of school and workplace contexts that surfaced during the "formal and informal orientation processes" of Anna's internship, particularly her need to subordinate an individualist rhetoric to a functional and organizational rhetoric. One of my former first-year students expressed a dissonance akin to Anna's: "In this writing I was representing another organization so I couldn't voice my own personal opinions. It was a pain. I couldn't wait to get it over with." Some Writing in Sport Management groups reported similar conflicts (like being frustrated with the "standard forms" or "nit-picking" of the agencies); but more groups reported a different kind of conflict—not being given *enough* directive instructions and guidelines by their agency contacts (especially in their initial meetings).

Chris M. Anson and L. Lee Forsberg tracked six "fairly competent" college writers in their movement between academic and workplace (mostly internship) contexts and discerned three broad stages of transition: "Expectation," "Disorientation," and "Transition and Resolution." What they observed in the cases was "an ongoing process of adapting to a social setting, involving not only the idiosyncratic textual features of a discourse community but a shifting array of political, managerial, and social influences as well" (225). The study also suggests "that the writer must first become a 'reader' of a context before he or she can be 'literate' within it. This literacy does not seem restricted to mutual knowledge of some intellectual domain but includes highly situational knowledge that can be gained only from participating in the context, which itself is in a constant state of change" (225). The stages described by Anson and Forsberg resonate with the end-of-semester summary oral reports on agency projects by the students in Gullion's class.

Members of several of Gullion's groups stated that they initially expected their projects to be "so easy" or "cake" (perhaps not only because brochures and manuals seem simple genres at first glance, but also because many students in the class had been involved in hometown recreation leagues like those being served in Amherst). For some groups, disorientation set in at the first meeting. One group doing a swimming-lessons brochure remarked, "We didn't know what we were getting into." For others, disorientation surfaced during the writing and revising process (most were surprised at the degree of revision they had to undertake, and that there was no room for error in final drafts). And for others, the collaboration process among group members was sometimes problematic.[1]

Ultimately, however, all groups related a success story, even if a qualified one. Below are some representative comments from course evaluations:

♦ "If we had to do it again, we might take on a smaller project, but we liked it."

♦ "We were satisfied with what we produced, although we would like to have gone into more depth and detail."

♦ "We did a pretty good job and we definitely had fun doing it."

♦ "I didn't want to do this at first, but then liked the design aspects of it."

Gullion's report to the Provost echoes the general findings of Anson and Forsberg, as well as the particulars of her initiative:

The students wrote that they felt rewarded by producing a useful written piece needed by an organization, they took their writing seriously because a real client was editing it, and they liked performing community service. However, they also experienced frustration and uncertainty in leaving the comfort of the classroom for a real-world situation (which I obviously see as more valuable than they did!) and in juggling the off-campus demands of their projects in light of athletic and work schedules.

In his essay "Bridging the Gap: Scenic Motives for Collaborative Writing in Workplace and School," James Reither proposes that to translate our social research perspective on nonacademic writing into classroom practice—particularly with respect to collaborative writing—we need to do more than simply import co-authoring and peer editing into our courses. He suggests that most writing college courses, even when they attempt to incorporate elements of social theory, fall short: "What is missing from these classrooms are the circumstances that make possible and (thus) motivate writing as a social process—the very conditions that make collaboration and cooperation appropriate, even necessary, in many business, governmental, and professional workplaces. What is missing are the rhetorical needs, aims, functions, and motives that organize and drive the production of written knowledge" (196).

Laurie Gullion speaks to just such missing circumstances when she remarks, "The biggest goal that I have is that students have an exposure to a real client relationship where they're tailoring their writing to an exceedingly clear audience." Reither admits that while "there is probably no point in pretending that classrooms can truly replicate . . . workplaces," we can "begin making our classrooms scenes that enable writing and knowing as social, collaborative, intertextual processes" (205). Drawing on Kenneth Burke, Reither believes that to do this we must

organize classrooms as places where students can experience the same kinds of motives for writing and collaborating that many people experience in many workplaces. Students (and teachers) need to know what happens when there is work to do and when writing is the way to do that work. Students need to experience scenes where writing and collaborating are central ways for people to define themselves and their relation-learning technical writing courses depart from traditional technical writing courses in that they focus exclusively on the nonprofit sector (in contrast to the usual emphasis on business and industry) and raise social justice concerns (in addition to the on-the-job ethical issues addressed by most technical writing textbooks).[2]

One notable disadvantage of service-learning projects, particularly in comparison with some cases cited above involving semester- or yearlong internships, is their brevity. Most writing-for-the-community projects account for only one part of a one-semester course—hardly enough time for novice writers to fully initiate themselves into an unfamiliar discourse community. Many of Gullion's students felt overwhelmed by the tasks before them, or simply did not have enough time to do as in-depth a project as they would have liked. In my own first-year composition class, I often embed a writing-for group project in a course focused primarily on the academic essay. Like Gullion's students, mine sometimes feel overwhelmed or rushed when a real-world project is slotted for completion in only a few weeks. This concern is reflected in the advice of many service-learning practitioners that instructors carefully select projects which do not require too much background knowledge or rhetorical sophistication, but which are still challenging and no less "real" (Bacon, "Community Service Writing"; Watters and Ford, *Guide*; Cooper and Julier, *Writing*). For the sake of both students and community partners, instructors need to filter out projects beyond the grasp of undergraduates; but this does not mean watering down the projects so that they look like tidy textbook assignments. Much like genuine workplace writing, writing for the community almost always brings with it some risk, uncertainty, and unpredictability. This needs to be viewed as an opportunity rather than a liability. As Dewey reminds us, student confusion in response to an unfamiliar situation is often the most productive starting point for learning.

Writing-for Projects and Nonacademic Writing Theory

Because writing-for-the-community projects generally demand that students compose documents for constituencies both inside and outside the academy, they raise complex issues addressed in current scholarly dialogues on nonacademic and professional writing. Over the past fifteen years, scholarship on nonacademic writing has flourished, deepening our understanding of relationships between academy and workplace, cognition and context, and theory and practice. Most notable among such scholarship is the trend toward social constructivist understandings of knowledge, language, writing, and rhetoric.

Certainly the "social perspective" can be discerned in the history of rhetoric, as Bruce Herzberg attests in tracing a genealogy of social constructivist rhetoric in the broad sweep of western intellectual history from the Greek sophists through Francis Bacon, Giambattista Vico, George Campbell, and Friedrich Nietzsche ("Rhetoric"). Within the scope of rhetoric and composition as an academic discipline, a fitting starting place is Lester Faigley's 1985 essay "Nonacademic Writing: The Social Perspective" in Lee Odell and Dixie Goswami's *Writing in Nonacademic Settings*, often cited as the first major book in composition studies attending to workplace discourses. Faigley distinguishes the "individual" and "textual" perspectives on language research from the "social" perspective, which investigates "how individual acts of communication define, organize and maintain social groups" (235). This theoretical orientation pervades more recent collections like Carolyn Matelene's *Worlds of Writing: Teaching and Learning in Discourse Communities of Work* (1989), Charles Bazerman and James Paradis's *Textual Dynamics of the Professions: Historical and Contemporary Studies of Writing in Professional Communities* (1991), Nancy Blyler and Charlotte Thralls's *Professional Communication: The Social Perspective* (1993), Rachel Spilka's *Writing in the Workplace: New Research Perspectives* (1993), and Katherine Staples and Cezar M. Ornatowski's *Foundations for Teaching Technical Communication: Theory, Practice, and Program Design* (1997).

Among the defining characteristics of the social perspective on writing research are a rejection of positivism and an embrace of rhetorically constructed linguistic communities, or discourse communities (see Blyler and Thralls 3–34). In a similar vein, Tyler Bouldin and Lee Odell have suggested "a systems theory perspective" on writing research in the workplace. This theoretical tion.[4] Furthermore, students need to read the culture of the agency and learn the protocol for meetings, dress, oral presentation, computer design, and follow-up on projects in process (c.f. Deans and Meyer-Goncalves; Lipson, "Technical" and "Teaching"). Gullion makes this need explicit to her students both in class and in individual conferences. It is also evident in the way she forms student assignment groups, attempting to balance both social and writerly proficiencies in work groups (i.e., both a "people person" and an able editor in each team), and insuring that each group of two or three has at least one computer-savvy member.

In our interview, Gullion noted that she sent students out into the community not simply as writers but as "representatives of the [sport management] department." She coached them "right down to the details of how to walk into a meeting," and was careful to state that they were, in her words, expected to function as professionals in human relations, even if not expert writers. These expectations, at least with respect to interpersonal relations, were "not pre-professional—we're talking about professional starting right now." Relating the story of a group of students feeling overdressed in the first meeting as an example of their anxiety in forming a professional client relationship for the first time, Gullion remarked in our interview that "those are small but important areas for them in terms of development."[5]

This is not to imply that Gullion downplays the teaching of textual conventions and skills—far from it. She devotes a large portion of the semester to teaching the genres and textual dimensions of nonacademic writing: résumé, cover letter, memo, proposal, publicity packet, personality profile, biographical sketch. She taught these genres, as well as some grammar and usage, before initiating the service-learning projects because, in her words, "I wanted to give them a good enough prep through all of those writing assignments" before risking the agency project. Thus Writing in Sport Management was about students learning textual conventions of professional documents, but also about novices entering, even if only temporarily, professional relationships and discourse communities.

The centrality of the social perspective on composing for nonacademic contexts is evidenced in Gullion's remark that students' success depended as much on their social interactions with agency contacts as on their writing skills. She explains: "If inter-actions with community contacts were not good, the projects were not good. . . . I think that one of the major things that makes these projects successful is how well people get along with their contacts." This conclusion was confirmed during student in-class group presentations at the end of the semester. All the groups devoted substantial presentation time to discussing their social interactions with agency contacts—some praising the dedi-cation of competence of their supervisors and collaborators, and others bemoaning their lack of availability or guidance. As a fur-ther indication of Gullion's attentiveness to the social perspective on composing, she cited social factors, like gender, as key factors in the writing process. For example, she noted that "the people who had difficulty with team members were the guys. And the people who were able to resolve conflicts were the women. . . . Guys rumbled in their logs, while the women benefited from the group-conflict-resolution class lecture." While Gullion did not pursue this line of thinking further, she did clearly recognize the importance of accounting for gender, an issue that merits more attention as service-learning scholarship matures (see Novek; Foos).

In concert with the major premises of contemporary nonaca-demic writing theory, Gullion's course, and her perceptions of it, reveal that comprehending the differences between academic and nonacademic *texts* is not enough; teachers and students must rec-ognize, and respond to, the movement between specific academic and workplace *contexts*.

Audience and Audiences

In my experience, the reason teachers most often cite for being initially attracted to service-learning writing pedagogies—particu-larly those which fall in the writing-for category—is the prospect of students writing for an authentic audience beyond the class-room. Indeed, this factor first attracted me to service-learning, and Laurie Gullion cites it as her primary justification for intro-ducing writing-for projects into her Writing in Sport Manage-ment course. Even for those like the founders of the Michigan

State Service-Learning Writing Project, who, in addition to audience, foreground other reasons including civic literacy, critical consciousness, and social change, audience remains a compelling justification for community-based learning. In this section I explore traditional understandings of audience in rhetoric and composition, analyze writing-for projects which articulate their main purpose as writing for "real" nonacademic audiences, and problematize conceptions of audience which rely too heavily on the nonacademic/academic, real/unreal binaries. My goal is to move beyond oversimple conceptions of audience and toward more textured understandings of audience in relation to community writing.

Early composition scholars like James Britton and James Moffett critiqued writing assignments void of personal investment or meaningful connection to audience—what they sometimes referred to as "dummy runs." As Moffett points out, "The dissociation in the minds of students between school stuff and writing for real is one of the deep and widespread symptoms that has made English teaching ripe for reform" (207). This remains a concern for compositionists today, particularly for service-learning advocates like those at Arizona State University, who celebrate community-based writing as a solution to "empty assignment syndrome" (Brack and Hall 143). I recognize the logic of such claims about audience, and I see them at work in my own students' evaluations of community writing projects in service-learning composition courses, where comments on audience surface repeatedly. For example, one student found the service-learning projects in my course different because they "would be seen by people other than my classmates." Another comments, "The main difference between the community service writing project and the other writing this semester is the audience. The process (revising, etc.) was the same, but I had to keep in mind that I was writing for a large, probably uninformed audience." And another, "Working to meet the standards of a professional magazine was much more challenging than regular essays. Knowing that my work was to be published in a magazine read by people around the world was difficult."

Since Aristotle, audience has been a favorite concern for rhetoricians, and contemporary writing theory ranges from arguments that student writers tend to be insufficiently cognizant of audience (Booth) or overly concerned with it too early in the writing process (Elbow, "Closing"). Lisa Ede, surveying theoretical and empirical scholarship from a variety of disciplines (rhetoric, cognitive psychology, composition, speech, communication, and philosophy), concludes that "the teacher of writing that would have a sophisticated, productive understanding of audience faces a large task" (153; also see Kroll). Ede provides an overview of the long-standing tradition of audience analysis, from Aristotle's prescriptions to sociological and psychological approaches. Such modes of audience analysis usually play a role in writing-for projects, as when instructors prompt students to analyze the differences between academic and workplace audiences as well as the demographics and characteristics of the client target audience.

Some service-learning advocates imply that if we only put our students in more "authentic" purpose-driven rhetorical situations (like writing for agencies), then audience will suddenly transform for novice writers from a general, anonymous academic concept to a clear and compelling singularity (the agency director, or the agency clients, for example). However, my own experience as a service-learning teacher and my observations of Gullion's course lead me to conclude that the most immediate outcome students experience when they suddenly switch from writing for an academic audience to writing for a nonacademic audience is not rhetorical but motivational. After the initial disorientation discussed earlier, students generally *feel* better about what they are doing and often articulate a renewed investment in their writing. Writing for a community agency often means more to students than writing for a teacher and jockeying for a good grade. Some of my former students have remarked on this effect in their course evaluations:

◆ "It felt good knowing it [the project] was for a good worthwhile cause."

◆ "This time, it is not a matter of A/B/C/D/F. Instead, it is a matter of a job I must do for a good cause. There is no room for error."

◆ "We had to please someone else with our writing other than our teacher. Our writing essays probably wouldn't be seen by anybody outside of class but my service project is going to be seen by many people."

Nora Bacon reports analogous findings in her perceptive study of students doing service-learning as part of a writing course. Upon reviewing the essays written by fifty students whose teachers had asked them, at semester's end, to reflect on their writing-for-the-community projects, she concludes: "Overwhelmingly, students discussed Community Service Writing as a social experience. Their essays barely touched on the creation of texts" (*Transition* 114). Instead, the students opted to discuss what they had learned about their community organizations, about themselves as members of a larger community, and about their "new, more authoritative" or "professional" roles.

A student I interviewed from Gullion's class offered similar reflections on his motivation for community-based writing in comparison to academic writing:

> Doing work for community [agencies] that need it—that's probably what makes it [the service-learning writing project] different. . . . Laurie saw that and said, "Look, this is a great opportunity for students to apply themselves and learn what they have to learn," and it's almost like, yeah, you can look at it and say, "Ahh, shit, I have to do this now, and I don't want to. Why can't I just get by with it." But it gives you a sense of reality. And at the same time, all those communities benefit from it. It's kind of like a plus/plus, win/win situation. . . . I think if you overall as a person can help the community, it's an overall plus.

In such self-reflections we catch glimpses of how a change in rhetorical exigency can dramatically affect a student's sense of investment.[6] This is no small matter. "Interest," or internal motivation, functions as a key concept in Dewey's theory of learning. Russian psychologist Lev Vygotsky also reminds us that we should not underestimate the power of motivation, which he describes as "the most secret internal plane of verbal thinking." Motivation is vital, Vygotsky claims, because it is so intimately bound to social context and because it serves as a precursor for cognition and learning: "Thought has its origins in the motivating sphere of consciousness, a sphere that includes our inclinations and needs, our interests and impulses, and our affect and emotion" (282). If we, like Vygotsky, acknowledge motivation as a key factor in learning, then community writing projects that spark student motivation deserve our attention.

Awareness of the differences between academic and nonacademic audiences and genres (and some general consequences that these differences hold for composing) is generally concurrent with or soon to follow changes in motivation. And while such meta-awareness of audience is valuable and helpful, students need just as much instruction and coaching (often more) to produce a rhetorically successful brochure as they need to produce a rhetorically successful academic essay. Although renewed motivation is a significant asset, the road to rhetorical competence in a new discourse community like a nonprofit agency is no less arduous than is the road to rhetorical competence in an academic discipline. The experience of Gullion's students and the thrust of Margaret Mansfield's essay "Real World Writing and the English Curriculum" remind us that changing the scene of student writing from classroom to workplace generally does *not* simplify notions of audience or the writing process.

Mansfield describes a course she taught, Writing for the Public, in which students reviewed the Writing Proficiency Exam (WPE) at the University of Massachusetts Boston (UMB) for a faculty senate committee. The project involved designing and conducting surveys, analyzing results, and writing a report. By the end of the course, Mansfield concluded that her students had questioned "the 'single audience' assumptions underlying most students' perceptions of the academic [and workplace] writing situation" and developed a "new awareness for multiple audiences," as suggested by the comment of one of her students: "We wrote for several different audiences—ourselves, our classmates, our professor, the UMB faculty, and the WPE Committee—with different purposes in mind: for self-discovery, for the sharing of ideas, for grades, for the collection of data, and for the approval of our superior, the WPE Committee" (73). Mansfield ultimately concludes, very much in the spirit of service-learning advocates, that "It was [the] interplay between 'real world' writing experience and academic reflection and analysis that provided the most valuable insights for my students and me" (71).

Another key essay which complicates any oversimple use of the term audience is Douglas B. Park's "The Meanings of 'Audience.'" Park unpacks the multiple meanings and abstract concepts gathered into the term and concludes that 'audience' essentially refers not to people as such but to those apparent aspects of knowledge and motivation in readers and listeners that form the contexts for discourse and the ends of discourse" (160). He distinguishes between meanings of audience that rely on people external to the text and those that stress how audience is implied or invoked by the text itself (a project carried out in depth by Ede and Lunsford, "Audience Addressed/Audience Invoked"). Park then goes further, delineating four particular meanings of audience in order to confirm the complexity and ambiguity of the term:

1. Anyone who happens to listen to or read a given discourse.

2. External readers or listeners as they are involved in the rhetorical situation.

3. The set of conceptions or awareness in the writer's consciousness that shape the discourse as something to be read or heard.

4. An ideal conception shadowed forth in the way the discourse itself defines and creates contexts for readers. (161)

Park closes his essay with an insight particularly pertinent to the theory and practice of writing-for-the-community projects: "[It] seems important to note that audience is elusive in much teaching of writing not only because the concept itself is difficult. A fully serious art of rhetoric and a concomitant sophistication with audience—like that found in the classical rhetorics—must grow from a clear understanding of the kinds of discourse to be served and their purpose in society. Our composition courses generally do not operate with such an understanding" (168).[7]

I find Park's observations convincing. In most college writing classrooms, students write essays at the prompting of the teacher, for the purpose of a grade, and for an audience of one (the teacher, in the case of many classrooms) or of peers (in the case of teachers who publish student writing). Only indirectly, through the rhetorical skills students will employ outside the classroom, does student writing usually find currency in the world of discourse beyond the curriculum. If we define rhetoric as practical and purposeful discourse that gets things done in authentic social situations, then service-learning writing projects can be a vital complement to the academic and expressive discourses generally included in writing courses—and even encourage the complex comprehension of audience that Park anticipates when assignments, like community writing assignments, "grow from a clear understanding of the kinds of discourse to be served and their purpose in society."

While not approximating the sophistication of Park's analysis, the understanding of audience demonstrated by Gullion's students included, and went beyond, simple audience analysis. Certainly, all the student writers had, and were aware of, a "target audience"—for example, inexperienced coaches who would be using the first-aid manual, or 13–16-year-old girls who would be reading a nutrition pamphlet. Through audience analysis, the student groups inferred predictable and helpful writing goals, such as the need to include very basic information and write in an accessible style ("we had to make it easy to read"). But audience matters became more complex as, like Mansfield's students, Gullion's students needed to consider multiple audiences—for example, "a brochure for children who fear summer camps, and also for parents." Attendant to all the projects was the fact (even if not always explicitly recognized) that the document would be written as much (perhaps more) for the agency contact person as for the agency constituency(ies). Gullion recognized this: "It's a dual audience—the coordinator they're working with, and the audience for the piece they're actually producing." Furthermore, students could not help but consider Laurie Gullion as an audience since, as their teacher, she would ultimately grade them.[8]

There were also instances in which students were prompted to "invoke" characteristics in their audience (Ong; Ede and Lunsford), as when a group was instructed to express in their brochure (and thus encourage in their readers) the "spirit and philosophy" of a sports league which was focused more on fun than on competition. Genre, particularly the brochure and manual formats, also shaped both writer and audience expectations. Although not often aware of it (and usually realizing it only after several agency meetings), students doing these writing-for projects were grappling with the multiple meanings and exigencies of audience as outlined by Park.

It is tempting to argue, as Paul Heilker does, that replacing traditional academic assignments with writing for "real" audiences will lead college writing to a more authentic rhetoric. To a degree, I concur. But, of course, what counts for "real" is relative. Some define anything nonacademic or non-ivory-tower as "real" (as in the "real world" students enter upon graduation); others argue that nothing could be more "real"—in the lives of students, that is—than school; and still others argue that creative and essayistic writing are more "real" (as in "really important") than memos, brochures, or reports. The experience of my own, Gullion's, and Mansfield's students suggests that although employing dichotomies such as real/unreal and nonacademic/academic can be useful in making broad initial distinctions and motivating students (and therefore should not be completely abandoned), such binaries must ultimately yield to more complex and textured understandings of audience and discourse. As Nora Bacon concludes about her experience teaching service-learning courses, "The distinction between the artificial classroom and the real world is overly simplistic; really, students are being asked to write for both a teacher and a community audience" ("Community Service Writing" 43). Whether writing an academic essay or a first-aid manual, the larger rhetorical questions persist for each writer: How do I read and participate in my social context? How should I respond to my multiple audiences? How do I (and my collaborators) define and solve the problem before me (us)? Which rhetorical strategies and textual conventions will serve me (us) well in this particular situation?

Heeding Dewey, an enemy of entrenched dichotomies, service-learning educators need to comprehend both the dialectic of and continuities between the academy and the workplace, school and society. The same goes for academic and nonacademic writing processes. Because it deliberately straddles the academy and community, service-learning writing as practiced in Writing in Sport Management—more than either academic or professional writing alone—stands poised to make the most of Dewey's school and society dialectic as well as Mansfield's "interplay" between academic and nonacademic conceptions of audience, writing, and learning.

Writing for the Community and the Ends of Service-Learning

If we agree with Shirley Brice Heath that "learners are preparing for adulthood in a world of work and public services that differs radically from that of the centuries in which our expectations of the essay originated" ("Rethinking" 107), then service-learning projects in the writing-for vein are particularly fitting for composition classrooms. They also steer classroom learning toward Dewey's goals of experiential learning and the closer alignment of school learning with contemporary social demands. And while at first glance this might seem to entail demoting a venerable belletristic heritage, service-learning can also be perceived as a return to the classical rhetorical tradition of employing pragmatic discourse toward the aim of participating in the public affairs of a community.

As charted in the typology in Chapter 1, and as confirmed in large measure by my study of Gullion's course, writing-for-the-community projects—like those undertaken at Stanford University (Watters and Ford, *Guide*; Bacon, "Instruction"), The University of Massachusetts (Deans and Meyer-Goncalves), Louisiana State University (Dorman and Dorman), Virginia Tech (Heilker), Michigan State University (Cooper and Julier, *Writing*), The University of Utah (Huckin), Southwest Missouri State University (Henson and Sutliff), and Winona State University (Eddy and Carducci), as well as many others—align with a paradigm in which the most important goals are that students learn nonacademic writing practices, compose a needed document for an agency client, and reflect on community needs. Workplace discourse is most highly valued; the movement between functional and academic literacies is required; the learning relationship between student and agency contact person is most emphasized (at least during the project); and the primary site for learning is off-campus at the nonprofit agency (again, for that portion of the semester devoted to the project).

As with all kinds of service-learning, it is important to acknowledge limits and shortcomings along with potentials and successes. In a review of several anthologies and monographs on nonacademic writing scholarship, Alan Gross points to the danger that in their "principled drift away from the humanities," workplace writing researchers leave themselves open to ignoring the "ethical, social and political implications of their work" (829). The same charge could be leveled at the instrumentalist bent of writing-for pedagogies—that is, while doing good work for community agencies, writing-for students function as subcontractors in a flawed social service system (c.f. McKnight). In fact, C. David Lisman criticizes this kind of service-learning as based on a consumerist "weak democracy" philosophy rather than a communitarian "strong democracy" philosophy. As I discuss in Chapter 4, Bruce Herzberg views the instrumental bent of writing-for pedagogies as potentially complicit in American conceptions of individualism and meritocracy that serve to mask the systemic causes of social injustice.

This line of critical thought is worth exploring. Among the kinds of community writing I address in this study, writing-for projects are generally the quickest to adapt to the dominant rhetorics and ideologies of the workplace. While service-learning approaches informed by Marxism or radical pedagogy tend to frown on such accommodation to the status quo in preference for an antihegemonic academic rhetoric (as we will see in Chapter 4), and those inspired by neopragmatism and intercultural collaboration tend to articulate a combination of social policy and language reform goals (as we will see in Chapter 5), writing-for advocates celebrate the emerging capacity of novice writers to effectively negotiate new, useful, and culturally privileged workplace discourses.

Rather than adopt cultural critique as the centerpiece of social action, writing-for courses generally prefer cooperation with established social service networks (nonprofit agencies) as the most appropriate means of social action. Of course, teachers need not see this as a stark "either/or" choice. One can emphasize both critique *and* nonprofit work, but the limits of university teaching (there's never enough time in one semester to do it all) dictate that instructors prioritize. Writing-for courses, complete with community partners waiting for the final products on deadline, tend to prioritize getting the project done, and done well. To draw on Deweyan and Freirean vocabularies, writing-for projects tend to align more closely with the Deweyan ideal of pursuing cooperative, project-based learning that participates in a reformist ideology than with the Freirean ideal of cultivating a critical consciousness that participates in a radical ideology.

While the rhetorical demands of writing for community agencies often crowd out time for extensive dialogue on structural change, they do still offer significant opportunities for ethical and civic reflection. Initiatives within the writing-for paradigm certainly vary in their ethical register and in their reflective goals. The Service-Learning Writing Project at Michigan State University, for example, pairs an agency project with extensive study of the American intellectual tradition of civic involvement and social change (see Cooper and Julier, *Writing* and "Democratic"). Such projects remind us that the goals of completing an agency project and fostering critical consciousness need not be exclusive or contradictory. Similarly, courses on many campuses complement agency projects with essay assignments and classroom discussions that extend the reflective domain beyond the rhetorical concerns of getting a real-world project done. However, some writing-for initiatives that focus almost exclusively on rhetorical goals trust that the experience of writing for an agency in need, combined with limited structured reflection (like a journal), are adequate for encouraging ethical reflection in students.

Writing in Sport Management illustrates how each instructor has a hand in deciding which kinds of reflection are likely to prevail in a particular course. Gullion devoted the bulk of her efforts to helping her students meet the rhetorical goals of negotiating professional relationships and composing quality products for nonacademic audiences. But she also hoped that the experience of venturing off-campus, working with committed agency personnel, and seeing their writing serve a practical purpose in the community would prompt students to reflect on the collaborative process, on community needs, and on the personal rewards of service—and indeed, most students did reflect on these issues in their journals and in class discussions. Gullion is committed to the notion that citizens should be actively involved in improving their communities, but she chose not to steer reflection toward the ideological concerns that advocates of critical pedagogy might prefer; instead she concentrated her teaching time on the projects themselves. Thus, when she asked students to discuss their perspectives on service in their final oral presentations, they did not display the kind of ready vocabulary for systemic social critique that is developed and encouraged in courses focused on ideology, critical reading, or cultural studies. Most groups opted to address the rhetorical and interpersonal aspects of their projects rather than larger questions of social justice.

Gullion's course tended to encourage reflection on the writing, learning, and collaborative processes. (How does writing for college courses differ from writing for your agency? What did you learn? How did your group function?) As noted in sections above, students reflected on changes in both motivational and rhetorical processes when they wrote for real-world audiences. Gullion reported such an account to me in an interview:

> A woman on the University of Massachusetts basketball team, a poor writer and shy student, helped create what evolved into a comprehensive coaching manual for the Amherst Youth Basketball League. She wrote movingly about being valued for her academic abilities, not just her "dumb jock" athletic abilities. Her knowledge of basketball gave her the confidence with content and helped her make her writing concise and clear.

Students in writing-for-the-community courses are also generally encouraged to reflect on community needs as defined by the agencies: Who does the agency serve, and how might we best meet the needs of that constituency? The following selected student reflections reveal a widening awareness of community needs:

> ◆ When I was growing up we never did too much in the community. . . . We never went out of our way. . . . But doing work for community things that need it—that's probably what makes it [the service-learning writing project] different.

◆ We learned that there are a lot of people in Amherst serving the community that we didn't know about.

Finally, students in writing-for courses tend to reflect on the personal and affective rewards of service: How did providing the agency with a useful document make you feel as a writer? As a citizen? When asked what makes service-learning writing different from technical writing done for profit, Gullion emphasized the *personal rewards* for students as writers and contributing citizens. She believed that working with for-profit organizations or corporations would have changed the character of the project. She reflected:

> I think—and from the writing logs—that students in the class felt genuinely rewarded by being able to help out an agency. These were not "make work" tasks. There was a legitimate need. And the fact that they knew they were dealing with some underfunded agencies was pretty apparent. And I think they were aware of it and felt good about being about to offer these particular services. I think there would have been a different slant on the project if it had been for a for-profit agency. . . . Student satisfaction was not only about the nature of the work but also about what they were providing.

Such reflections also loop back and confirm my earlier analysis of writing for community agency audiences as a motivational (as well as a textual) matter.

Writing-for courses, therefore, generally reflect on the learning process, on community needs, and on personal rewards. In contrast, as will be evident in later chapters, writing-about courses tend to reflect abstractly on the nature of systemic social and ideological forces (class, race, gender), and writing-with courses tend to reflect on strategic local change and the rhetoric of collaboration.

In addition to advancing compelling rhetorical goals, the writing-for-the-community approach to college composition encourages meaningful connections between school and society, knowledge and experience, and individual and community. Many argue that writing for the community is the most effective, most pragmatic, most needed version of service-learning. It tends to de-emphasize the abstract cultural critique of writing-about initiatives and the intercultural rhetoric of writing-with efforts; but it moves students quickly into new discourse communities where they can provide immediate and useful service to understaffed agencies in genuine need. Furthermore, the documents students produce advance the missions of the agencies and move readily into the public sphere. In the classroom, writing for nonprofit agencies opens an opportunity for meta-discourse about audience and about differences among discourse communities. The writing-for approach also helps students learn vital social competencies (reading audiences and work cultures, adopting professional codes, collaborating with peers and supervisors) and textual skills which will serve them well in their lives after college (adapting to new genres, employing concise language, integrating text and graphics).

Well-designed and well-executed programs like Gullion's also tend to be applauded not only by students but also by community partners. In fact, a recent nationwide study of service-learning at twenty-eight institutions reveals that, on the whole, host agencies were "extremely satisfied" with the contributions of student volunteers (Gray, Ondaatje, and Zakaras vi). The following comments are characteristic of Gullion's written community partner evaluations:

- ◆ This was a wonderful project. I was left with 2 informative brochures for the summer program.

- ◆ [The product was] very professionally designed; well organized handbook.

- ◆ Overall, the program is a good one. For all 3 projects that I have, it is a good step in the right direction. None of the final projects will be distributed, but will be used as guidelines/blueprints for the products that will be given out.

- ◆ This [coaching manual] (with a few minor changes) will be used this season!

As evident from the two latter statements (and confirmed by my own experience), even the best programs will result in some projects that are subpar in quality or which remain unfinished or unused. Students are still students, after all, and not professional writers.[9]

Despite generally favorable reviews by teachers, students, and community partners, writing-for initiatives still face several key challenges if they are to flourish beyond the experiments currently under way. The three most pressing challenges include institutional support, the matching of student ability to project difficulty, and assessment.

At the institutional level, one must consider the basic feasibility of writing-for initiatives in the university, including English departments, as currently configured. Such courses tend to be praised by students and the general public, and the current surge of interest in service-learning among faculty and administrators is encouraging. But such courses also require a great deal of extra faculty effort and time, which presents a problem to instructors already pressed for time. There are also serious questions about whether institutional support will be sustained over the long term (Zlotkowski, "Linking"; Deans, "Writing Across the Curriculum"; Morton, "Issues"). Will community-based writing instruction be the latest educational fad or a meaningful part of the curriculum? The grant that launched the service-learning component of the Writing in Sport Management course not only prompted Gullion to experiment with a new pedagogy but also allowed her to hire a teaching assistant. As is often repeated by service-learning educators, such forms of institutional support—funding (beyond soft money), additional personnel to initiate and maintain relations with community partners, and a well-staffed community outreach office on campus—are critical to long-term program viability. Because writing-for courses venture beyond the traditional curriculum, they also require more time for planning, more time for building and maintaining relationships with community partners, and more time to troubleshoot the many unanticipated exigencies that surface when students work off-campus and write beyond the curriculum. Because Gullion did not have the funding for a teaching assistant during the semesters following the one studied here, she had neither the time nor the staff to properly plan a course with multiple agency projects and was (to her disappointment) forced to drastically limit the service-learning component of subsequent Writing in Sport Management sections.[10] A more fitting institutional support structure is evident (as will be discussed in the following chapter) in the Bentley College Service-Learning Project, which helps instructors initiate and maintain community relationships, offers advice for first-time practitioners, and provides curriculum materials, financial backing, and the encouragement of like-minded colleagues.

Another key challenge for writing-for-the-community pedagogies is finding the right "fit" between student abilities and agency needs. First-year composition remains the most-taught course in U.S. higher education and the place where most service-learning writing initiatives are launched. For this student cohort, new to the university community and often lacking in writing competency, taking on real-world agency projects, even when supported by instructors and patient agency contacts, can exceed their rhetorical means. Certainly there are success stories; but I fear that our failures are less acknowledged than they should be, and I maintain that college writing instructors should be careful not to draw on the time (and good intentions) of community partners without offering a readily useful document in return. Recently I spoke with a community agency contact who had sponsored several projects from University of Massachusetts writing courses (including my own), and she was quite explicit in how much more useful a junior from an upper-division writing course had been in comparison to any of the first-year students.

Based on my experience in teaching several versions of first-year and upper-division service-learning courses, as well as my review of Gullion's course and others like it, it is my judgment that the writing-for approach can work quite well in first-year courses, so long as instructors follow a few key guidelines: filter out overly difficult projects (or break them down into manageable components); match students well with their interests (and with each other in groups); and monitor progress regularly, insuring that agencies are well served. Still, I believe writing-for projects are generally better suited to settings like the WAC course studied in this chapter, as well as to upper-level technical writing classes (see also Henson and Sutliff, who recommend writing-for projects as most fitting for upper-division courses). Such courses most often include students in their junior or senior years, and by then students have matured in both their writing and social abilities, have become more knowledgeable in their chosen areas of study, and stand poised to enter professional as well as disciplinary discourse communities.

Once service-learning courses are under way, assessment stands out as another major challenge. Since the kinds of documents students produce depart from the conventional essay—and the ways students go about completing projects often departs from conventional teaching protocol—the introduction of service-learning can upset the traditional student-teacher relation as well as standard modes of assessment. Even without the addition of a community-based or nonacademic component, writing assessment is a complex, uncertain, and difficult task. Yet if we are to partner in a spirit of reciprocity with community agencies, they must be given authority in the assessment process, which further complicates assessment. Many knotty questions then surface, such as: To what standards do we hold students undertaking difficult projects in new genres? How do academic teachers evaluate nonacademic writing? What formal or informal role should the community agencies play in grading? What happens when the evaluations from the teacher and the community partner conflict? For me, assessment is still a work in progress, most often taking the form of a hybrid of traditional academic grading and agency input (through both formal written evaluations and informal conversations).

Based on my experience with service-learning composition courses, the testimony of other teachers, and Gullion's Writing in Sport Management course, I see continued promise in writing-for-the-community initiatives. They not only have a surprising motivational effect on students but also are consistent with the trajectory of socially-focused writing theory. They offer students complex and purposeful rhetorical tasks, enrich experiential learning, widen the diversity of discourses included in our curricula, and make material contributions to the needs of local communities.

Writing about the Community: Critical Pedagogy, Academic Literacy, and First-Year Composition

In some sense, in the simplest sense, all I'm doing is trying to make sure that when they [my students] write these papers, they don't isolate things—they don't isolate the topic as a purely academic exercise.

BRUCE HERZBERG, personal interview

When visiting Bruce Herzberg's Expository Writing I: Summary and Synthesis course at Bentley College, I arrived early and found a few students milling about. In the minutes before Herzberg and the other students arrived, I introduced myself and asked them to share any initial thoughts on whether this course differed from others they were taking. One woman remarked, "In this class, we do more critical thinking."

This chapter discusses Bruce Herzberg's Bentley College composition courses as exemplars of service-learning courses designed to write *about* the community—that is, courses which ask students to do community service and then reflect on their community-based experiences in writing. The kinds of outreach students do vary widely (tutoring youth is a favorite) but the service itself generally does not involve writing (as with the writing-for-the-community approach). The kinds of reflection prompted by the instructor also vary widely, from a focus on processing the powerful emotions prompted by community involvement to critical analysis of the root social forces that put people in need.

Herzberg's writing-about-the-community course is centered on critical analysis. It includes community service work, emphasizes a rhetoric of cultural critique, and aims for improved academic and critical literacies. In contrast to the writing-for projects discussed in the previous chapter, Herzberg's students do not perform writing *as* service for nonacademic audiences. Rather, they tutor at a local elementary school and bring their experiences, like texts ripe for analysis, into composition classes focused on themes of literacy and schooling.

The empirical material for this chapter is gathered from interviews with Herzberg, visits to his class, email interviews with several of his students, and a review of his course materials. I also include the scholarship Herzberg has published on his own service-learning courses. The conceptual dimensions of the chapter are drawn from the traditions of critical pedagogy and critical theory, including some figures with whom Herzberg self-identifies, and others I introduce because they contextualize and illuminate writing-about-the-community practices. I situate my analysis of the courses in relation to Dewey and Freire, proponents of critical pedagogy (like James Berlin, Ira Shor, and Henry Giroux), and debates in composition studies over the role of academic discourse.

The Bentley College service-learning courses I study follow a two-semester sequence and are part of a "learning community" through which the same group of students takes Herzberg's first-year courses in conjunction with a philosophy course in the fall and a sociology course in the spring. Before discussing Herzberg's writing-about-the-community courses, it is helpful to understand his institutional context, in brief. Bentley is a private, business-oriented college in suburban Boston. Starting in 1990, the college moved to make a serious institutional commitment to service-learning by establishing the Bentley College Service-Learning Project (BSLP), a cross-curricular effort to integrate academic study and community outreach. By 1995–96, service-learning had become "a campus culture," with forty service-learning courses across the curriculum, twelve of sixteen departments sponsoring or recognizing some kind of discipline-based service-learning, and over fifty full-time faculty participating. To support these activities, the college established a nationally recognized administrative support system, with the BSLP office at its center. Its staff includes a faculty director, a volunteer center coordinator, an internship coordinator, an administrative assistant, an administrative coordinator, graduate assistants, student assistants, and community service scholarship students.

According to it own publications, "the primary goal of the BSLP is educational; namely, to enhance our students' ability to function as liberally educated business professionals." More particularly, "it seeks to provide learning opportunities in the community" where students can

- ◆ get hands-on experience that both complements and supplements skills, techniques, and methodologies to which they have been introduced in the classroom;

- ◆ become sensitized to a variety of socioeconomic circumstances as well as a diverse population of individuals so that they are better able to function as citizens and business professionals in a complex, multicultural society;

- ◆ learn to appreciate the practical interconnectedness of the disciplines they study;

- ◆ develop a broader appreciation of the personal and professional value of their Bentley education, as well as habits of inquiry and action that will enable them to continue to learn and grow after graduation.

In addition, the BSLP articulates two "social goals":

- ◆ to help partnering organizations in Waltham and nearby communities serve their constituencies as effectively as possible,

- ◆ and to promote a more cohesive sense of on-campus community—not only by linking academic and nonacademic programs but also by actively encouraging all Bentley departments and all Bentley employees to become involved in community-based activities. (*Bentley*)

As an institution, Bentley offers a great deal of support for cross-curricular service-learning and welcomes a range of approaches. According to Jim Ostrow, Director of BSLP, faculty approaches to integrating service with disciplinary learning at Bentley are "wildly different." In order to keep a range of faculty involved, there is no quest for a "unified field theory" of service-learning. Some instructors, like Herzberg, emphasize cultural critique; others focus on civic virtue; still others prefer "hands-on" or "real world" projects.

Composition and the Tradition of Critique

Herzberg identifies his theoretical stance as rooted in the Left, influenced by such figures as Marx, Lukács, Foucault, Freire, and Eagleton. His approach to teaching resonates with critical pedagogy, which has its roots in neo-Marxist philosophy and educational theory. In this section I discuss critical pedagogy, and in particular the intersections of critical pedagogy and service-learning; in the next section I return to a detailed analysis of the Bentley sequence of service-learning composition courses.

The most cited figure in the scholarship of critical pedagogy is Paulo Freire, a kind of grandfather to the movement who has significantly influenced the work of such theorists as Henry Giroux, Stanley Aronowitz, Ira Shor, Donald Macedo, James Berlin, Peter McClaren, bell hooks, C. H. Knoblauch, and Lil Brannon. Because I have discussed Freire in Chapter 2, I will not revisit his educational philosophy in detail. Rather, I consider here the applications and implications of Freirean thought and of critical pedagogy for first-year college composition courses, particularly those with service-learning components.

Critical pedagogy adopts a radical perspective, departing not only from liberal humanism but also from popular conceptions of literacy instruction. In *Critical Teaching and the Idea of Literacy*, C. H. Knoblauch and Lil Brannon articulate four categories of literacy: functional, academic, cultural, and critical. Functional literacy aims to help learners assimilate dominant language and cultural practices (as in the call for "basic skills" and "job skills"); academic literacy aims to have students adopt the rhetoric of the university; and cultural literacy aims to have citizens learn dominant cultural knowledge and habits. Critical literacy, in contrast, concerns itself with power relations and the critique of oppressive cultural institutions and practices. C. H. Knoblauch explains:

Its agenda is to identify reading and writing abilities with a critical consciousness of the social conditions in which people find themselves, recognizing the extent to which language practices objectify and rationalize these conditions and the extent to which people with the authority to name the world dominate others whose voices they have been able to suppress. Literacy, therefore, constitutes a means to power, a way to seek political enfranchisement—not with the naive expectation that merely being literate is sufficient to change the distribution of prerogatives but with the belief that the ability to speak alone enables entrance to the arena in which power is contested. At stake, from this point of view, is, in principle, the eventual reconstituting of the class structure of American life, specifically a change of those capitalist economic practices that assist the dominance of particular groups. ("Literacy" 79)

Thus, the development of a Freirean "critical consciousness" that assists students in "reading the world and the word" is chief among the aims of critical pedagogy. Also woven into Knoblauch's pedagogy—and, as we will see, into Herzberg's as well—is what Freire terms "utopianism as a dialectical relationship between denouncing the present and announcing the future" (Shor and Freire 187).

Critical pedagogy, with its insistence on analysis of social context, is particularly concerned with its own social setting—the school. It relies heavily on theories of cultural reproduction that view the school as an institution that serves the interests of the dominant culture. However, most critical pedagogies offer the possibility of resistance, the possibility that, through critical teaching and learning, educators and students might participate in what Freire calls "the unveiling of reality." Greta Nemiroff notes that while critical pedagogues are certainly not uniform in their thinking, there is "virtual consensus" among them on the following:

1. The schools represent a powerful force of social, intellectual, and personal oppression.

2. The reasons for such oppression are rooted in the culture's history.

3. They represent a number of deeply held cultural values—hierarchy, conformity, success, materialism, control.

4. What is required for significant changes in the schools amounts to a fundamental transformation of the culture's consciousness. (Nemiroff 55; see also Purpel 19–20)

The idea that schools are sites for reproducing the dominant culture is certainly a major theme in Freire's work. Likewise, schooling and literacy constitute the central themes of Herzberg's courses Expository Writing I: Summary and Synthesis and Expository Writing II: Research and Rhetoric, which include student community service at a local public elementary school along with a pedagogy that encourages critiques of education through careful observation, classroom discussion, student writing and research, and the reading of such works as Mike Rose's *Lives on the Boundary* and Jonathan Kozol's *Savage Inequalities*. While skeptical that two first-year courses can denaturalize or, in Freire's term, desocialize prevailing myths of the American meritocracy and introduce students to the fullness of Freirean critical consciousness, Herzberg remarked in our interview: "Freire would be ideal, if we can get the students to a point where we can get students to think about their own education and their own social circumstances and see the way they themselves have been constrained by social forces—then that would be a Freirean moment." Even though the "Freirean moment" may not happen often, critical thinking in a Freirean vein is evident in the design and workings of the Bentley courses.

Because critical pedagogues hold to a bleak assessment of schooling as an institution, much hope is placed in the individual teacher. From the perspective of critical literacy, teachers must be "transformative intellectuals" who are not only interested in student success but also, according to Henry Giroux, "concerned in their teaching with linking empowerment—the ability to think and act critically—to a concept of social transformation." Giroux insists that "teaching for social transformation means educating students to take risks and to alter the grounds upon which life is lived. . . . [They must perceive the classrooms] as active sites of public intervention, where students and teachers learn to redefine the nature of critical learning and practice outside the imperatives of the corporate marketplace" ("Educational" 179).

Critical pedagogy has garnered a following in composition

studies, with many writing teachers looking to Freire or one of his many American interpreters. In its translation from a Third World practice to a U.S. practice, and then to the particular context of the college writing classroom (not to mention its melding with feminist pedagogy, cultural studies, and mainstream teaching methods), critical pedagogy has assumed many permutations. Ann Berthoff, one of Freire's earliest proponents in composition studies, emphasizes his phenomenology and its implications for writing and teaching processes ("Reading"). Later interpreters, such as James Berlin ("Freirean"), Patricia Bizzell, Victor Villanueva, and C. H. Knoblauch and Lil Brannon (*Critical*) focus on the ideological and curricular implications of Freire's work, as well as the connections between academic discourse and critical consciousness.

Nearly all composition courses (except those focused exclusively on grammar and usage), and nearly all service-learning composition courses, name "critical thinking" as a goal. "Critical" is a slippery adjective, and can stand for many things.[1] As noted in Chapter 3, the critically reflective component of writing-for courses is often more trained on discerning differences between academic and nonacademic contexts and discourses than on the social and political concerns of critical pedagogy. Certainly in community-based courses, where the realities of social injustice are immediate to students, some degree of reflection will follow. But as the next section demonstrates, Bruce Herzberg has a specific and deliberate idea of what constitutes critical reflection in his writing-about-the-community service-learning composition courses. His classes are designed not only to teach academic discourse but also to encourage new college students to critique dominant social institutions (particularly schools) and dominant attitudes (particularly the ubiquitous American faith in individualism and meritocracy).

Serving Academic and Critical Literacies: Expository Writing I and II at Bentley College

The syllabus for Herzberg's Expository Writing I: Summary and Synthesis informs students that the main goal of the course is "to help you learn how to read and write 'academic discourse,' the type of writing that occurs in the academic disciplines." The syllabus for Expository Writing II: Research and Rhetoric reads, "We continue our work on education in America with the goal of producing substantial individual research reports." In our interview, Herzberg characterized the classes as "basically standard research and argument" courses.

In the preceding chapters, I cite several justifications for expanding the college writing curriculum beyond the bounds of teaching academic discourse. Yet this is not a priority for Herzberg. With respect to first-year composition, he is little interested in such curricular arrangements. Referring to the Stanford University service-learning approach (which is somewhat similar to Gullion's Writing in Sport Management course and which falls under the writing-for-the-community paradigm), Herzberg commented: "I remain uninterested in the audience concerns of the Stanford model. . . . That may be an incorrect or ungenerous characterization because they certainly do some good things. But it may partly be that we're at Bentley, and the instrumental approach that's at the base of the Stanford model would play too much into the students' expectations at Bentley. . . . And I don't think that [first-year] Bentley students could do a very good job [for the agencies]." He goes on to justify his focus on academic discourse, stating that, "I can't *not* teach academic discourse. . . . They [college students] have to learn how to handle it." The emphasis on academic discourse is evident in the syllabi: exercises in summary, paraphrase, and synthesis; prompts for close readings of abstract sources; directed journal entries; instruction in academic research methods; and academic essay assignments.

The focus on academic discourse is also evident in student assessments of the courses. One student remarks, "[The] most important [things] learned, I guess, would be practicing writing papers and summaries." And another first-year student:

> The most important things we learned are definitely the skills that we will need in our coming years at Bentley. These are things such as learning to refute arguments, the organization of research papers, and carefully analyzing and dissecting complex statements in some of the books we read. I know this will

benefit me because I will need to know how to do these things next year and beyond.

Herzberg is a critical teacher, and as such he remains concerned about more than equipping students with academic discourse. His stance resonates with the philosophical commitments of critical literacy. In an essay reviewing the suspect history of schooling and curriculum, Herzberg points to critical and hopeful possibilities for composition: "Critical consciousness has been and continues to be a goal of the profession. Composition theory has itself become an exercise in critical consciousness, drawing the hidden curriculum into the open and facing its consequences. The contradictions of the curriculum and the society it serves are becoming familiar as themes in composition courses. This is as it should be" ("Composition" 116). Certainly, in his service-learning composition course, critical reflection on the role of schooling is a "familiar theme."

Aiming to nudge his students toward critical consciousness, Herzberg coaches them to widen their apprehension of social context, particularly with respect to understanding schools and educational policy. He explains: "They [students] know perfectly well that academic discourse doesn't directly intervene in public policy. . . . I want them to see that these issues are not purely academic, that there is a public policy issue at stake that affects actual lives." As with all service-learning courses, Herzberg works at constructing a bridge between the academic and public spheres—but the connection he pursues is primarily a *conceptual* one. Commenting in our interview on the relation of academic discourse goals to critical teaching goals, he articulated an inclination to move beyond academic discourse: "In some sense, in the simplest sense, all I'm doing is trying to make sure that when they [my students] write these papers, they don't isolate things—they don't isolate the topic as a purely academic exercise."

A similar motive for community-based learning is advanced by service-learning advocates at Arizona State University (ASU), who cite an analogous fear of "isolated" student writing—what they label "empty assignment syndrome."[2] Their experience suggests that connecting composition to the tutoring of at-risk youth remedies students' lack of engagement with course material (Brack and Hall; Hall). While both the Bentley and ASU courses fall squarely in the writing-about-the-community category, they value different literacies and work toward different goals. Both curricula aim at helping students to recognize the connections between the academic and social spheres. With respect to cognitive goals, however, Herzberg is most concerned with having students grasp the abstractions and then critically apply them to the social scene—working from the classroom *outward* to the community. In contrast, the ASU program is more concerned with remedying "empty assignment syndrome" by bringing community experiences into the classroom—working from the community experience *inward* to the classroom. ASU instructors find in community service the source of promising topics for student writing (as well as increased student motivation), while Herzberg sees the community-based portion of his course as a potential site, among others (like course readings), for the development of critical consciousness and academic discourse skills. Furthermore, Herzberg emphasizes that his course is not primarily intended to prepare better tutors (this is done, but outside of class time); at ASU, tutor training is a major goal of the courses (program administrators emphasize how the quality of student tutoring is improved through the coursework).

Herzberg's teaching goals pair academic literacy with critical literacy. I suspect that this was his stance long before integrating service-learning into his courses, and as a result he does not rely on community service to "bring an epiphany of critical consciousness" ("Community" 315). As he remarks in an essay based on his own service-learning courses, "I don't believe that questions about social structures, ideology and social justice are automatically raised by community service. From my own experience, I am quite sure they are not" ("Community" 309).

Facilitating critical literacy entails helping learners comprehend the social forces—among them class, gender, race, and ideology—that shape both our culture and the lives of individuals. Herzberg gives most attention to class issues. He explained this preference: "I think here [at Bentley] it is very hard for my students to talk about class. So if there is an essential cultural concern, I think for me it begins with class." Through critical readings of Mike Rose's *Lives on the Boundary*, Jonathan Kozol's *Savage*

Inequalities, and E. D. Hirsch's Cultural Literacy, as well as class discussion, directed writing assignments, and final research projects, he unpacks the social dimensions of literacy and schooling from a largely neo-Marxist perspective. "What I hope to focus on here," he writes, "is how difficult my students find it to transcend their own deeply ingrained belief in individualism and meritocracy in their analysis of the reasons for the illiteracy they see" ("Community" 311). This is, essentially, performing what Freire terms "desocialization," a key component of critical literacy. And while there is, as Herzberg writes, "no guarantee that students will go beyond the individual and symptomatic" assessment of social issues ("Community" 309), at least they will seriously and deliberately inquire into the social dimensions of literacy, schooling, and the topic each chooses for the final research paper which constitutes the culmination of the Expository Writing II: Research and Rhetoric course.

When I visited the service-learning section of Expository Writing I at Bentley in November 1996, the class members were discussing observations from one of their first sessions at Hamilton Elementary School in nearby Brighton. Sitting in a circle, students shared reflections from their journal writing. One student described his work with a Pakistani youngster who had communication problems. Another commented on seeing an all–African American kindergarten class—far from his own experience in rural New Hampshire. He also remarked on the strict orderliness of the class, in response to which Herzberg prompted the class to make a connection to Mike Rose's discussion of urban schooling in Lives on the Boundary. Other students shared reflections on special-education classes they observed. They described the "busy-work" handouts the children were assigned and the yawning and fidgeting of the kids; they also suggested that some children who were too capable for special reading classes were still being assigned there.

Herzberg prompted the students to compare their own grade-school experiences with what they observed at Hamilton. This discussion wandered through topics of student aggression, Attention Deficit Disorder (ADD), tracking, discipline, and a music class that seemed pointless. Herzberg flagged some topics— remediation, tracking, ADD—as ones that students might want to take up later as major research projects. He also steered students away from simply blaming teachers for the shortcomings they observed, suggesting that broader factors such as large class size and school funding were also factors. In an interview later that day, Herzberg commented, "They don't know just how good a discussion they had." Such discussions constitute the beginning stages of exploring what Freire would call a generative theme—in this case schooling—and are similar to the classroom discussions Ira Shor describes (and encourages) in *Critical Teaching and Everyday Life*.

On the surface, students seemed to be touching on a collection of matter-of-fact observations of school life in the United States. By the end of the following semester, the same students, having tutored weekly at the Hamilton School and participated further in their own ongoing writing instruction (paired with philosophy and sociology instruction), were undertaking major research projects that critically analyzed pressing social issues. Among the students with whom I communicated, paper topics included inquiry into the inequities in school funding, multicultural curriculum design, Ebonics, ADD, funding for Head Start programs, and busing as a response to racial segregation in schools. Although Herzberg does not require (or even encourage) students to do research projects related to their tutoring experiences, these research topics seem to be motivated by the community service experience and to draw directly on that experience as a primary source. The students undertake in-depth, critical-consciousness-oriented projects that require them to integrate primary, secondary, and popular media sources. One first-year student reflects:

> I am writing my paper on the topic of Ebonics or African-American Vernacular English (AAVE). So far it is going well, I am only waiting for my first-hand research from the Hamilton school so that I might complete my paper. I asked the teachers if Ebonics instruction could be used in the Boston area. Is there actually a linguistic problem locally, and would this type of teaching help? . . . Since we are only working on one paper this semester, a lot of effort is put into it. For example, I have used over forty sources for this paper, which is different than high school or any other class at Bentley.

In his much-cited essay "Community Service and Critical Teaching," Herzberg describes an earlier version of his service-learning composition course, also focused on the theme of literacy, but in which the service component involved tutoring adults at a homeless shelter rather than children at an elementary school. For that course, Herzberg writes, "Most of the students did not incorporate the tutoring experience into the research papers they wrote or my class." He goes on to assert, "This was as it should be: The goal of the course was not . . . to facilitate the tutoring experience but to investigate the social and cultural existence of illiteracy—the reasons, in other words, that the students needed to perform the valuable service they were engaged in" (316).

Student research projects for the Expository II: Research and Rhetoric course are perhaps the most visible manifestation of student investigation into the "social and cultural existence of illiteracy." Unlike the writing-for projects described in Chapter 3, or the writing-with projects to be analyzed in the next chapter, these research papers are *not* public documents. They are *about* pressing social issues, but written in a rhetoric of academic critique and argument, and intended for an academic audience, primarily the teacher.

As the student's comment about using more than forty sources suggests, the research papers Herzberg assigns tend to be more complex and lengthy than ordinary first-year composition essays. Students devote the bulk of the Expository II: Research and Rhetoric course to crafting one research paper that is "an analysis of a problem in education in America." Six of the seven assignments for the semester (a proposal, two drafts, two oral presentations, and the final essay) are part of the main research project, and the other (called "Going Public" and discussed in the following section) is based on it.

Because Expository Writing II: Research and Rhetoric is paired with Sociology 101, field research and sociological methods of analysis are part of the research program. (In fact, the same final paper is submitted to both instructors.) Instructions for the first draft of the paper cover familiar academic territory: thesis paragraph, outline of issues, supporting research, bibliography. As the semester moves on, students are instructed to include at least three "levels of research": professional, popular, and public. (These levels are undertaken in addition to firsthand field research.) The professional category includes academic books and journals; the popular includes the work of experts and serious journalists writing to interested readers (like the Rose and Kozol books); and the public includes news reporting, editorials, and popular magazines. Students are also invited to consider fiction and Internet sources.

Herzberg admits that his students "don't really have the tools to evaluate it [their topic]. . . . They're just freshmen, but they'll have some way of understanding." Certainly, many are testing new schemas of abstract thinking as they concurrently learn about their topics and the codes of academic writing. As they negotiate academic discourse, Herzberg also steers his students toward thinking about the public implications of their academic research, as he stressed in our interview: "I want them to see the relationship there, how these three types of discourse [professional, popular, public] affect public policy. That's the place where I'm trying to focus."

Reflecting on his earlier version of the service-learning composition sequence, Herzberg concludes, "The final research papers for the composition course show a growing sophistication about the social forces at work in the creation of illiteracy" ("Community" 65). He supports this view by citing examples of students who strengthened their intellectual grasp of social context in analyzing such topics as tracking in schools and education in prisons. This conclusion is also supported by comments that students made in response to my inquiries. For example, one student from the spring 1997 course reflects:

> The most important thing I have learned is that writing is not just something people read or write for amusement, but a powerful medium used to portray important messages that affect our children's education in this country everyday. Writing can make a difference. It can show people what inequalities exist in our educational system and maybe even show them how they can help solve these problems. I think that this course has definitely helped improve my writing style and informed me on the educational issues that exist in this country. It has shown me the different views on curriculum, school funding, ebonics,

and much more. I never even cared about these issues before this course. Now that I am more informed I feel that it is partly my duty to get involved in some of these topics and to help inform people. Often people make a judgment before they know all the facts.

This student researched the inequalities in school funding and resource distribution, and, like the first-year student quoted earlier who researched Ebonics, she combines the recognition of her improvement in academic discourse with a newfound capacity to engage in cultural critique. Not every student in the course arrived at such an appreciation of cultural critique; in fact, almost half reported that they valued the course more because it prepared them for the challenges of their college coursework, with little mention of its impact on their lives as critical citizens. Still, all of them did research on some aspect of literacy or schooling and all grappled with academic sources and their relation to public policy.

The application of such academic and critical habits to social issues is of paramount importance to Herzberg. He reflected in our interview: "I am working on this academic discourse as the most highly valued discourse. . . . I think that what I am trying to develop is a sense how academic discourse—I don't have the right metaphor yet—for the connection between academic discourse and public discourse about a public policy issue." The connection between academic discourse and public discourse, always a concern for service-learning, is considered more intensively in the following section.

"Going Public": Critique and the Nature of Public Intervention

One of the most common and compelling claims made by service-learning advocates is that through service-learning students make an *intervention* in the world beyond the academy. The nature of that intervention is a primary concern of this study—in particular, the different interpretations of how students can intervene in the community through service-learning. "Going public" using writing and rhetoric is the primary imperative of writing-for and writing-with programs, and marks the most telling distinction between initiatives like Herzberg's and those aligned with other community writing paradigms. As noted earlier, Herzberg remains uninterested in having students intervene in contexts beyond the classroom by writing for nonacademic audiences (like nonprofit agencies or their clients). Rather, as he explained in our interview, "I get at it [the public connection] from the other direction. . . . They're not necessarily going to do research on something at Hamilton School. That I found was a limitation." Herzberg asks his students to research a pressing public problem related to literacy and enriched by—but not necessarily directly drawn from—the experience of tutoring at the school. Herzberg noted an example: "For example, they might look into prison education—that still requires 'on-site research' as well as academic research. . . . One of the things they will discover [while doing the prison project] is that a huge majority of those who are incarcerated for more than a year are deeply illiterate. . . . They will learn from Rose and Kozol and the work at the school how someone can go through the public school and still be illiterate." Thus, his students engage in research and analysis that asks them not only to consider relationships among public policy, literacy, and their own opinions, but also to grapple with several sources, including course reading, traditional academic research, popular press accounts, interviews, and personal experience in the community. Students' primary tasks here are familiar to academic writers—synthesis and analysis.

The manner in which Herzberg teaches his course prompts students to question and critique how our culture structures schooling and literacy. This pedagogical approach itself marks an intervention in the world, a disruption of dominant public discourses, casting Herzberg in the role of critical teacher and transformative intellectual. Yet Herzberg admits, "The way they [his students] write to actually make an intervention is still problematic." The "Going Public" assignment in the Expository Writing II: Research and Rhetoric course gestures at something more than critique. The "Going Public" assignment reads:

Going Public

How would someone who was interested in your topic and had a point of view get involved in the public debate on the issue?

a) In what media (talk, radio, newspaper, editorials, books, discussion groups on the Web, etc.) does the debate take place? List all that you know about or think likely.

b) Are there public forums (school board meetings, city council meetings, public lectures, rallies, etc.) at which there is debate on your issue? Again, list.

How would you express your point of view or make an argument on your topic? Pick one of the media or forums of debate, collect several examples of contributions to that debate in that medium, and answer the following questions about them:

Who are the writers/speakers?
Who is the audience?
How long are the statements?
What sort of evidence is presented to support positions?
Are sources of any kind used?
Which one of the examples you found is the most persuasive? Why?

With this assignment, Herzberg wants to raise in the minds of his students such questions as, "If answers to questions like tracking and prison education are so universally agreed upon by academics, why is public policy so contrary to such recommendations?" In his 1996 MLA presentation, "Service Learning and Public Discourse," he suggested that "we need to [help our students] conceptualize the gap between the academic and public spheres." His inclination for intervening "in the gap" seems intended to brainstorm ways of using rhetoric to bring the public sphere closer to the academic—essentially, asking students to imagine themselves as academic emissaries to the public. He asks students to think rhetorically and to analyze the various constraints of public discourse. His students need to locate a viable public forum in which to voice their concerns—the editorial page of the paper, a Web site, a radio spot. They then need to analyze the opportunities and constraints of such a forum and adjust their rhetorical stances with respect to genre, audience, ethos, accepted conventions, and so on. For example, a student might come to learn that crafting a piece for National Public Radio means being very brief and adopting a register quite different from that of academic analysis—something hard to do without losing the depth of analysis of the research essay. Thus the "Going Public" assignment is well suited to raising important rhetorical concerns. It includes all the components of the classical rhetorical process except actual delivery to a public audience outside the classroom.

As such, "Going Public" can be an important rhetorical learning experience for students; but as an intervention, it remains *conceptual*. While the assignment prompts students to venture outside academic rhetorical territory, what the student writes remains hypothetical—an imagined rhetorical performance for an imagined audience. Also notable is that the assignment counts for fifteen points within the grading distribution, less than one-fifth of the research paper's eight-five points. Herzberg's students certainly provide a valuable and tangible service in their weekly tutoring sessions; they also grow in their capacity to manage academic discourse and analyze various forms of public discourse. Yet the "Going Public" assignment remains largely an academic exercise rather than a purpose-driven rhetorical performance that moves readily into the public sphere (as do writing-for projects). However, Herzberg indicated that he might rethink this part of his course and consider other possibilities for students to insert themselves into public discourse. In writing-for-the-community initiatives, "Going Public" means adopting a nonacademic rhetoric to actively participate in public and workplace discourses. For Herzberg's writing-about course (or at least for this incarnation of it), "Going Public" means conceptualizing the gap between academic and popular spheres and imagining how one might employ rhetoric to insert a critical perspective into public discourse.

Writing *about* the Community and the Ends of Service-Learning

Service-learning initiatives that write about the community vary enormously, and Herzberg's courses constitute but one example.

Some writing-about versions simply yoke service work to journal writing, trusting that journaling will lead to fruitful reflection. Many instructors find that such undirected student writing about community service often focuses on the personal and emotive aspects of the event rather than on social and conceptual dimensions and implications of the experience. For some, this is perfectly acceptable, even encouraged. Outreach experiences can prompt compelling personal narratives, lively renderings filled with sensory description and other forms of expressive discourse.

In fact, most service-learning courses include opportunities for writing about community service experiences to help students in processing the powerful affective and frequently disquieting experiences they often undergo when doing outreach work in contexts far from their comfort zones. Some teachers see expressive discourses that favor personal narrative and reflection as important modes of writing in and of themselves, while some avoid the personal altogether. But many prefer to use personal writing as a bridge to analytical writing. Much personal reflection in service-learning courses takes the form of journaling, whether freestyle or with directive prompts. I've come to prefer an interactive or dialogic journal in which students record and reflect on their community experiences, followed by teacher response and reflection, and continuing back and forth as a structured written dialogue.

Robert Coles, a figure often invoked by service-learning advocates, prefers the use of literary texts as vehicles for reflection. Commenting on what seems the most popular type of community service in service-learning—college students tutoring disadvantaged youth—Coles remarks:

> Our colleges and universities could be of great help to students engaged in community service if they tried more consistently and diligently to help students connect their experiences in such work with their academic courses. Students need more opportunity for moral and social reflection on the problems that they have seen at first hand, and such intellectual work would surely strengthen both their academic lives and their lives as volunteers. Students need the chance to directly connect books to experience, ideas and introspection to continuing activity—through discussion groups in which the thoughts and ideas that

are so suggestively conveyed in fiction and essays are brought to bear on the particular individuals who inhabit a world of hardship and pain. ("Putting" 24)

The kind of reflection Coles suggests here is primarily personal—the student figuring out what the powerful community experience means for his or her own life by reading narratives of real or fictional people dealing with similar issues and themes. Thus, writing about an outside text (fiction or nonfiction that centers on social justice or community-oriented topics) is another important way that students can write *about* the community (see also Comstock; Coles, *Call*).

Herzberg recognizes that students need to process personal experience through narrative; but more important to him is that they use the service experience as a text (alongside other texts like those by Kozol and Rose) to be reflected upon with critical rigor. He is wary of reflection limited to the personal and affective. He asserts, "Writing personal responses to community service experiences is an important part of processing that experience, but it is not sufficient to raise critical or cultural consciousness" ("Community" 309). Similarly, he insists, "Writing about the actual experience of doing community service, then, does not seem to me to be the primary work to be done in a composition course like mine. Instead, we study literacy and schooling and write about that" (309–310). Clearly, he structures his course in a way that encourages deep critical reflection about pressing cultural issues, and he coaches students in how to express such critique in academic rhetoric.

The options available for writing about the community are almost without limit, ranging from the personal/affective to the social/analytical—as well as, which is perhaps more important, all the generative possibilities for combining diverse ways of knowing. (We don't want to fall back into the dualisms between the personal and the social that Dewey and Freire work so hard to bridge.) For example, Zan Goncalves at the University of Massachusetts supplements journal writing by using such methods as guided visualization exercises, which help students recall key moments, people, and narratives from their service experiences and render them in rich sensory detail. Later, students return to consider how such personal narratives fit into more social and critical understandings of related social problems. She also includes "write arounds," through which students role-play (in writing) a number of personas in order to make more audible the multiple (and often conflicting) voices and political perspectives of the many persons who have a stake in a complex issue like homelessness or poverty. Goncalves uses these in-class assignments, along with course readings, as invention strategies for essays that creatively combine personal and analytical strands.

Brock Haussaman describes a service-learning composition course at Raritan Valley Community College through which students volunteer at local retirement homes during the semester and later draw on that experience as they write biographies of the residents. In this case, the biography writing is tied to other significant course goals, such as research, because students integrate the narratives gathered on-site at the nursing homes with information from library sources that reveal other perspectives on particular historical moments of importance to the nursing home residents' lives. Such an assignment carries the obvious value of teaching important narrative and analytical writing strategies and conventions, but Haussaman, drawing on the work of Benjamin Barber, sees the service-learning component as prompting two other distinct benefits: students learn to listen, because they "must pay careful attention to the unfamiliar words they hear from unfamiliar people they work with"; and they learn imagination, since students must "stretch their vision in their study of people from different backgrounds, and such imagining, the capacity for informed social empathy, is a critical art in democracy" (196–97).[3]

For those who wish to move students beyond personal reflection and toward critical consciousness, Herzberg's approach is instructive—but it is not the only option for writing-about courses that encourage social and critical analysis. There are, of course, many ways to guide students toward critical reflection through directed journal prompts, in-class writings, and essay assignments (see Anson, "Reflection;" Eyler, Giles, and Schmiede, *Guide*; Greco). We can also look to a variety of well-structured writing-about-the-community service-learning courses (each with its own specific literacy goals) at a number of colleges and universities across the nation. Note a few examples:

- Ilona McGuiness of Loyola College in Maryland asks students to draw on their community service experiences as they write essays in response to a range of fiction and nonfiction texts that center on themes of social justice, race, class, and identity. The outreach work, she finds, helps "soften" the often rigid beliefs that students bring to class and helps deepen their understandings of social issues. She reports that the service-learning experience enlarges "the parameters in which they negotiate and construct meaning" as they write about the community (8).

- Likewise, Cynthia Cornell Novak and Lorie J. Goodman describe how in a first-semester composition course at Pepperdine University—Choosing Civility and Peace: Critical Thinking, Reading, and Writing in an Age of Violence—service-learning often helps students to step beyond simplistic or polarized debates on social issues. They report that service-learning encourages a tone of "shared inquiry" among students and creates "a safe/r contact zone for critical thinking and writing because students focus their energy on processing new, often baffling experiences they share together rather than prematurely facing-off with each other on a given subject" (67).

- Rosemary Arca underscores the potential value of service-learning in basic writing courses. As Arca's basic writing students at Foothill College perform various kinds of formal and informal service in the community, she invites them, through a series of writing assignments, to "explore an ever expanding circle of responsibility relationships—the family and community, self and community, society and community" (135). Arca finds in service-learning "a road to authority for basic writers" not only because of the immediate connection with readers opened by service-learning but also because "community service writing prompts basic writers to think of how they are 'connected' to their world and creates opportunities for students to operationalize those connections" (135; see also Linda Adler-Kassner, "Digging," on the value of service-learning in basic writing).

In my own service-learning writing courses, I sometimes include a community-based research assignment (such as writing a profile of a local community organization). More often, I include a major writing-about-the-community academic essay assignment toward the beginning of the semester for both its own merits and as a prelude to a writing-for-the-community or writing-with-the-community project assigned later in the semester. As does Herzberg, I ask students to compose academic essays that investigate pressing social problems which affect the local community (although, because my students are not devoting the bulk of the semester to this essay, their research is less comprehensive than that of Herzberg's students). For example, a student has researched care options for Alzheimer's Disease patients, drawing on personal experiences with a grandparent with Alzheimer's, an interview with the director of the local Alzheimer's Association, and library sources. Later in the semester, this student (with two collaborators) partnered with the local chapter of the Alzheimer's Association to undertake a writing-for project requested by the organization (a survey and analysis of current college student attitudes toward Alzheimer's, the results of which were published in their newsletter). Another student investigated local water pollution problems, drawing on library, personal, and interview sources; later in the semester, that student (in a student group) wrote a newsletter article for a local environmental group (see Deans and Meyer-Goncalves). I discuss this course, and others that combine strands of the writing *for*, *about*, and *with* paradigms, in Chapter 6.

As charted in Chapter 1, and as supported by my inquiry into Herzberg's course, the writing-about-the-community paradigm generally values academic and critical literacies, as well as academic and personal discourses, and it maintains the classroom as the primary site of learning. Writing-about-the-community courses are in many ways the most attractive to college teachers since they generally do not disrupt the dominant rhetorical practices of the academy. The focus on critique and academic discourse is certainly not contrary to practice within the academy—in fact, it supports the kind of abstract thinking and writing valued across the curriculum. And as for those teachers committed to expressive writing, they can easily integrate personal writing opportunities into the writing-about service-learning model, often with promising results since the personal writings generally emerge from emotionally charged outreach experiences.

While the requirement or option of doing community service in connection with a composition course is certainly new and still rather rare, the *rhetorics* and *genres* of student writing in writing-about-the-community courses remain largely familiar—the academic essay and the journal. Such courses also align nicely with a traditional function of first-year composition—initiation into the academic discourse community—and with traditional modes of assessment. However, while genres and rhetorical practices remain much the same, writing-about practices are potentially the most disruptive of all service-learning approaches to broad patterns of cultural oppression. As Herzberg explains, drawing partly on C. H. Knoblauch's language, such a pedagogy can encourage students in developing a "social imagination":

> The effort to reach into the composition class with a curriculum aimed at democracy and social justice is an attempt to make schools function . . . as radically democratic institutions, with the goal not only of making individual students more successful but also of making better citizens, citizens in the strongest sense of those who take responsibility for communal welfare. These efforts belong in the composition class because of the rhetorical as well as practical nature of citizenship and social transformation. . . . Students will not critically question a world that seems natural, inevitable, given; instead they will strategize about their position in it. Developing a social imagination makes it possible not only to question and analyze the world but also to imagine transforming it. ("Community" 317)

Critical teachers are generally skeptical of the power of everyday experience or community service alone to foster critical consciousness. As Herzberg remarks, "The community service experience doesn't bring an epiphany of critical consciousness" ("Community" 315). The outreach experience must be incorporated into a larger project of sustained and critical reading, analysis, dialogue, and inquiry (see Lisman).

However, it is worth noting that critical pedagogy advocates tend to assume that if students perform ideological analysis and critical literacy in the classroom, they will parlay that critical consciousness into concrete civic action later in their lives. I suspect that this faith in a movement from critical consciousness to grounded action is not altogether misplaced. Writing instructors who prefer writing-for and writing-with approaches often share this belief, as well. However, they prefer methods of intervention that ask students—as writers—to move more quickly and tangibly into public discourse. Herzberg's students tutored weekly at a local school, which marked a meaningful community service, even if it had little influence on their development as writers until processed in class and integrated with their academic work. As noted in the "Going Public" section of this chapter, there remains the possibility that a focus on critique can shortchange active community intervention in the community in the form of public rhetorical acts. Conversely, there remains the possibility that writing-for and writing-with projects can shortchange critical reflection on root causes of social injustice by devoting the bulk of their energies to immediate intervention in the public sphere.

Ultimately, Herzberg remains committed to his approach to service-learning, as well as critically aware of his practice. He maintains, "I'm going to stick with the notion of critique—and academic discourse is the safest place to be. It is an appropriate thing to do because clearly one of our missions is to prepare students in academic discourse." Along with those committed to critical pedagogy, he trusts in the power of critique to transform society and shares in the spirit of what Freire calls "social dreaming." In closing our interview, Herzberg reflected: "I really do take a progressive social position on this. I want to change the world. . . . I am committed to social justice and to actual change. It's all this stuff, some of which is deeply held personal commitment, which makes service-learning, and this particular angle on service-learning, so attractive."

Writing with *the Community:* Social Cognitive Rhetoric, Intercultural Discourses, and the Community Literacy Center

I want them to control multiple discourses. . . .My sense is that we're doing the same thing with them [the college student mentors] as we do with the teens: giving them multiple discourses that they can handle.

LINDA FLOWER, personal interview

Perhaps the most visible and well-researched university–community partnership under the writing-with-the-community paradigm is the Community Literacy Center (CLC), a partnership of Carnegie Mellon University (CMU) and Community House in Pittsburgh. The CLC describes itself, in brief, as follows:

> The Community Literacy Center (CLC) is a community/university collaborative of Pittsburgh's 80 year old Community House and the Center for the Study of Writing and Literacy at Carnegie Mellon University (CMU). At the CLC, writing lets community members take action, build consensus, and be heard on a broad range of issues. Working together, CMU college mentors and CLC teens develop skills in intercultural collaboration, problem-solving, and writing. CLC projects culminate in Community Conversations, which bring the voices from the neighborhood, city and university to a common table. (CLC, *Working* 16)

The goal of the CLC is community literacy, which cofounder Wayne Campbell Peck describes as "first and foremost a response of urban residents to dilemmas and opportunities in their lives" (20). He maintains that "community literate practices are rooted in the life struggles of urban residents and are best understood as transactions or responses of people addressing dilemmas through writing" (20). CLC leaders assert four guiding aims of community literacy: social change, intercultural conversation, strategic approach, and inquiry/research (Peck, Flower, and Higgins).

The CLC is located at Community House, a six-story brick building in the North Side section of Pittsburgh, a primarily African American inner-city neighborhood. Community House was founded in 1916 as part of the settlement house movement of the early 1900s. Settlement houses where "laboratories for social change" in urban neighborhoods; they predated modern social service systems and were "motivated by a vision of social change through inquiry and politically self-conscious cultural interaction" (Peck, Flower, and Higgins 201). Community House also includes a Presbyterian Church, and Wayne Peck, Director of Community House and a key member of the CLC staff, serves as pastor there. The partnership between Carnegie Mellon, a research university on the other side of town, and Community House was initiated by Wayne Peck while both director there and a doctoral student in rhetoric at Carnegie Mellon. He recruited Linda Flower as his partner in reinventing the tradition of the settlement house by moving Community House from a primarily recreational center to a site of literacy work. (This initiative marks a departure from the way most college community writing projects begin. Usually the first move is an overture from university faculty or administrators, as in the two previous case studies.)

The Community House–Carnegie Mellon partnership through the Community Literacy Center reflects a multifaceted, long-term relationship supported by the university and community. Most service-learning initiatives hinge on an academic course—instructors pairing academic learning goals for classes with work in the local community—and, certainly, the Carnegie Mellon undergraduate/graduate course Community Literacy and Intercultural Interpretation constitutes an integral part of CLC activity. But it is only one part. There are also weekly tutoring sessions on-site at Community House; student video productions;

ongoing research projects; and pubic gatherings, called Community Conversations, that bring local residents, urban teens, university people, and city officials together to address local community issues.

The partnership among local teens, college mentors, and CLC staff is central to the CLC. Their collaborative activity is aimed at addressing pressing community problems by means of oral and written intercultural communication, problem-solving strategies, and rhetorical performance—what CLC researchers gather under the term *literate social action*. Examples of literate social action include the writing and publication of a magazine co-authored by urban teens and college mentors in response to the imposition of a curfew on Pittsburgh youth in 1996; a teen video production dramatizing both potential troubles resulting from the curfew and alternate solutions to dealing with teen behavior; and a public Community Conversation at which teens and mentors performed their previously unheard perspectives on the curfew to a room filled with local residents, city officials, university people, and police officers. Rather than a revamped college composition course, the CLC is a comprehensive social change effort with rhetoric at its center. The CLC also distances itself from the term "service-learning," preferring the terms "literate social action" and "intercultural inquiry," with their emphasis on literacy and their avoidance of associations with "community service." Still, it clearly falls under the broad definition for service-learning that I employ in this book.

I contextualize my reading of the CLC with three strains of research and theory: John Dewey's pragmatic tradition, including Cornel West's prophetic pragmatism; rhetorical theory, especially social cognitive and problem-solving rhetorics as articulated by Linda Flower; and intercultural literacy, which is integral to CLC practice and serves as the central topic of the CMU course taken by the college mentors. These three bodies of knowledge—pragmatism, rhetoric, and intercultural literacy—serve to explicate the aims and assumptions of the CLC, as well as to advance my goal of contextualizing and clarifying distinctions among university–community writing projects. The following section on Dewey offers a broad philosophical context for the CLC; the cognitive rhetoric section moves closer to the action of the CLC and engages more directly the discourse of rhetoric and composition studies; and the section on intercultural collaboration attends to the intellectual and material dimensions of the college mentor–urban teen relation. The final part of the chapter examines the Carnegie Mellon course Community Literacy and Intercultural Interpretation, housed in its English department.

Because I gather my information from material published by scholars connected with the CLC, on-site observations, and interviews with CLC staff and Carnegie Mellon students, I cannot claim to fairly represent the perspective of the urban teens who work with the CLC. Certainly a more comprehensive study should include their voices; here I do that only to a limited degree. Rather, in keeping with my research agenda, I focus on the work of the CLC as it informs our understanding of college writers, emerging models of community-based writing courses, and the discourse of composition studies.

Deweyan Pragmatism and the Community Literacy Center

During his time as a professor at the University of Chicago, John Dewey worked with Jane Addams at Hull House, part of the same national settlement house movement that would later lead to the founding of Community House in Pittsburgh. Hull House in Chicago was a community center and "a place that was whatever need dictated: a maternity hospital when a single mother went into labor and could get no help from the stalwart Irish matrons who thought she deserved all she got; a terminal ward when one of the regulars died of consumption; a refuge for battered wives; a mutual training shop for immigrant boys; a library; a self-help probation service; and so on" (Ryan 151). In his lecture "The School as Social Centre," delivered to the National Education Association in 1902, Dewey celebrated the settlement as a place of education that responded especially well to such turn-of-the-century challenges as poverty, immigration, violence, and the ever-changing demands of the workplace (Ryan 152).

The CLC claims a similar pragmatic social and educational philosophy as one rationale for its work. The founders cite Dewey as an early exemplar of their approach to learning and literacy (Peck, Flower, and Higgins 199). Moreover, in our interview, Linda Flower described her attraction to pragmatism, sparked by her reading of pioneering pragmatist (and a major influence on Dewey) William James. She said that "some of our [CLC] work is driven by that pragmatic experimental approach to knowing . . . that the meaning of something is in the consequences and in the conditions it takes to create it. And that you can't just do academic analysis." Certainly, her words and ideas are aligned with those of James in his landmark lecture series on pragmatism. James writes: "The pragmatic method . . . is to try to interpret each notion by tracing its respective practical consequences" (28). For James, pragmatism is a "attitude of orientation" that not only banishes "the pretense of finality in truth," but also seeks the "practical cash-value" of principles, and assumes the posture "of looking away from first things, principles, 'categories,' supposed necessities; and of looking toward last things, fruits, consequences, facts" (31–32). As Flower recognizes, these core Jamesian pragmatic tenets also characterize the work of John Dewey. In a recent essay, Flower cites Dewey and his inclination, like her own, to adopt methods that measure the value of theories, policies, and beliefs not by "the normal academic test of comfort and certainty (i.e., by their internal elaboration and consistency)," but by results as perceptibly *experienced* ("Partners" 101). In our discussion, she also remarked, "Instead of talking about the causes of problems with kids, we're trying to help them look at those problems and deal with them themselves . . . trying to put out a sense of the substance of that knowledge in the larger community. . . . Looking at social issues in terms of their implications—it's really straight Dewey—it's saying that the meaning of the things we are doing is tied into the consequences. . . . The ideology is figuring out where you can get some leverage [to make a change]. . . . Broadcasting the need for change *is* necessary, but a lot of that work stays in the academy and that, it seems to me, is not adequate."

For Dewey and for the CLC, the pragmatic consequences of community work might be the solving of a pressing local problem (for example, misunderstandings between police and teens that often result in brutality). Yet a meaningful consequence is also to be found in exploring the problem more deeply (what Dewey termed "inquiry"), and initiating a strategic dialogue among those involved, taking particular care that marginalized voices are heard (urban teens, for example).[1]

As discussed in Chapter 2, Dewey's pragmatic philosophy intertwines action and reflection; it also prefers a communitarian approach to democracy. Alan Ryan notes that Dewey's approach "does not offer to give us large and general rules; it is going to encourage us in the sensitive exploration of contextual problems" (231). For the CLC, the problem is literacy and the context is inner-city Pittsburgh; the means of "sensitive exploration" is a university–community partnership centered on tutoring in writing and rhetorical action in the spirit of intercultural conversation and negotiation.

Dewey sees democracy not as a political apparatus but as a vigorous and open dialogue, as free communication, as "the very idea of community itself" (*Public* 148). It is not surprising then that of the four guiding aims of the CLC (social change, intercultural dialogue, strategic approach, and inquiry/research), intercultural dialogue was the most prominently featured both at the Community Conversation I observed in 1996 and in the syllabus for the Carnegie Mellon mentor course. While a pragmatic orientation calls for an accounting of actual consequences, Deweyan theory still supports the emphasis of Community Conversations on dialogue, on *being heard*, rather than only on bringing about a prescribed change in a particular city policy. Of course, political change may happen through teens being heard by city officials and others with power, but the "end in view" (to borrow a term from Dewey) for the Community Conversation is the rhetorical performance of the teens—a robust, problem-solving conversation (which happens concurrently with the dissemination of a teen/mentor-authored publication on the topic at hand). The immediate focus of the CLC is on opening a rhetorical forum for multiple perspectives rather than on advocating for a particular city policy.

This emphasis on the process of dialogue presents a tension pointed out to me by CLC Director Elenore Long. She mentioned that some CLC staff have at times claimed that Community Conversations won't change, for example, the unjust ways that the police actually treat the teens, which suggests that a more organized political response may be necessary. I heard similar opinions from parents and community members during discussion at the November 1996 Community Conversation, pointing to a tension between open dialogue and organized political action. For instance, only hours before the scheduled Community Conversation on a recently imposed teen curfew in Pittsburgh, a decision in a highly publicized, racially charged trial was announced. White police officers were acquitted of responsibility for the death of Jonny Gammage, an African American motorist who had died in police custody. Many in the black community (and many at the CLC) were disappointed and outraged upon hearing of the acquittal. The Community Conversation, because of its focus on police–teen relations, could not escape connection with the trial and its racial reverberations. The Community Conversation went forward with its dialogue on the curfew and teen–police relations at Community House while activists simultaneously protested the Gammage trial verdict at the city courthouse.

The CLC puts a premium on intercultural conversation, and the staff kept this aim in focus during the Community Conversation. For example, during the discussion after the teen performances, city councilman and local African American leader Sala Udin registered his strong opposition to the curfew before departing to join the courthouse protest. Soon after, several in the audience pressed a representative from the mayor's office to justify the curfew policy. The representative got defensive, and the conversation started to drift toward a more entrenched, oppositional dialectic (outraged citizens versus the official power structure). Joyce Baskins (who is on the CLC staff) and Linda Flower stepped in to redirect the interaction toward voicing perspectives rather than taking sides. In this scene two strands of rhetoric were at play: a rhetoric of dialogue, of sharing perspectives (launched by the sharing of the underrepresented perspectives of urban teens), and a rhetoric of political activism (moving to march on the courthouse and refuting the representative from the mayor's office).

In terms of Deweyan and Freirean frames of reference, Freirean theory certainly endorses the dialogic nature of the Community Conversation but also embraces the activist turn, the inclination to mobilize collective political action. Dewey's stance encourages keeping the focus on communication, exchange, dialogue—especially since the constituencies present (teens, parents, police, city officials, legislators, community activists, local citizens, university representatives) rarely, if ever, participate in dialogue that is as robust and meaningful as the one I witnessed at the Community Conversation. Here we see one concrete example of how Dewey's pragmatist faith in experiential, provisional outcomes stands in contrast Freire's utopian faith in revolutionary outcomes. Dewey writes of working pragmatically toward "ends in view" that then serve as pivots for further action (*MW* 9: 112). Each Community Conversation is an end in view, an eight-week collaborative effort to strategically address an issue through literate social action—that is, through rhetorical performance (oral and written). And when that aim is reached, a Deweyan reassessment and realignment of aims follows. The hopeful, strategic process of intercultural conversation and negotiation, rather than a political process focused on a prescribed policy outcome, is the focus. Outcomes, in the spirit of Dewey, are always conditional, ripe for critical reflection and revision. According to Dewey, "All general conceptions (ideas, theories, thought) are hypothetical. . . . [T]hey have to be tested by the consequences they define and direct" (*LW* 4: 132). A driving motivation for the CLC is Dewey's radically democratic *process of inquiry*.

Linda Flower and Elenore Long note that Cornel West's "prophetic pragmatism," an extension of Deweyan pragmatism into the arenas of postmodern cultural criticism, race relations, religion, and radical democratic action, has also served as a major theoretical influence on CLC thinking, planning, and practice. Long credits Wayne Peck with bringing West into CLC discourse. In our interview, Flower noted that Cornel West's prophetic pragmatism "is the place where I would like to be standing." She is drawn to West's approach because he "recognizes the injustice that is there and looks for opportunities for transformational praxis" while not losing focus on "the agency of marginalized people." Prophetic pragmatism, as articulated by West, marks a "reconception of philosophy as a form of cultural criticism that attempts to transform linguistic, social, cultural and political traditions for the purposes of increasing the scope of individual development and democratic operations" (*American* 230). West sees prophetic pragmatism as "a child of Protestant Christianity wedded to left romanticism" (227) that is "discursively situated between John Dewey's radical liberal version of socialism and Antonio Gramsci's absolute historicist conception of Marxism" (215). As does Dewey, West insists that philosophy and cultural critique should support grounded action. West explains:

> Human struggle sits at the center of prophetic pragmatism, a struggle guided by a democratic and libertarian vision, sustained by moral courage and existential integrity, and tempered by the recognition of human finitude and frailty. . . . The strategies are never to become ends-in-themselves, but rather to remain means through which are channeled moral outrage and human desperation in the face of prevailing forms of evil in human societies and in human lives. . . . Prophetic pragmatism attempts to keep alive the sense of alternative ways of life and of struggle based on the best in the past. In this sense, the praxis of prophetic pragmatism is tragic union with revolutionary intent, usually reformist consequences, and always visionary outlook. (*American* 229)

Although West's intellect probes various theorists and his voice soars in almost evangelical fervor, he is careful to connect his theoretical discourse to strategic action—an important overlap with the goals of the CLC and with Linda Flower's social cognitive rhetoric. West insists that prophetic pragmatists "move directly to strategic and tactical modes of thinking and acting" (*American* 226). This echoes Flower, who throughout her writings returns to, in her words, "the direct attention to strategic thinking found in cognitive rhetoric, with its focus on the writer's goals, strategies and metacognitive awareness" (*Construction* 108). Her social cognitive theory of writing is pragmatic in spirit and strategic in practice: "[A] social cognitive conception of literacy embeds texts within contexts and purposes; texts and text features are means to an end, not an end in themselves. Moreover, they turn out to be mutable, adaptive features that reflect rhetorical and intellectual responses to social exigencies" (16).

Flower and the CLC staff deliberately distance their strategic pragmatist approach from the school of radical pedagogy. Recalling words she attributes to Wayne Peck, she remarks: "You don't need to tell kids on the street that they are oppressed." In an article on the CLC, Peck, Flower, and Lorraine Higgins speak to the limitations of liberatory pedagogy, what they term "the literacy of social and cultural critique." They remark that "the discourse of critique offers few strategies for change beyond resisting the dominant discourse practices with the promise that the victors will somehow be more just than their predecessors. Critique is necessary but insufficient on its own terms for building a just society. Without a clear strategy for constructing more participatory practices, critique alone can not articulate the 'somehow' of this promise" (205). Flower also finds the radical critique approach of such scholars as James Berlin limited because it remains primarily a dialogue among academics. She resists approaches that insist only on problem posing; her preference is for a balance between problem posing and problem solving (although problem solving gets much more attention in her scholarship). As she noted in our interview, "Instead of talking about the causes of problems with kids, we're trying to help them look at those problems and deal with them themselves."[2] The stance of Flower and other CLC leaders with respect to community literacy resonates with what Jay Robinson, also an admirer of Dewey, terms civic literacy: "A civic literacy must make use of the languages of critique that Marxist oriented theorists have urged upon literacy workers. But civic literacy must extend beyond a language of critique to languages of construction and of possibility, to ways of thinking and speaking that are adequate to the complexities of collective living and problem solving, to modes of listening and of responding that are sensitive to the multiple voices and minds of those who have stakes in civic issues and those who are affected by the solutions that are proposed for difficult problems" (14).

My own sense is that the CLC staff is drawn to Deweyan pragmatism and West's prophetic pragmatism because they supply not only a compelling philosophical rationale for an action-oriented, intercultural program, but also an ethical warrant for an emphasis on individual agency and a strategic approach. In composition studies, advocates of radical pedagogy have long claimed the ethical high ground (from which they have at times thrown rocks at cognitive rhetoric). Dewey and West provide the

CLC with not only a theoretical foundation for strategic action but also with a moral authority and vocabulary.

Cognitive Rhetoric and the CLC

Work at an inner-city community center may seem far from the research in cognitive rhetoric for which Linda Flower became widely recognized in the 1980s. In fact, it both is and isn't. The major tenets of cognitive rhetoric—individual agency, problem solving, strategic thinking, and metacognition—are evident throughout CLC practice and particularly in the composing process for the CLC publications co-authored by teens and mentors. Flower remarked in our interview that "cognitive rhetoric is part of the grounding" of the CLC because such rhetoric "looks at writing as a force in the world." Problem solving, the mantra of cognitive rhetoric, surfaces throughout the discourse of community literacy. This section focuses on problem-solving cognitive rhetoric as it relates to the guiding theory and grounded practice of the CLC. This focus is aligned most closely with the strategic approach goal of community literacy. Flower remarked: "Getting kids to be problem solvers in their own lives—this is where most of our energies go." As noted earlier, she avoids paradigms of critique (like the critical pedagogy focus evident in Herzberg's classroom) because they often fail to account for pragmatic intervention in the world. She also steers away from expressive paradigms (even while acknowledging their value) because she wants the teens (and college students) not simply to develop their voices but also to strategically insert them into public spheres. Flower hopes that both CLC teens and the college student mentors will use writing to produce texts that do not simply critique or express, but also problem-solve, instigate social action, and intervene in the world. She says, in a pragmatic spirit, that CLC documents "have got to work."

In the preface to the first edition of her *Problem-Solving Strategies for Writing* (a later edition of which she uses in her course for CLC mentors), Flower describes cognitive psychology as "a young field—a reaction, in part against the assumptions of behaviorism. In the tradition of William James, it is concerned with the process of cognition, and, like the field of English, with the nature and process of creative thought" (vii). And in the landmark essay "A Cognitive Process Theory of Writing," co-authored by Flower and John Hayes, they outline a cognitive process theory of writing based on the following assumptions: (1) that writing is best understood as a set of distinctive thinking processes which writers orchestrate during the act of composing; (2) that these processes have a hierarchical and highly embedded organization; (3) that the act of composing is a goal-directed thinking process; and (4) that writers create their own goals (366).

As cognitive rhetoric gained prominence in the field of rhetoric and composition in the 1970s and 1980s, its emphasis on individual agency and individual decision making prompted critique from such scholars as Patricia Bizzell, James Berlin, and David Bartholomae, all finding it suspect for its relative dismissal of the importance of social context or for its presumed conservative ideology. In keeping with the social turn in composition studies, Flower has revised her early theories on the individual cognition of writers, giving much more attention to social context. Yet revision should not be taken as a recantation. Flower remains committed to cognitive rhetoric and insists that personal agency must be at the fore of writing instruction. The CLC bears the stamp of a *social cognitive* approach, which is evident not only in the recurring themes of problem solving, strategic thinking, and metacognition, but also in the emphasis on a dialectic between individual cognition and cultural context.

Flower's extended articulation of her theoretical stance, *The Construction of Negotiated Meaning: A Social Cognitive Theory of Writing,* addresses the traditional concerns of cognitive rhetoric (how writers represent problems to themselves and act on those representations to solve problems); but it also explores the multilayered circumstances which form the social contexts for writing. A social cognitive conception of literacy assumes that texts are situated, purposeful, and adaptive. Flower conceives of writing as a series of complex "literate acts." Her role as a researcher is to observe writers in action and "trace that constructive process in students across different academic contexts" and shed light on "the logic of [those] literate negotiations" (35). While her extensive study focuses on college classrooms as contexts for writing, Flower invites writing outside the classroom under her definition of what constitutes a "literate act."

A review of Flower's recent work confirms the shift to more context-sensitive understandings of writing, or what she terms a "a social cognitive view." Compare the four major claims Flower and Hayes make in their 1981 "Cognitive Process" essay to the following claims she makes about literacy in 1994 in *The Construction of Negotiated Meaning*: (1) literacy is an action performed as part of a rhetorical, social, and cultural situation; (2) literacy is a move within a discourse practice, within a "flexible social script for how such things are normally done"; (3) becoming literate depends on knowledge of social conventions and on individual problem solving; and (4) literate action opens the door to metacognitive and social awareness (20–30). These four guiding claims both draw upon and extend the four claims Flower and Hayes make in 1981. However, a *social cognitive* perspective, in contrast to the earlier *cognitive* perspective, affirms and explores the roles of personal identity, collaboration, conflict, dialogue, and negotiation in the writing process.

In contextualizing the CLC, Peck, Flower, and Higgins describe the influence of rhetoric as follows: "Cognitive rhetoric treats writing as a both a strategic, social act and an individual thinking process that invites study, teaching and learning. In this paradigm community literacy can become a goal-directed process dedicated to social change—a form of action in both the community and the lives of the writers. . . . Text is not an end in itself but a performance measured by its personal and public consequences" (208). The college mentors working with the teens at the CLC felt the press of a goal-driven cognitive rhetoric in their collaborative work on writing projects. As one reflected in an e-mail interview:

> Although we [mentors] were creating a written document with these teens, the focus of our relationship was to produce a finished text, not to explore the process of invention and composition. We were working under tight time constraints in order to organize and present the teens' opinions to the community. The coordinators were interested in developing the teens' writing abilities, but they [CLC staff] were more concerned that the teens produce a document instigating social action. They

allocated their time and energy to having something in hand, a hard copy of the teens' ideas.

This mentor's reflection recalls Flower's imperative that CLC documents "have got to work."[3] The social cognitive rhetoric outlined in Flower's theories and experienced by this mentor is pragmatic in spirit; moreover, it affirms the *personal agency* of urban teens and college mentors as writers, problem solvers, and strategic users of literacy for social change. This stance, taken within the context of a project rooted in community concerns, constitutes one form of writing with the community. Operating out of a rhetorical orientation which emphasizes situated and strategic problem solving, the CLC brings cognitive rhetoric to the inner city.

College Mentors and Teen Writers at the CLC

Cognitive rhetoric is often associated with the thinking and decision-making processes of the individual mind as it strategically represents a task and composes a text. Yet community literacy is premised on *collaborative* social action, and thus collaborative writing; furthermore, an inter-city setting entails *intercultural* collaboration, particularly the interaction of predominantly White middle-class college students and predominantly African American working-class and poor urban residents. According to Elenore Long, Director of the CLC, one of the guiding questions for the CLC staff is "how to be involved in an intercultural living space." Community House and Carnegie Mellon stand not only in different sections of Pittsburgh but in different cultural spheres with respect to history, race, class, and discourse practices.

Intercultural collaboration is one of the four tenets of community literacy, and the title of the Carnegie Mellon course for mentors, Community Literacy and Intercultural Interpretation, signals its centrality. Linda Flower asserts:

> If community/university relations are to be based on the logic
> of inquiry, the first issue to put on the table is the problem and
> potential of cultural difference. Difference exists not just in
> simple distinctions such as town/gown, rich/poor, black/white,

but in the alternative discourses, literate practices, goals, and values brought to an inquiry. When people doing this hypothesis making, testing, and judging live much of their lives in different worlds, talking different languages, they may indeed struggle to be understood at times. But when they come to the table as collaborative equals (where everyone's discourse, practices, and goals are recognized) those differences can produce an explosion of knowledge. ("Partners" 102)

Describing how the CLC departs from "multiculturalism," Peck, Flower, and Higgins articulate their vision of *inter*culturalism as consisting of "boundary-crossing encounters that go beyond mere conversation to the delicate exploration of difference and conflict toward the construction of a negotiated meaning. In this negotiation (which is going on both within and among individual writers), intercultural collaboration is a strategy for making something—a new understanding, a document, a public, literate act" (211). The kind of collaborative social action they envision "emerges from a sense of conflict and a willingness to negotiate social and cultural differences through collaborative literate action" (212). I recognized intercultural dialogue happening on multiple levels at the CLC: at the institutional level, as a university and community work together; in daily interpersonal relations at Community House; through the collaborative problem-solving and writing processes of teens and mentors; in the discourse of the teen/mentor publications; in the drama and dialogue of the Community Conversations; as a matter of academic debate in readings for the Community Literacy and Intercultural Interpretation course at Carnegie Mellon; and in the electronic bulletin board and student "inquiry" papers for that course.

This section focuses in particular on the college student mentors—how they collaborate with teen writers and how they conceptualize this intercultural collaboration. I observed the mentors working toward the aims of an intercultural collaborative rhetoric (as they concurrently accommodated a cognitive rhetoric framework) in two main ways: collaborating as writers with teens at Community House to produce both publications and skits for the Community Conversations; and reading, discussing, and writing about intercultural literacy in a college classroom setting (the Community Literacy and Intercultural Interpretation course).

In her doctoral dissertation, CLC Director Elenore Long contextualizes, documents, and analyzes the collaborative processes of mentors and teens in one of the initial years of the CLC. Working from a wealth of on-site observations, interviews, mentor self-interviews, and other empirical data, she explores how literacy and social action unfold in the praxis of the CLC, and how CLC practice relates to rhetorical theory. She tracks several college student mentors over the course of sixteen weeks as they navigate multiple discourses, conflicts, priorities, and values at the CLC while under the pressure to act. Long concludes that mentors ultimately arrive, via different routes, at "negotiated images of literate social action." I make no claim of replicating Long's fine-grained examination of CLC life. Rather, my analysis is largely comparative, juxtaposing the CLC's writing-*with*-the-community approach and the writing-*for* and writing-*about* approaches.

Collaboration in the Teen–Mentor Writing Process

Intercultural collaboration is evident in the strategies that mentors and teens undertake as they draft texts for CLC publications. *How to Be Heard: A Handbook for Community Literacy* outlines the five main CLC rhetorical strategies:

- ◆ collaborative planning
- ◆ telling the story behind the story
- ◆ rivaling
- ◆ options and outcomes
- ◆ revising for readers

Telling the story behind the story is a strategy for invention, but it also prompts analysis of the "hidden logic behind what teenagers do" (*How to Be Heard* 7). Rivaling, also a combination of invention and analysis, is a process of generating rival hypotheses, "alternative ways of reading a situation, alternative ways of defining a problem, or alternative solutions" (10). Intended as both an interpersonal and (eventually) an internalized process, rivaling prompts teens and mentors to consider multiple perspectives in a complex, strategic problem-solving process. In turn, the focus on options and outcomes prompts teens and mentors to analyze alternatives and consequences, thus moving the writers further along in their problem solving, negotiation, and decision making. All of these strategies, according to Flower, "immerse students in a larger, more intercultural space, in more richly represented problems and issues, and in the human reality of those issues" ("Partners" 112). Revising for readers shifts the focus to audience, persuasion, arrangement, and textual features. These strategies, with the teens as writers and the mentors as supporters, grow out of the central tenets of cognitive rhetoric (individual agency, problem solving, strategic thinking, and metacognition) married to an emphasis on collaboration.

When Carnegie Mellon mentors sit down with teens (the mentor is usually at a computer keyboard transcribing for and supporting the teen writer), the strategies of telling the story behind the story, rivaling, and considering options and outcomes serve as both invention exercises and templates for literate social action. The CLC imagines the ideal collaboration as an egalitarian partnership of experts (in both invention and composing) moving through episodes of conversation and negotiation and toward a pragmatic outcome—often a document to be published and disseminated publicly in booklet form.

College mentor and urban teen collaborations/negotiations result in written contributions to CLC publications which are intended to voice multiple perspectives on pressing local problems for a diverse public audience. The following passage is excerpted from "The Curfew Center: Relocating the Problem," an article by CLC teen Elliot Mitchell that appears, with several others, in the 1996 CLC publication *Raising the Curtain on Curfew*. It illustrates an end product of the teen–mentor composing process.

From "The Curfew Center: Relocating the Problem"
A mixed crowd is going to be at the curfew center. The city thinks that they're going to keep the kids safe by taking them

off the streets and taking them somewhere else, but it's going to cause more trouble. All they are doing is relocating the problem.

There are going to be people from different neighborhoods and there will be rival gangs taken to the curfew center. Most of the kids that are going to be taken to the center are going to be the ones that don't care about the rules, and that is why they were out past curfew. There are going to be trouble makers down there, and the good kids won't know what to expect . . . .

Riots could break out. You never know what they're going to do. And how are the cops going to control it? What will they do? Billy club everybody? If the cops are mean, the kids are going to be tough back. They're going to start arguing. It's going to be really wild. Fights will break out. Girls are going to be down there, and people are going to hook up and get together. There are going to be problems.

It's not like they are going to have separate buildings for the different neighborhoods. What about males and females? Are they going to be together? There should be a way to separate the good kids from the trouble-makers. But it's hard to know who is good and who is not. It's like judging a book by its cover. It's not right. There's no way to tell. Gangs don't wear that bandanna stuff anymore, and the good kids are going to get slapped around.

This passage represents the insider perspective of a teen anticipating problems at the curfew detention center, as well as popular teen discourse strategies like short staccato sentences and the word choices "hooking up" and "Gangs don't wear that bandanna stuff anymore." Yet it also includes academic strategies, like leading paragraphs with topic sentences, and summarizing and abstracting with a thesis: "All they are doing is relocating the problem." As well, the discourse has been edited to follow, even if not slavishly, the syntax and usage of standard written English. One can trace the intermingling of academic and teen discourses in the text, reflecting the collaborative and intercultural process by which it was constructed. It is just the kind of collaborative and strategic "public literate act" hoped for by the CLC.

Mentors are aware of the collaborative ideal, as is evident in the care they take to respect the ideas, voices, and discourses of the teens. Yet mentors also quickly experience how difficult it is to realize the ideal of intercultural collaboration in practice. Finding ways to craft dialogic and hybrid written texts through teen–mentor collaboration is a high priority for the CLC. One undergraduate described her CLC experience, both the mentoring and the college course, as unlike anything she had done before. In particular, she singled out the collaborative writing processes—on-site at the CLC and in the Carnegie Mellon course—as distinguishing factors. Echoing the guiding theories of the CLC, she spoke of interaction with her teen writer using the vocabulary of cognitive rhetoric and collaboration. She had a defined goal—to help her teen write a piece for the *Raising the Curtain on Curfew* CLC publication. According to the mentor, the process "made me think about writing strategy . . . how the audience enters into it—things that I did [in my own writing] but never realized I did before." Here is evident an emphasis on the strategic approach and metacognitive awareness goals of cognitive rhetoric, as well as the conversation and negotiation goals of collaborative rhetoric. The mentor spoke of the importance of CLC methods of invention (e.g., rivaling), as well as her response to the teen–mentor dynamic. At the keyboard she had to resist the temptation to "automatically translate" what the teen was saying to "how I might have wanted it." Beyond the ideas, she and her teen also grappled with genre. She originally assumed they would write an essay, journalistic piece, or narrative. But the teen resisted. The mentor suggested a dramatic script—and the teen also rejected that idea at first, but later agreed. Self-conscious of this process of negotiation, the mentor reflects: "When you are steering him toward something, you may not be steering him toward something better, but toward what you want." She noted that the teen "definitely had his own ideas"; however, when the process moved beyond the brainstorming and the choice of genre, the teen generally acquiesced to the mentor's suggestions on wording and language.

In contrast, the same mentor describes a different process of collaboration with a different teen. With the second CLC teen, the writing process "was more of a mixture"—in other words, more of a shared process in both invention and composing. In this case, the teen was more assertive in both the choice of ideas *and* the style of writing. In the mentor's words, "No one was in charge." Eventually this document, like the one with the first teen, was completed, revised, copyedited, and published. In this mentor's experience, both teen–mentor writing processes were collaborative and strategic, but the second, in which the teen asserted his voice on both content and textual features, is clearly closer to the CLC ideal. The mentor was optimistic about her collaboration experience with the CLC, and her reflections resonate with those of the CLC staff.

Certainly, not all teen–mentor collaborations are this productive. Some prove problematic. In particular, there are times when cognitive rhetoric's mandate to "get the writing done" collides with the priority to engage in collaboration. Also, sometimes mentor expectations depart from those of the CLC leaders. For example, one mentor's reflections evince both conflicts:

> The further we progressed, the better I understood that my perception of the program differed greatly from that of the coordinators. Although we were creating a written document with these teens, the focus of our relationship was to produce a finished text, not to explore the process of invention and composition. We were working under tight time constraints in order to organize and present the teens' opinions to the community. The coordinators were interested in developing the teens' writing abilities, but they were more concerned that the teens produce a document instigating social action. They allocated their time and energy to having something in hand, a hard copy of the teens' ideas. I was more concerned with exploring the challenges and frustrations of composing and revising. We were approaching the task from two different perspectives, and working toward different, although not contradictory, objectives.

This mentor, a graduate student, experiences dissonance because she must simultaneously serve a goal-driven rhetoric and a collaborative rhetoric, and because she prioritizes project goals differently than do CLC staff as she represents them. My observations of the CLC suggest that the combination of cognitive rhetoric and intercultural collaboration can result in complex intellectual explorations, effective problem-solving publications, and compelling public events; but potential side effects can include, at least in the short term for some mentors, frustration and confusion. The mentor quoted above did in fact bend to accommodate CLC policy and successfully assisted one of the teens in composing and publishing a piece in *Raising the Curtain on Curfew;* but she also retained her personal allegiance to a more expressivist and process-oriented approach to writing instruction.

Flower addresses this matter of differing aims and values explicitly in her scholarship, emphasizing that, for her, collaboration includes conflict, hard choices, and the imperative move from dialogue to directed action. Collaboration, she notes, should not be equated with conversation. Even though many voices may be invited to the table, the pressure to act in the world will force pragmatic choices and compromises which consequently foreclose some options at strategic points in the composing process. She acknowledges that the *conversational* model of free exchange and egalitarian sharing is valuable; yet she ultimately opts for a model of collaboration premised on *negotiation,* emphasizing the goal-directed and problem-solving nature of exchange among interlocutors (*Construction*). Such a vision incorporates the open exchange that is characteristic of conversation, but it also asserts that conversational sharing must progress into a pragmatic, strategic process, ending in what she terms the "construction of negotiated meaning."

Collaboration through the Community Conversation

The "talking around the table" metaphor is central to CLC. It is represented visually in the graphics of CLC publications and training manuals and is evident in phrases that repeatedly surface in CLC discourse: "bringing more voices to the table"; "the problem on the table"; "creating a table in your own mind." Intercultural dialogue occurs most visibly at the CLC when individuals and constituencies from various cultural, ethnic, political, professional, and generational groups gather at Community House several times a year for Community Conversations, also known as "community problem-solving dialogues." The goal of these public, performative "literate acts" is "to go beyond knowledge based on academic research alone or on contact solely with the community's professional representatives and bureaucracies. And it is to go beyond transferring knowledge to the community, by moving to inquiry *with* the community" (Flowers, "Partners" 106).

The *Raising the Curtain on Curfew* publication and its companion Community Conversation were the culmination of an eight-week agenda. At the end of the eight weeks, teens, in collaboration with their college mentors, had met the challenge of crafting a purpose-driven hybrid document and staging public performances in which they dramatized their perspectives on the curfew through skits and a video. I observed as key players in the problem (teens, university faculty and students, city officials, parents, local citizens, the district's congressman, a police sergeant) participated actively in the Community Conversation and read the newly published *Raising the Curtain on Curfew*, which included articles on teen strategies for making curfew safer, narratives of potentially dangerous scenarios between teens and police, advice on how to diffuse teen–police conflicts before they escalate, and explanations of unintended consequences of the curfew law (like Elliot Mitchell's, excerpted above). During the Community Conversation, teens and mentors dramatized scenarios related to curfew. After the skits and a teen-produced video, there was vigorous dialogue among members of the audience. In all, the Conversation marked an impressive mix of oral, written, and dialogic rhetorical performances.

During the open conversation after the teen/mentor performances, dialogue was animated, at times even verging on angry, but, throughout, civil. City Councilman Sala Udin, as noted earlier, registered his opposition to the curfew and advised the teens on how they could utilize "escape routes" from the policy while still obeying the law. In contrast, a city official (from the mayor's office, which was involved in administering the curfew) represented the curfew as a "safety zone" for teens. Several skeptical parents and teens countered this representation—they stood up and refuted the city official (at other times they spoke quietly and sometimes resentfully among themselves in the back of the room). They saw the curfew as an unwarranted police action, as unjustified and unfair. There was no denying the conflict and tension in the room—particularly in the skeptical words and gazes addressed to the representative from mayor's office. Playing off both the curfew discussion and the Gammage court decision, several members in the audience spoke of their discontent with police–community relations. The representative from the police department listened as CLC staff person Joyce Baskins moderated the discussion, ensuring that all would have an opportunity to speak. Linda Flower closed the dialogue with a call for ongoing reflection.

If the larger strategic goal of the CLC is to create a context for public dialogue, that aim was met—even if the larger social problems remained. Essentially, the CLC Community Conversations are oral expressions of the same collaborative and strategic processes which characterize the teen–mentor writing process and CLC publications. They are unique among community-based college writing initiatives that I have encountered because, alongside the text-based composing strategies that are key to publishing the CLC booklets (like *Raising the Curtain on Curfew*), Community Conversations emphasize, true to the classical origins of rhetoric, oral public performances in the interest of the civic good.

Mentors as College Students: Academic Theories, Hybrid Discourses, and Inquiries

While most CLC activity takes place at Community House, important learning also happens on campus at Carnegie Mellon. As a companion to their work at the CLC, the college student mentors take a course, Community Literacy and Intercultural Interpretation. As Mentor Coordinator Jennifer Flach noted, the course is "aimed at keeping the intellectual part, the theoretical part, in the community, so it's not just all feel good, but there's some other types of learning going on." One mentor commented, "I think the readings [for the course] serve as background for things I wouldn't have picked up on."

While all service-learning courses connect academic thinking to experience in the community, and many confront issues of cultural difference, this course also investigates the theory and practice of intercultural literacy. The course combines the intellectual with the experiential, insisting that participants include in their written texts multiple voices (personal/expressive voice, teens' voices, academic voices) and cultural perspectives (those of the primarily White, middle-class CMU students; the urban, primarily African American teens with whom they work; and an array of traditional academic scholarship). In our interview, Flower emphasized her key goal for the mentors: "I want them to control multiple discourses. . . . My sense is that we're doing the same thing with [the mentors] as we do with the teens: giving them multiple discourses that they can handle." The multiple discourses include academic discourse, community discourses (in this case, African American urban discourse), and creative combinations of these, which she terms "hybrid discourses."

The course is divided into three phases. The first focuses on research and theory in community literacy and intercultural discourse; the second includes the on-site mentoring work at the CLC described in earlier sections of this chapter; and the third returns mentors to campus to do more reading and complete a major research project. Much of the reading for the course includes scholarship on literacy. For example, students are asked to self-select a number of essays from Kintgen, Kroll, and Rose's *Perspectives on Literacy.* They also read scholarly articles on linguistics, cultural difference, and schooling. Moreover, students read texts, like Mike Rose's *Lives on the Boundary*, that combine narrative and analysis, and they study practical approaches to teaching writing (using Flower's *Problem-Solving Strategies for Writing*). There is also a prominent place reserved for polyvocal, hybrid texts, including Keith Gilyard's *Voices of the Self*, which alternates between autobiographical and academic discourses, and Alice Childress's *A Hero Ain't Nothin' but a Sandwich*, a novel for adolescents which shuttles among several voices.

Carnegie Mellon tutors are expected not only to read hybrid texts but also to write them. As discussed earlier in the chapter, they help write the CLC publications (i.e., *Raising the Curtain on Curfew*) in collaboration with teens and in hybrid discourses. As part of the on-campus Carnegie Mellon course, they write to an electronic bulletin board, which mentor coordinator Jennifer Flach describes as "a conversational space" for mentors and faculty. Finally, they undertake a major research paper. The project is termed an "inquiry," an experimental, hybrid genre on a topic emerging from the mentor's experience, requiring empirical research (interviews, data collection) and representing multiple voices (college students, urban teens, popular culture, academic scholarship). This inquiry project, initially disconcerting to the undergraduate and graduate students alike, is a distinguishing feature of the Carnegie Mellon course. The inquiry projects, true to Deweyan principles, emanate from the mentors' experience on site at the CLC, that is, from a lived curiosity, problem, or quandary. As one mentor commented, "My inquiry was more sparked from my teen. Now I'm going to be struggling with getting readings. . . . They didn't force you [to pick a topic based on reading]."

Characteristic of student response to service-learning across the board in higher education is a perception that such courses are markedly different from others. So too at Carnegie Mellon. All the mentors with whom I spoke commented on how this course represents a departure—in content and structure—from any other they had taken. One undergraduate remarked in our interview:

> There are aspects of this course that are completely different from anything I've ever done before, [including the inquiry, which is] of a different nature [than past research papers]. Most of the times when you do a research paper it is assimilating what you have learned, what you have read. . . . The argument you make is dictated by the information you have. In this case it's a nice one because it is your own ideas and then you are going out and testing those ideas. . . . It's very different. It's a matter of what we think and then testing what we think. . . . It's adding to the body of knowledge rather than just using it. I'm just starting to see that.

A graduate student mentor similarly reflects: "It's definitely different [from other classes]. . . . I don't think there's a pulling and stretching like in other courses where you're trying to make things fit. I think you just go, and it fits. . . . I think it's also different because you're not going to come up with an answer." There is less "assimilation of what you have learned" and less "pulling and stretching to make things fit" because the course, and particularly the inquiry projects, are premised on what Flower terms "observation-based theory building."

Observation-based theory building stands in contrast to the dominant approach to theory building in English studies, in which a theory is generally valued for its historical authority, internal consistency, rhetorical elegance, or capacity to offer a novel interpretation of a text. In the spirit of Deweyan pragmatism and empirical composition research, observation-based theory is "built from the union of two sources of evidence: it springs in part from an intuition or an argument and in part from the complementary evidence of close, systematic observation and data" (Flower, "Observation-Based" 172). Flower champions inductive reasoning that starts with observing events in action, with problems as experienced in real life rather than as explained by authoritative theorists. This approach has apparently been internalized by the undergraduate quoted above: "It's a matter of what we think and then testing what we think. It's adding to the body of knowledge rather than just using it."

Observation-based theory building is readily apparent in the student inquiry projects. The term *inquiry* is borrowed from Dewey's lexicon, and true to his experiential and experimental philosophy of learning, the projects emerge from grounded experience and are forwarded as tentative (though serious and useful) renderings of meaning. I analyzed three inquiry projects—one in an early draft by a graduate student exploring her felt conflict between the CLC's rhetoric on collaboration and her experience of pushing teens to produce a publishable text; another, "'Nigger'—As Bad as it Sounds?", written by an undergraduate in 1995; and the third, "Responses to Uncertainty in Mentoring at the CLC: Implementation of Structure or Support," by a pair of undergraduates. Each text is a complex interweaving of sources and discourses.

Also key to the inquiry projects is the problem-solving imperative of cognitive rhetoric. As evident in the graduate student inquiry (untitled at the time I read it) and "Responses to Uncertainty in Mentoring at the CLC," many students identify a problem in the mentoring process, assert their own perspective, consider alternate perspectives using empirical data gathered at the CLC (observations, interviews), weave in academic scholarship, and propose a solution. Likewise, the "'Nigger'—As Bad as it Sounds?" inquiry started with a problem—a student's confusion over the multiple meanings and uses of the word "nigger" among urban youth. (He was, of course, familiar with the word as a term of denigration but was intrigued by how young African Americans used it as a term of affiliation or affection.) His inquiry brings several sources to bear on the matter (his opinions, interviews with CLC teens, interviews with African American and White adults, course readings, academic scholarship on linguistics, and excerpts from popular films and magazines) and concludes with a complex analysis of reversal strategies and the context-driven nature of language.

While some service-learning courses (like Herzberg's) and some quarters of English studies (like cultural studies) similarly draw on a wide range of popular and scholarly sources in their research methodology, almost all (with some forms of progressive feminist scholarship a notable exception) continue to disseminate their research in the well-established academic genre of the traditional critical essay. In this respect, the Carnegie Mellon inquiries depart. Earlier in this chapter I discussed the hybridity of the mentor/teen publications and the Community Conversations. Hybrid discourse is likewise a key element of the inquiries, except that for these research projects, the Carnegie Mellon student must gather multiple perspectives and discourses and integrate them into his or her research paper. Just as the "discourse of a community problem-solving dialogue is not going to be anybody's home discourse" (Flower, "Partners" 107), the discourse of the inquiry cannot be entirely in the "home" discourse of the academy, that is, standard academic discourse.[4] Although they take the form of a text written for school, inquiry projects—crafted in a hybrid discourse and accounting for multiple perspectives—nonetheless constitute another space for intercultural collaboration.

Unlike writing-*for*-the-community projects, the inquiry projects do not readily abandon academic genres for workplace discourses. And unlike the writing-*about*-the-community projects of Bruce Herzberg's Bentley College students, the Carnegie Mellon inquiries still depart from, or at least creatively revise, academic discourse. They are essay-like but betray some of the conventions of the traditional humanistic essay: they work from experience toward theory, rather than apply theory to experience; they advance tentative claims rather than assert confident theses; they adopt report-like text features rather than aspire to a seamless elegance; and they value a diverse range of sources (especially observations on-site) rather than privilege only traditional "authoritative" texts. The inquiry projects include slang and include not only bibliographies but also multiple appendices with interview transcripts and empirical data. Pragmatist William James would say that the projects have "cash value," a usefulness to the ongoing work of the CLC (they are read by CLC staff, mentors, and future mentors to better understand the CLC context and amend policy). They mark a phenomenon rare in college courses—an organic, experimental genre emerging from a deliberate mingling of the academic with the nonacademic, of White with Black, of dominant discourses with marginalized voices.

Writing with the Community and the Ends of Literate Social Action

The CLC's practices mark a departure from business as usual in the English department. As a pioneering program, the CLC generates excitement and innovative thinking. However, because it disrupts expected modes of teaching, learning, collaboration, and writing, some find it disconcerting. The CLC emphasizes a new context for learning (far from the comfort of campus), hybrid discourses (a departure from the familiarity of academic discourse), intercultural collaboration (Who's the expert here anyway?), unforeseen practical problems (What happens when teens abandon CLC projects for the start of basketball season?), and uncharted assessment issues (How does one assess the deliberately unfamiliar discourse of college student inquiry projects and teen publications, and how does one measure social change in the community?). As Jennifer Flach, CLC mentor coordinator, reflected: "I think there is a lot of craziness about the CLC, which I think is part of what you need to understand about any kind of community–university collaboration. Communities, thank God, do not work like universities—that's part of the strength of having something like this. There are days when things go so badly—but they pick up, and something good comes out of it and you have to take a big breath and realize that it will all work."

In the work of the CLC is manifest the potential of the academy to partner with local communities in a spirit of cooperation and strategic action across lines of culture, race, class, and discourse. In collaboration with the residents of the north side of Pittsburgh, Carnegie Mellon works toward social justice in the Deweyan sense of facilitating more open communication across boundaries and in the Freirean sense of encouraging democratic participation among those traditionally devalued, excluded, or overlooked (here African American urban teens). It puts writing, rhetoric, and problem solving at the center of such an initiative, opening more venues for oral and written rhetorical performance to address pressing community problems. Without being mediated by nonprofit agency bureaucracies (like many service-learning initiatives, particularly writing-for projects) or by schools (like many writing-about courses that focus on tutoring), the CLC realizes pragmatic possibilities for partnering directly with marginalized constituencies to help them exercise their writerly voices in the public sphere. The CLC meanwhile prompts privileged college students to risk stepping beyond the comforts of both campus and academic discourse. Moreover, it emphasizes the potential of writing and rhetoric to imagine and enact alternative modes of inquiry and action through the generative process of creating intercultural spaces, performances, and discourses.

The CLC/Carnegie Mellon initiative stands as an exemplar of the writing-with-the-community paradigm in my charting of community-based writing programs. According to the typology, writing-with initiatives are distinguished from writing-for and writing-about programs by their goals and by how they value distinctly different discourses, sites for learning, literacies, assessment measures, and learning relationships. As for goals, the CLC works collaboratively and strategically, using rhetoric to identify, explore, and address local problems; it encourages intercultural collaboration and the forging of hybrid discourses; and it supports shared inquiry and research. Its most highly valued discourse is characterized by its adaptability to local circumstances and its hybridity (in contrast to the academic essay or established workplace discourses), and the primary site for learning is the community center (rather than the classroom or the nonprofit agency). The most highly valued learning relationship is that of mentor and teen, a significant departure from writing-for projects (where the primary learning relationship involves the student and the agency contact) and from writing-about projects (where the primary learning relationship involves the student and the teacher), both of which often result in interaction between college students and community partners of similar racial, class, and educational backgrounds.

While this study examines only one program that follows the writing-with paradigm, many other community–university partnerships also fall under this rubric. While each differs in many ways from the CLC, all are innovative grassroots partnerships that hinge on writing and are largely unmediated by nonprofit agencies. A few examples:

◆ The Write for Your Life Project, a joint venture of Michigan State University and secondary school teachers and students, is aimed at developing and implementing a writing curriculum that starts with themes generated from both student experience and community needs. It creatively combines personal, research, and public discourses in service to the community (see Stock and Swenson).

◆ Brian Conniff and Betty Rogers Youngkin describe the Dayton Literacy Project, which involves faculty, graduate students, and undergraduates in grassroots literacy work and writing workshops with women on public assistance. Meanwhile, they undertake collaborative research.

◆ Ellen Cushman, in her "Rhetorician as Agent of Social Change," echoes Flower's view on the limits of classroom-based cultural critique and then goes on to describe how an individual ethnographer can forge reciprocal relationships with less privileged community members while undertaking research.

◆ Sandra Stotsky describes programs that center on "participatory writing" (often letter writing), highlighting the ways that "the ability to write facilitates participation in the civic process" ("Participatory" 236), particularly the use of writing to express civic identity, obtain information or help, provide a public service, or evaluate a public service, political structure, or public official.

◆ Aaron Schultz and Anne Ruggles Gere describe what they call "public" service-learning, which asks students to solve pressing campus or local problems through writing. Although the service-learning projects they discuss are ones through which students address problems in the *campus* community (like gender equity in college athletics or a university policy perceived as racially biased or otherwise unjust), the problem-solving ethos of the course that Schultz and Gere discuss best fits the writing-with paradigm.

Finally, the experiment in community self-expression described in Ross Talarico's *Spreading the Word: Poetry and the Survival of Community in America,* while not technically a university–community partnership, stands as an example, like the CLC, of the power that writing can have when practiced by inner-city residents. Talarico describes how he uses his experience as a poet and professor to do writing with the community—mostly poetry and autobiography—in the interest of marginalized voices.

The CLC is the result of a constellation of forces which, unfortunately, are not often readily available in most university–community pairings: significant commitments of senior university faculty and key community members; a respected community center with which to work; a long-term, stable partnership of two institutions; funding from without (foundation grants) and within (university commitments of personnel and resources); and a companion graduate program to supply a cadre of graduate students who provide able management and research assistance. It is these prerequisites, in part, that make possible the richness and depth of the CLC program—but they also make it difficult to launch at other colleges or universities. Still, although a full-scale CLC would be difficult to replicate, many of its concepts and strategies are portable. Some of Flower's recent work suggests how composition teachers can create community problem-solving dialogues in their own classrooms (see "Partners"). She also devotes chapters in her latest textbook, *Problem-Solving Strategies for Writing in College and Community*, to guiding students through such a process.

As a comprehensive social action effort with writing and rhetoric at its center, rather than a retooled composition course, the Community Literacy Center's efforts at writing with the community present both an exemplar for and a complex challenge to rhetoric and composition as a field. While all three kinds of community writing programs I analyze in this study are progressive and experimental in terms of pedagogy and curriculum, the CLC, unlike the others, is also progressive and experimental in the forms of discourse produced. Deliberately prompting alternatives to dominant rhetorics and genres, the CLC makes possible the kinds of innovative hybrid discourses we rarely find in largely static academic, workplace, and political discourses. By strategically channeling such creative literate practices to the exploration of local community problems, the CLC stands as a bench mark for writing with the community.

Prospects for Service-Learning in Composition

If the academy is to be more responsive to community concerns, institutions themselves must become less imitative and more creative. . . . What I'm describing might be called the "New American College," an institution that celebrates teaching and selectively supports research, while also taking special pride in its capacity to connect thought to action, theory to practice. . . . Undergraduates at the college would participate in field projects, relating ideas to real life. Classrooms and laboratories would be extended to include health clinics, youth centers, schools, and government offices. . . . The New American College, as a concerned institution, would be committed to improving, in a very intentional way, the human condition. As clusters of such colleges formed, a new model of excellence in higher education would emerge, one that would enrich the campus, renew communities and give new dignity and status to the scholarship of service.

ERNEST L. BOYER, *"Creating the New American College"*

A first-aid manual (written and desktop-published by a collaborative student group) for a local swimming league. An in-depth academic research essay (enriched by on-site tutoring experience) on Ebonics as it relates to schooling and literacy in America. An observation-based research project (in an experimental hybrid genre) on the nature of African American language use. These final student projects for service-learning courses mark three distinct kinds of writing and perform three distinct kinds of literacy. In addition, taken together, students in the courses I have examined in this study produce a diversity of other documents: personal, reflective, and analytical essays; reading and reflection journals; summaries and interpretations of class readings; personal narratives based on powerful community experiences; project logs, business letters, and memos to nonprofit agencies; dialogic electronic bulletin board postings; and collaborative publications. Certainly these documents constitute an impressive spectrum of writing, ranging from the personal to the academic to the public.

As I have noted in previous chapters, some of these genres and literacies are already well represented in college composition classrooms. For example, students in technical writing classes regularly compose manuals and brochures like the first-aid manual from the Sport Management writing-for-the-community course; and students in critical pedagogy–oriented composition courses write essays similar to the Ebonics or ADD essays from Herzberg's writing-about course. Furthermore, in the academy, cultural studies continues to problematize the same fundamental separation of academic inquiry and social action that service-learning is bridging. Yet while some of the practices in service-learning courses mirror those of other English courses, we must acknowledge several key departures. Most technical writing courses look to the corporate rather than the nonprofit community for motivation and models, and both critical pedagogy and cultural studies courses practice cultural critique as a classroom-based and reading-based academic pursuit rather than as a pragmatic writing-based intervention in the community.

Despite the differences I have discerned among community writing paradigms, all three share characteristics that distinguish them as a whole from current practice in college writing instruction: an emphasis on experiential learning, an insistence on living out a dialectical relationship between action and reflection, a synergistic pairing of community work with academic study, a folding of community outreach experiences into research and writing, and a commitment to addressing community problems and social justice through writing and rhetoric. Given this combination of characteristics, something genuinely new is afoot in rhetoric and composition, even if service-learning inherits many of its theoretical foundations.

The Community Writing Typology as a Heuristic

I began this study by naming and charting three community writing paradigms. Such sorting serves the immediate purposes of helping us apprehend the diversity of community-based writing initiatives and of giving us handy generalizations from which to launch discussions of service-learning. Yet the typology's most significant function is heuristic in nature—particularly its use in sharpening our vision of the distinctions among (even within) programs and paradigms. Consequently, the typology can help us make more informed choices about pedagogy and curriculum. It helps us answer those most fundamental teaching questions: What do we want our writing courses to *do*? What kinds of literacy should we most value in our curricula? *What kind of writer do we hope to encourage through our teaching?* The typology assists us not only in asking these questions, but also in translating them into practice by matching literacy and social action priorities with specific teaching strategies.

In one sense, this study is an extended inquiry into the kind of dissonance Bruce Herzberg overheard among participants at a 1996 CCCC roundtable at which presenters (myself among them) were describing their experiences of teaching writing-for-the-community pilot courses. Herzberg, observing that both the presenters and audience seemed confused about the goals and outcomes of the courses being discussed, commented later: "They [the University of Massachusetts presenters] were using the *Stanford approach* and the audience was wondering why they weren't achieving the *Bentley effect*." In other words, many in the audience sensed a disjunction between the writing-for-the-community approach being presented and discussed and the writing-about-the-community outcomes and effects that they generally favored. Yet none of us had a vocabulary for making such distinctions or for readily discerning the relationship of particular service-learning approaches to particular literacies, discourses, pedagogical arrangements, and learning goals. The chart of community writing paradigms offers the beginnings of such a vocabulary. The typology, given its heuristic function, helps us to align the specific approaches with the specific effects of service-learning programs (and, one hopes, helps us to recognize when they are mismatched). As noted at the outset, the typology is *not* intended as an argument for any single program or paradigm as most effective, most worthy, most just. Rather, it lays out options and allows individual teachers to make informed choices based on their own values and in light of the opportunities and constraints of their own particular community and institutional contexts. The typology helps curriculum planners to see the implications of their choices, and it helps instructors to align specific teaching practices with their chosen visions of literacy and social action.

The mark of a good typology is its continuing flexibility and usefulness. The *for, about, with* schema that I charted in Chapter 1 can be pressed into further service by simply changing the variable in the left column and then fleshing out how that variable is manifested in each of the three paradigms. I am most interested in literacy outcomes, discourses, learning relationships, and goals. Thus I inserted those in the left column and traced their manifestations and consequences for each paradigm. Others may have different priorities. For example, another variable could turn on an important question such as *Who defines community needs?* By considering this question in relation to community writing practices and analyzing it in the context of the typology, important distinctions can be readily identified (see Figure 1).

One discovers that in defining community needs, writing-for programs generally rely on the expertise of local nonprofit agencies: "We, the agency staff, need the first-aid manual, which we will in turn use to meet community needs as we define them and respond to them." Writing-about programs do much the same concerning the direct (nonwriting) community service work (i.e., tutoring), while the classroom component of a course like Herzberg's prompts students to engage in academic research about systemic causes of social injustice: "I, the teacher, help students explore systemic causes of community needs through dialogue

	Writing *for* the Community	Writing *about* the Community	Writing *with* the Community
Definition of Community Needs	For service component, nonprofit agency staffs define community needs and what documents are required.	For service component, local community agencies or school administrators define needs and tasks (i.e., helping at a homeless shelter, or tutoring at a local school).	For service component, community residents, together with university people, name pressing local problems.
Response	For writing component, students respond by composing workplace documents in collaboration with the agency contact person, to his or her specifications.	For writing component, students respond by composing essays for teacher that analyze the root social and institutional forces that put people in need.	For writing component, students respond by composing problem-solving public documents in collaboration with local residents.

FIGURE 1. *Definition of and response to community needs in the three community writing paradigms.*

and critical analysis." A writing-with project like the CLC generally brings university people together with community residents in a grassroots setting to name a local problem and to employ strategic methods in solving the problem: "We local residents believe that the recently imposed teen curfew creates a community need to which we should respond." Thus, writing-for programs define community need primarily according to agency needs; writing-about programs define need primarily as a topic to be analyzed abstractly in academic discourse (and, implicitly, as an issue to be addressed in the long term as students leave college to become more critical citizens in their lives); and writing-with programs define need primarily as a problem identified by local residents. One can also extend the analysis to suggest the kinds of texts most appropriate to meeting the needs manifested in each paradigm.

The typology could help draw similar distinctions with respect to other variables, and such distinctions can help us better understand what we are doing and why we are doing it. The distinctions are both descriptive and instrumental—descriptive in that they help us comprehend the range and variation of community writing programs, and instrumental in that they help us interrogate and refine the assumptions, ideologies, and implications embedded in particular pedagogical practices.

Programs that Cross Categories

What happens, however, when a service-learning initiative does not fit any of the categories I've defined—or, more likely, when it incorporates elements of more than one paradigm? My own experiences in teaching a variety of service-learning courses and my observations of other teachers lead me to affirm that generative combinations of paradigms within the same writing course are certainly possible, and by all indications quite promising. However, in referring to generative combinations I do not mean courses that meld multiple pedagogies into a single new amalgam, but instead those that weave distinct but complementary strands of the three paradigms. Successful combinations of paradigms are not those that haphazardly stir different approaches into a pedagogical melting pot, but rather those that weave a fabric of distinct yet related pedagogies to address distinct yet related literacy goals.

For example, my own teaching often combines writing-for-the-community and writing-about-the-community approaches. My initial interest in service-learning was sparked by a desire to have students undertake "real-world" writing projects for audiences outside the academy (primary concerns of both the Writing in Sport Management course studied here and writing-for pedagogies in general). What I found in my own classroom, much as I found in studying Gullion's, is that this pedagogy immerses students in meaningful nonacademic writing experiences and prompts them to grapple with workplace literacies which are markedly different from those usually demanded by traditional essay-focused composition courses. I also, as did Gullion, noticed a refreshing surge in motivation as student writers were challenged with community projects for someone other than the teacher. Now, as then, I believe that this is a fruitful pedagogy.

Yet during the first few semesters after adopting a writing-for service-learning pedagogy, I also grew concerned that my students, while doing (mostly) good work for nonprofit agencies, were often overlooking important social and ethical issues attendant on outreach work. I feared that while the writing-for service-learning component was a productive rhetorical addition to my course, there was too much sentimental emoting ("I feel good about helping the less fortunate") and not enough critical thought and reflection devoted to the complex ethics of community and service. In other words, my concerns mirrored those of Herzberg, who posits that instrumental service-learning projects often skirt an analysis of fundamental issues such as social class and institutional injustice. Unwilling to forego either the workplace literacy goals valued by a writing-for approach or the critical literacy goals valued by a writing-about approach, I have attempted to weave both into the same course. The danger of this compromise is that one semester is too short a time in which to pack these dual goals (*plus* all the other instruction generally expected of composition teachers, such as teaching academic discourse, research methods, and grammar; allowing opportunities for personal writing; building the classroom community; and so on). Particularly in first-year writing courses, instructors who want to include more than one paradigm run the risk of rushing to fit everything in, but doing no single thing well.

Despite this danger, I believe that weaving multiple paradigms into a single course is possible. My own solution has been to keep the writing-for assignments in my syllabus but to limit their scope so that groups of students can complete smaller projects within a few weeks rather than pursue large projects over the course of the entire semester. I have also learned to make the writing-about and writing-for elements of the course more complementary. For example, I use a writing-about essay not only to teach academic discourse but also to help students prepare for their writing-for project later in the semester.

An outline of the assignments for my Expository Writing III: Writing in College and Community course illustrates my approach (see Appendix A for syllabus). This is a class for upper-division students, but I also teach a pared down version of it for first-year composition. The first assignment for this course will look familiar—the academic research essay. One of my primary goals is to teach academic discourse (the essay genre, research methods, analysis, synthesis, use of sources, documentation, and so on). I do so, in large part, through this assignment. For the essay assignment, I emphasize to my students that we will be researching, arguing, and writing like academics. Meanwhile, I have two ulterior motives: to discover which kinds of social problems are of most concern to the class (so that I can seek out fitting community partners later in the semester), and to invite students to get invested in, and more familiar with, their chosen topics.

RESEARCH ESSAY ON A SOCIAL CONCERN
This assignment asks you to write an essay that investigates a particular social problem of your choice, preferably one that affects our local community. You are required to bring current research to bear on the topic through traditional library research, interviews, and/or electronic resources. You are also encouraged to weave your own experience and perspective into the essay.

Due Dates:
Proposal due	Sept. __
Exploratory Writing due	Sept. __
Mid-Draft due	Sept. __
Final Draft due	Sept. __

The Basics:
6–10 pages
Must include at least 4 reliable sources

The Proposal: The proposal is a tentative plan. It should run 1–2 pages (typed and double-spaced) and include a statement of the particular problem you intend to investigate, and your specific *research question*. You should also indicate *why* you wish to pursue this topic, *how* you expect to gather information, and *who* your target audience is. What you write in the proposal is not set in stone—your plans may change as you move through the writing and research process, and that is fine. However, if you intend a wholesale change of topic you need to discuss that with me and write another proposal.

Exploratory Writing: This writing should be at least 3 pages, but it can be in rough form (handwritten; lists; questions; plans;

scattered ideas; summaries of potential sources). Here you will want to include what you already know about your topic, and how you predict the essay will unfold (either in outline or narrative format). You should include your understanding of the "rhetorical situation" for this essay (see Flower). You must also make at least one visit to the library to survey potential sources. Please include *at least 5 potential sources*, whether they are books, articles, people to interview, government documents, Internet sites, etc. Along with the titles of the sources, include documentation (e.g., publishers, Internet addresses).

Mid-Draft: This should run at least 5 pages and be typed. Your ideas should be taking coherent shape, and your focus clear. You should be weaving in several of your sources, *and you must include in-text citations and a "Works Cited" list in accord with MLA or APA conventions*. These drafts will be reviewed by your classmates and submitted to the instructor.

Final Draft: This draft should represent your best work. Your ideas should be focused, developed, and supported; your organization finalized; and your language and syntax polished.

The research questions that students select vary with their majors and personal concerns, and my hope is that they emerge from a Deweyan starting place for learning that emphasizes experience and interest. Some recent research questions have included: Why doesn't our town have a curbside recycling program? Do senior citizens get adequate care at long-term care facilities? What strategies do chain stores use to draw business away from small-town retailers? Is technology evenly distributed among schools in our region? How much of a problem is gambling on campus? What resources are available to pregnant teens in the local area?

Students do library research, draw on their personal experience, and interview campus personnel and/or local people who deal directly with the chosen essay topic. Even though they have not yet ventured into the community to do service, the students are writing *about* the community and conducting community-based research. Through their research and writing, interviews with community contacts, class discussions, and conferences with me, they are also (with varying degrees of success) gaining a greater critical grasp of both the nature of the problem and the social forces which shape that problem. (See Appendix A for samples.)

Next, I ask the students to recast the essay in a different genre and for a different audience—an old saw of an assignment, but still effective. The assignment reads as follows:

REVISING THE RESEARCH ESSAY FOR A DIFFERENT AUDIENCE

Now that you have investigated a social problem in depth, it is important to communicate your findings to other, particularly popular, audiences. You may have written your essay with one or more audiences already in mind (the instructor, the academic community, local townspeople, government officials, etc.), but you still had to write in the genre of the academic research paper. That genre is often not the most appropriate one for reaching audiences beyond the academy.

For this assignment you will need to choose a particular audience and genre and then revise your essay as appropriate. You might opt to transform your research essay into a journalistic article or a letter to the editor so that it can reach a wider audience. If so, select a particular newspaper (*The Collegian? The Manhattan Mercury? The Kansas City Star?*). Then get more specific: Which section of the paper? (News? Features?) You might opt to write a letter to a very specific person, group, regulatory agency, or town board. You might opt to create a Web page for an Internet audience. If you can think of a more fitting audience or genre for your work, please let me know.

Oct. __ Statement of audience and genre due (in writing). Also include a list of characteristics for your new document *based on a review of similar writings.* For example, if you are writing for the *Manhattan Mercury*, will it be a news or features story? Who do you expect your typical reader will be? What will that audience expect of you, the writer? How long is the typical article? What is the style? What is the tone, voice, and ethos of most articles? What special conventions will you need to follow? How will you handle references to outside sources? And so on.

Oct. __ Draft due. Peer and instructor review.

Oct. __ Final draft due.

Most choose the journalistic article genre and imagine writing for the campus or local paper, while a few opt for a specialized magazine or professional journal. Others choose letters to

the editor or letters directly to those who have power to influence the given problem. This assignment, much like Herzberg's
Going Public project, encourages rhetorical thinking—particularly audience analysis—and allows further practice in revision
and editing. Meanwhile, I again have an eye on the community
writing project that will follow. While teaching this assignment, I
build a vocabulary for talking about writing as a social process
and as audience directed, which proves essential later when coaching students through the writing-for project (e.g., "reading the
context," "adapting to different audiences," "changing your voice
to fit a particular audience," "entering a new discourse community"). Students also practice adopting, or at least mimicking, a
new discourse as they first study the features of the genre they
will adopt. (How long is the usual editorial? Is there a conventional structure? What is the tone? Does it require different documentation than your research essay?) The revision of the research
essay for a nonacademic audience assignment also gives students
a trial run in code switching and genre switching, in moving between academic and nonacademic modes of writing, which is
something else they will need to negotiate in the writing-for-the-
community project that follows.

During the weeks in which students are occupied with these
first two assignments (which for me is the first third of the semester), I am contacting nonprofit agency directors and others in
the local community who deal, on a day-to-day basis, with the
problems that my students are investigating. I explain my teaching goals and inquire whether they have any writing or research
projects that need doing (parts of grant research? a newsletter
article? a survey and analysis? a Web page?). Most are eager to
collaborate, even after my cautions that the students are novice
writers who will need a good deal of guidance. (And the agency
contacts certainly need to understand that coaching the students
will take several meetings and lots of patience.) Based on my
experience, a good deal rides on these initial conversations with
agency contacts. Projects that are too clerical need to be avoided.
("I'm sorry, but simply posting your already written publicity
materials on the Web is more a technical than a writing matter.")
Likewise, projects that are too challenging need to be set aside or
divided into manageable tasks. ("No, I don't think the student

group could write such a grant; but they could, with your coaching, do the research for one particular part of the proposal.") Some seasoned service-learning teachers recommend that students themselves should make these initial arrangements with the agencies, thus emphasizing their responsibility for the project and their need to cultivate skills of self-promotion (Huckin; Henson and Sutliff). But I prefer to take a more active role in shaping the projects and orienting the contact people. After this initial intervention, I step back as much as possible from direct involvement in the day-to-day work of the projects, adopting the role of coach and consultant rather than instructor and grader.

Before students have completed the Different Audience assignment, I have, in consultation with local nonprofits, compiled a menu of potential projects resonating with their research essay topics and covering a range of social issues. Students then select their preferences. (Service-learning research suggests greater success when students can choose their own projects [Waterman, "Role"].) I encourage them to opt for a project related to their just-completed research. Most do so, or select projects that connect with their majors, prior community service, prior employment experience, or personal history. Any way that students can get some traction on their potential project can help: a nursing student, for example, wanting to work with a public health organization; a student who is already a Big Brother asking to work with that organization; a student with job experience in a long-term care facility opting to collaborate with the Alzheimer's Association; a student whose close friend in high school became pregnant wanting to work with a planned parenting organization. I have found that such connections to a project, whether personal or academic, are helpful since students with more background knowledge in a particular area are usually better equipped to work with agencies in that area. Similarly, in her study of service-learning, Nora Bacon notes greater success among students with prior relationships to their partner organizations (*Transition* 129).

After students rank their choices, I then cluster them into project groups (usually teams of two to four, depending on the scope and difficulty of the project), taking into consideration their preferences, prior experiences, and skills. For example, I try to get at least one able editor, one good people person, and one technology-savvy person in each group, if possible.

COMMUNITY WRITING PROJECT

The goal of this project is for you to become a more experienced and versatile writer who can use writing to address social and community problems. Our parallel goal is to craft high-quality documents that meet the specific needs of local community agencies.

While each project will be different, all will share a few common expectations. Working as a team, each group must do the following:

◆ Meet as a group to plan for the initial interview with your agency contact person. List the questions you intend to pose. See what particular strengths each member brings to the group. (Who's a good interviewer? Who's a good editor? Who has a facility with computers and/or desktop publishing? Who's a good researcher? And so on.)

◆ Keep an individual Project Log/Dialogic Journal (I'll collect them weekly). This should include updates on your progress and reflections on the process.

◆ Schedule and conduct your initial meeting. Introduce selves, gather information for the Agency Profile assignment, and discuss the proposed project. (We will practice this in class.) It is also a good idea to schedule your next meeting during this one. Most projects require 3 or 4 off-campus meetings with your community partner. A few regular classes will be canceled to make time for those meetings.

◆ As a group, write a letter that both thanks your contact person for the first meeting and reviews the parameters of the project (confirm basic expectations, deadlines for drafts and project completion, time and date of next meeting). I must see this letter before you send it. Due within 3 days after your meeting.

◆ As a group, write the Agency Profile Report. Due Oct. __. See separate instructions.

◆ As a group, meet with me to map your timeline for this project.

- Hold **at least** one draft/revise/update meeting with your community contact person between your first meeting and the final meeting. You may need more, depending on the project. I must see your drafts before you share them with your community partners.

- Complete projects by December __.

- Keep me informed of progress and any problems.

The project counts for 40 points, and grading will be based on the quality of the final document as evaluated by both the community partner and the instructor. It will be a team grade, with plus or minus adjustments to individuals only if there are extenuating circumstances. The Project Log/Dialogic Journal counts for 6 points and will be evaluated based on the regularity of your updates and, more significantly, on the quality of reflective inquiry demonstrated in your entries.

Changing gears from the writing-about paradigm to the writing-for paradigm can be jarring, especially for novices (students and teachers alike). Although throughout the semester the class has been oscillating between reflection and action in a Deweyan and Freirean spirit (i.e., reflectively discussing topics in class, then actively writing and critiquing; reflectively researching and drafting, then actively sharing in peer groups; and so on), this moment in the semester brings the terms of the action–reflection dialectic more dramatically into relief. As students embark on the writing-for projects and look beyond campus for the assignment (and beyond the teacher for instruction), the whole feel of the class changes. While most embrace this change, not everyone does, particularly those students especially attached to the familiar expectations of school rituals and school writing. Whereas peer response groups had previously been one step in the composing process for individual academic essays, the small peer project teams suddenly become *the* centers of activity at each in- class, homework, and agency meeting. Whereas the expectations of where and how learning would take place had gone much as anticipated (according to the timeline on the syllabus and the dictates of the instructor), now students are nudged into unfamiliar territory beyond the bounds of tidy assignments. Whereas the instructor had been the sole assigner and judge of coursework, now community partners assign and evaluate. As a consequence, the teacher often gets decentered, assuming coach and project manager roles rather than instructor and judge roles, particularly as groups look more and more to their new community partners for guidance. On a practical note, I cancel several classes so that project groups can meet on their own, with their community partners on-site at the agency, and with me in student group conferences. I also do this to signal that their time at the agencies is just as important as time in class.

As a first step, I require students to write an Agency Profile, which I assign for a number of reasons. Most importantly, the Agency Profile underscores that one cannot write for an organization until one knows something about that organization (again, emphasizing the social and context-driven nature of writing). The profile marks my limited (perhaps too limited) response to an important question that Nora Bacon has raised about assigning writing-for projects: "Recognizing, even insisting, that texts are embedded in their social contexts, how can we introduce students to a community agency one week and expect them to write in its voice the next?" She then goes on to observe, "We know that full, productive participation in a discourse community comes with time and practice; it requires a period of apprenticeship that involves not only acquiring topic knowledge but also growing comfortable with one's own role in the community" ("Community" 47). The Agency Profile is my attempt to start the process whereby students become familiar with at least the main characteristics of a new discourse community.

I also want students to have a safe opportunity to practice group interaction skills and to test-run what for many will be the unfamiliar experience of collaborative writing. In my experience, while most students report having done group projects before, many also bemoan how the group dynamics were less than ideal, and often downright frustrating. Like Laurie Gullion, I find it imperative to spend a class session or two teaching, discussing, and role-playing successful (and unsuccessful) small group dynamics. Dewey celebrates cooperation, but he very seldom accounts for the fact that cooperation needs to be modeled and taught. Thus, in addition to the opportunity for students to gather contextual information about their community partner, the Agency Profile gives them a relatively safe space in which to experience collaborative work before embarking on the high-risk process of doing an agency project. In technical or professional communication service-learning courses, the Agency Profile assignment, if modified, also presents the opportunity to teach the formal report genre.

AGENCY PROFILE

We can't work well with an organization until we get to know that organization. The purpose of the Agency Profile is to help you better understand the community partner organization with which you will work; it also will give you experience in collaborative and report writing.

The report should be a concise description and analysis of your community partner organization: Its mission? The nature of the organization? Its size? How old? Why founded? Government-related? All-volunteer? How funded? The nature of the audience for your future writing project? And so on. Much of the information for the profile will come from your initial interview. Still, you will want to gather written information from the agency (if possible), and do some library research.

You should also include some reference to the *social context* of this organization: What needs is the organization responding to? How does it relate to your findings in your research essay? Who defines those needs and how they should be met? What are the root social forces of the problems that the organization addresses? Are there alternative ways of addressing those problems? (3–4 pages won't allow adequate time to get to all these questions, so some can carry over as prompts for Log/Journal entries.)

Length: 3–4 double-spaced pages
Features: Title; subheadings, if appropriate; supplementary
            materials in an appendix, if appropriate.
Due: Oct. __

Students also keep a log (to keep me informed of progress), and a dialogic journal (to provide a window on group dynamics and to encourage continued reflection). The instructions read as follows:

PROJECT LOG/DIALOGIC JOURNAL

Starting this week you should keep a Project Log/Dialogic Journal and update it regularly (at least once a week). As suggested by its name, the Log/Journal serves two purposes.

◆ Log your project progress so that I can stay appraised of how the group (and each individual) is making headway. Be sure to log all group meetings, community partner meetings, due dates for drafts, and your particular responsibilities. Also comment briefly on these entries: How did the meeting go? Why did you get assigned particular duties within the group? How much time and effort did you commit to the project this week?

◆ In the Dialogic Journal you are invited to reflect both on the project and on the issues it raises for you. This can be informal and free-flowing (grammar doesn't count for anything here) but should involve serious thinking, too. I'm most concerned with the depth of your inquiry—how ardently you grapple with problems and pursue ideas that surface during the course of the project. Log/Journals will be read only by me and are not shared with team members, except with your permission. Therefore, you should feel free to bring up any problems or concerns you have with your team.

Questions to prompt thinking about the project include: How are the group dynamics working out? How does your work style gel (or conflict) with that of the others? Which parts of the project are most challenging? Are there times when you are feeling confused? Where do you think that confusion is coming from? Questions to prompt social inquiry include: What issues are surfacing in your mind as you work on this project? Why work on this topic? How does it relate to your own values and interests? How does your work relate to your findings in the research essay? What are you noticing about your community agency? Which events are most memorable for you? (Describe them, interpret them.) How does your work or the organization's work contribute to social justice? What are some of the root causes of the problems with which your agency deals?

Keep your Log and Journal entries in a separate notebook (or on pages you can remove). You can also, if you prefer, do them online and send them to me via email. I will collect Log/Journals regularly and will respond to your reflections. In turn, you are invited to respond to my entries.

I will not delve into the details of how this writing-for section of the course unfolds since the issues that surface are remarkably similar to those I have already explicated in Chapter 3. I will note, however, that I have opened the door to a variation on the community writing project that allows some student groups to work within the writing-with-the-community paradigm. Sometimes the social concern research essays will explore problems that students can better address *without* the aid of a nonprofit agency, leaving students to pursue a more grassroots approach. In a recent example, one student, prompted by the high teen pregnancy rate she saw in rural schools in her home region, wrote a research essay that investigated how high schools in the region were (and were not) teaching sexual education. She discovered that state law mandated sexual education and that while many schools were doing a good job, many others were skirting the mandate and teaching little or no sex ed. Rather than partner with a nonprofit agency on a writing-for initiative for the community writing project, she worked with two other students to survey a wide range of schools, and the students then used that data to write a report to the state board of education. In a spirit of problem solving rather than finger pointing, the report outlined the problem and suggested methods by which the board might address it. (Appendix A includes the full texts for this project.) Likewise, this approach to the community project is often fitting when students take up on-campus problems which they hope to remedy through writing, often by means of proposals to those who have the authority to change the situation (see Schultz and Gere). To close my Writing in College and Community course, I switch gears again (shuttling from active doing to reflective thinking), as students are asked to write a short capstone essay in which they reflect on their experiences both as writers moving between discourses and as agents acting in the community.

A similar example of weaving strands of different paradigms into one course can be found in the Service-Learning Writing Project (SLWP) at Michigan State University. While I have not observed this project firsthand, I have reviewed research describing and analyzing it and spoken with its directors. Based on a curriculum that combines writing-for-the-community projects with an American Studies tradition of introducing first-year students to critical reading of key American texts, the SLWP aspires to "civic literacy." SLWP founders David Cooper and Laura Julier define the three philosophical foundations of civic literacy as follows:

> (1) Rhetorical strategies made available to students through service-learning placements in non-profit civic-minded organizations support effective writing pedagogy. (2) Writing projects assigned to students in conjunction with such community service placements advance higher-order-academic discourse skills. (3) The combination of writing for a public service agency and the intellectual experience gained through carefully studying primary cultural source materials is a particularly effective way of advancing civic education. ("Democratic" 82).

The SLWP sees civic literacy as "a craft of social inquiry as well as an important mode of public discourse" ("Democratic" 83). Further recognizing two distinct but interrelated and complementary literacy practices (one instrumental, one critical), they remark: "Service-learning functions, then, at two levels: It helps make students more effective participants in public life, and it encourages them to be more competent witnesses to our troubled times" (92). Thus, the SLWP structures its curriculum accordingly—part devoted to critical interpretation of cultural texts in academic discourse (writing-about assignments); part devoted to undertaking real-world projects *for* nonprofit community organizations in public and workplace discourses (e.g., a newsletter article for Michigan Literacy, Inc., and a pamphlet for a community mental health board); and part devoted to relating these two modes of learning to each other.

Another example of a composition sequence similarly divided between the writing-about and writing-for paradigms is described by Floyd Ogburn and Barbara Wallace. In their first-year composition service-learning course sequence at the University of Cincinnati, students study important national social issues (like homelessness) through critical reading, Internet research, and process writing. And then, in a separate but coordinated follow-up course, they devote their skills and energies to writing profiles of local social service agencies. Selected profiles are then published on the Web, providing students with a public audience for their writing and serving the local community by publicizing community resources.

I expect that many—perhaps most—service-learning courses draw on more than one of the three *(for, about,* and *with)* paradigms. Discerning and explicating the multiple literacies embedded in such combinations insures that they are deliberate and that they complement one another. While this book offers a framework for such analysis, more research into programs that combine community writing paradigms is needed, as is more qualitative research that accounts for student experiences of service-learning.

Writing Across the Curriculum and Writing Across the Community

A recent study of Learn and Serve America grant recipients concludes that four factors are key to sustaining a service-learning program in the long term: (1) an institutional tradition of service, (2) leadership of a single individual, (3) faculty support, and (4) the presence of service centers (Gray, Ondaatje, and Zakaras vi). Also important, I believe, is an understanding of how community initiatives are shaped by their particular institutional and community contexts. The courses and programs I describe in Chapters 3, 4, and 5 are in large measure a result of the teaching values and theoretical commitments of their principal architects—Laurie Gullion, Bruce Herzberg, and Linda Flower. Yet these initiatives are also products of their institutional and local community contexts, and each such context constitutes a complex (and often conflicted) nexus of forces. For example, Gullion's initiative is housed in a sport studies department, an applied discipline with a history of outreach efforts and with a faculty generally supportive of community-oriented work. As she remarked in our interview, "I was made freshly aware of the fact that we [in Sport Studies] have a lot of faculty who believe in this type of program. That helps to make it work." That department, in turn, is part of a public land-grant university founded, in large part, on a mission of public service. These contextual factors, in addition to her being granted a faculty fellowship to support the course, suggest that Gullion's efforts and her instrumental approach to service-learning go with the grain of her institutional context. Still, ironically, several powerful forces at a land-grant university like the University of Massachusetts Amherst, which values its identity as a research institution, act in opposition to initiatives like Gullion's and can choke the long-term growth of community-based writing pedagogies. For example, the large and fragmented structure of the university mitigates against cross-curricular reform efforts like service-learning. Moreover, funding can be fleeting, as evident in fellowships that cover only one year, and research, rather than teaching and service, usually dominates faculty concerns as well as promotion and tenure decisions.

Similarly, Bruce Herzberg's course at a small, private, business-oriented college marks a response to its institutional context—a curious blend of assent and dissent. At a business college, working with nonprofit rather than for-profit ventures marks a fundamental departure from expectations. Yet, over several years, Bentley faculty have succeeded in making community–academic connections a valued part of the campus culture due to an ambitious cross-curricular service-learning program. Herzberg's course is one of the many at Bentley which integrates community action with academic course goals. However, his particular approach, as detailed in Chapter 4, marks a deliberate challenge to his institution and his students. Most service-learning courses at Bentley, according to Bentley Service-Learning Project Director Jim Ostrow, adopt an ideology of service closer to the writing-for paradigm—i.e., students offering practical help to struggling nonprofits, meanwhile learning functional (rather than critical) literacies. Herzberg's students *do* in fact provide a needed, functional service by tutoring at local schools; but he balks at the writing-for approach. Herzberg's pedagogy is grounded in the critical and rhetorical theories which he marshals to critique the capitalist ideology in which his students are steeped, and on which a business college generally thrives. He makes his students think and talk and write about class and privilege on a campus (and in a larger culture) that resists open dialogue about class and privilege. While his initial choice to implement service-learning is very much with the grain of his institution, his particular approach of cultural critique works against the ideological grain of a business college.

In the case of the Community Literacy Center of Pittsburgh, while some form of public service has always taken place at major research universities like Carnegie Mellon, it has often been, particularly within the humanities, co-curricular, or, at best, peripheral to academic teaching and scholarship. Since the CLC relocates the site of learning from classroom to community center and pairs community-based literacy work with academic research, it certainly marks a departure from the dominant ideology of the institution. However, a closer look reveals that the CLC also reflects some values of both Carnegie Mellon and its local context. Notice that the CLC is the only program examined in this study to make race a priority and to involve graduate students. Its geographical context (a large multicultural city) and institutional context (Carnegie Mellon) shape the goals and practices of the CLC at least as much as Linda Flower's preference for cognitive rhetoric or Wayne Peck's approach to community activism do. One simply cannot be seriously involved in community work in the inner city without confronting issues of race; consequently, intercultural communication surfaces as one of the defining goals of the CLC. As well, the CLC places a higher priority on generating research than the other programs studied here and involves graduate students in its research efforts. This should not be a surprise when we consider that Carnegie Mellon is an elite research university which, like other institutions of its kind, places high priority on graduate study and the production of scholarship. Here too is revealed how the CLC, despite being something of an anomaly at Carnegie Mellon, works with the grain of its institutional context. From the institutional perspective, in fact, the CLC serves as a counterpoint to Herzberg's efforts at Bentley: Herzberg's choice to initiate service-learning was not out of the norm at Bentley, but his particular practices were at odds with the college's prevailing market-oriented values. Conversely, Flower and Peck's choice to initiate the CLC marked a departure from the norm at Carnegie Mellon, but CLC practice still aligns, in some key ways, with the university's research priorities. Thus, whether with the grain or against it (or both), all community writing programs are in large measure products of their home institutional cultures. It should come as no surprise, then, that the better program organizers understand not only the complexities of their local communities but also the dynamics of their home institutions. Anyone contemplating a service-learning initiative must read those contexts carefully and strategically.

Furthermore, service-learning advocates should not only read their institutional and local contexts, but also attend to the histories of educational movements that share core values with service-learning. These include the extension movement spurred by land-grant universities after the 1860s, the progressive education movement of earlier in this century (as evident in Dewey's work), and the activist movements of the 1960s.[1] More particular to composition studies is the writing across the curriculum movement of the last twenty years. To my mind, service-learning programs could benefit from capitalizing on parallels with writing across the curriculum (WAC). While many community-based writing initiatives, such as the CLC, have no significant link to WAC, the Writing in Sport Management course at the University of Massachusetts is, in fact, a junior-year WAC course. While there is no formal institutional relationship between the well-established WAC program at the University of Massachusetts and the provost's efforts to encourage service-learning across the curriculum, one of Gullion's primary reasons for introducing service-learning—that students need to experience the professional community which they will soon enter—mirrors the rationale for many WAC programs, that is, that students need real experience in writing within the disciplinary discourse community they are entering.

Likewise, Bruce Herzberg's service-learning courses, Expository Writing I: Summary and Synthesis, and Expository Writing II: Research and Rhetoric, while not part of a formal WAC program, have much in common with the writing-to-learn and writing-in-the-disciplines strands of WAC research and practice. As noted in Chapter 4, Herzberg pairs each of his service-learning composition courses with a course from another discipline. He explains: "We have a number of service-learning course clusters, in which students are enrolled in two courses simultaneously and 'share' the service-learning project. Often, one of the courses is composition, and my impression is that there is a good deal of shared writing or the sharing of information about writing. This is the case in my own service-learning cluster." Clustering a writing course with a sociology course one semester and with a philosophy course the following semester emphasizes the notion of writing as modulated to particular disciplinary communities. Thus learning to write, as in WAC, is associated with learning to write for particular disciplinary communities. The community outreach work (and academic writing assignments) shared by both courses underscore a link between community service and writing-in-the-disciplines, particularly as both Herzberg and the sociology and philosophy instructors ask students to integrate their community work (and writing about that work) with disciplinary ways of knowing and writing. These links between WAC and community writing, along with similar affinities I have encountered in my own teaching, suggest a correspondence between WAC and service-learning writing.

Some parallels between service-learning and WAC relate to pedagogy and student learning, and some relate to institutional politics—and both kinds can be marshaled to support the argument that service-learning should be moved from a marginal to an integral part of the college writing curriculum. Both WAC and service-learning are reform movements that aim to improve teaching and learning at the university. Both value active learning, collaborative learning, contextualized learning, constructed knowing, and authentic assessment. Studies suggest that writing-to-learn can aid student learning in general (Emig, "Writing"; Ackerman), and in particular disciplinary contexts (Bazerman and Russell). Likewise, as discussed earlier in this book, several studies suggest that service-learning enhances student learning, particularly with respect to intellectual and social development. In this sense, service is "instrumental" to learning (to use language that Christopher Thaiss employs to describe writing as a mode of learning) rather than a trendy course add-on (94). If faculty can be convinced of the cognitive and pedagogical value of service-learning, as many have been persuaded of the cognitive and pedagogical value of WAC, then the prospects for community writing projects will be brighter.

With respect to institutional politics, parallels important to increasing faculty participation in service-learning include the fact that there is no standard service-learning writing pedagogy to be imposed on a discipline or course. While some general pedagogical principles can be used as guides (see Mintz and Hesser), each instructor is free to adapt community-based strategies to match particular disciplinary and institutional contexts. Despite this flexibility, advocates for service-learning across the curriculum must recognize that WAC and service-learning are cross-disciplinary, which can be a precarious status in fragmented modern universities that organize themselves by insular departmental and disciplinary bunkers. Moreover, WAC and service-learning, while generally highly valued by a small core group of faculty and viewed as worthwhile by the university administration (and, notably, students, parents, and the larger culture), are perceived as low-prestige activities by much of the faculty. Both fall on the losing side of the prevailing value binaries of the modern university: generalist knowledge/specialist knowledge; teaching/scholarship; "soft" service/"hard" research. (Such dichotomies are especially persistent at research universities.) As a consequence, WAC and service-learning often meet not only with attitudes unfriendly to their propagation, but also, more significantly, with promotion and tenure systems that devalue them (and, in fact, actively discourage them since both WAC and service-learning are time-intensive activities—time which could otherwise be devoted to the "hard" research more valued by tenure committees). Since composition studies as a whole abides in a similarly marginal institutional space, it tends to be more affirming of community-based writing initiatives, as suggested by the relatively high representation of composition specialists among faculty invested in service-learning, the growing presence of service-learning research at professional conferences in rhetoric and composition, and the fact that the first book published in the American Association for Higher Education Series on Service-Learning in the Disciplines focused on composition (Adler-Kassner, Crooks, and Watters's *Writing the Community*).

To further interrogate these initial correspondences between the two movements, I turn to the history of WAC and what it might mean for the future of service-learning in composition. As David Russell chronicles in *Writing in the Disciplines 1870–1990: A Curricular History*, student writing has always played some role, even if often misunderstood or marginalized, in U.S. higher education. Public service has also been central to the missions of many universities, whether public, private, religious, or otherwise.

Yet the history of writing in the disciplines should give service-learning advocates in composition pause. Russell's history documents again and again how the modern university resists change, especially the cross-disciplinary sort championed by WAC and service-learning adherents. Despite the enthusiasm and vision of a committed few, efforts at increasing and reforming student writing across the disciplines have been repeatedly resisted and thwarted, even when well intentioned, well designed, and well funded.[2] Russell explains: "[Cross-curricular writing] programs failed not because they lacked substance but because they could not overcome institutional inertia, which the differentiated structure of mass education creates. Cross-curricular writing instruction goes against the grain of the modern university, with its research orientation, specialized elective curriculum and insular departmental structure—all of which makes it extremely difficult to change faculty attitudes toward writing instruction" (268). Russell goes on to suggest that because the academic community is fragmented, "there is thus no permanent defense against the slow erosion of programs under the pressure of well-defined departmental interests" (298). Therefore, WAC programs, like service-learning programs, often end up in an "institutional no-man's land" (298) or a "professional vacuum" (Zlotkowski, "Linking" 23). While Bentley College has avoided this dynamic because it worked so hard to institutionalize service-learning, and while the CLC has been able to thrive in large part because of Linda Flower's high-profile investment in the project, the "slow erosion" of Laurie Gullion's service-learning efforts were evident in the year following the one studied. She had to scale back her service-learning efforts not because of a lack of interest or commitment on her part, but because she did not have the support of a service-learning office of any kind and did not receive institutional funding for a teaching assistant to help with community contacts beyond the one-year span of her initial grant.

Still, the history of WAC also suggests some cause for optimism. Today, WAC is in a relatively healthy state, with a footing in at least 427 U.S. and Canadian colleges and universities, or 38 percent of those who responded to a 1987 survey (McLeod, *Strengthening* 103). Among those programs, there is dizzying variety and innovation. According to Susan McLeod, "A reform movement which began little more than a decade ago (a microsecond in institutional terms) seems well on its way to becoming part of the established order" ("Second Stage" 242). There is already a strong base of WAC scholarship (see Bazerman and Russell; Herrington and Moran, *Writing;* Bizzell and Herzberg; Ackerman), with continuing inquiry and dissemination of theory and practice through graduate programs, book-length studies, textbooks, academic journal articles, conferences, and networks (personal, professional, and electronic). The turn toward more systematic research has helped WAC gain footing in institutions where research is highly valued, and advocates for service-learning in composition are likewise beginning to understand the importance of research for their institutional longevity.

As seems to now be happening with service-learning, WAC started through recruiting faculty to attend voluntary workshops, slowly building on the enthusiasm and word-of-mouth success of the "early adopters" (to use a phrase Barbara Walvoord borrows from sociology to describe early WAC adherents). As WAC faculty and administrators gained more secure places in the academy, early research in support of WAC, such as Janet Emig's and James Britton's, was recognized, and new research on all aspects of WAC burgeoned (and continues to do so). Community-based writing advocates should note the grassroots approach of the emergent WAC days and read the literature on those workshops, noting especially that the programs which tended to be more successful modulated their approach to particular institutional contexts and garnered faculty as well as administrative support.[3]

With her *College English* article "The Future of WAC," Barbara Walvoord reflects on the prospects for WAC. (For earlier predictions about WAC, see Thaiss; McLeod, "Second Stage"; Herrington and Moran, "Prospect.") Walvoord suggests that WAC adopt a "social movement organization" ethos and engage several "micro" and "macro" challenges. According to Walvoord, the first macro challenge for WAC, if it is to grow and thrive, is to work with other movements and organizations which share WAC's reform agenda. She mentions such organizations as the American Association for Higher Education (a notable supporter of service-learning), university-based higher education research centers, funding agencies, and governing bodies. Susan McLeod sets a similar agenda for WAC, emphasizing the need to "braid WAC into ongoing issues" like assessment, technology, and general education reform ("Century's End" 72). Walvoord predicts that "the most likely scenario over the coming decade is for a multitude of educational reform programs to coexist in a shifting kaleidoscope, with some programs disappearing as they can no longer draw funds or faculty, and new programs arising" (69). She also comments, "Another possible collaborative role for WAC is what the movement literature calls dissemination of tactics or personnel, or becoming a network through which other movements form" (70). Certainly service-learning could share in, and contribute to, WAC's kaleidoscopic and collaborative vision. This notion echoes Christopher Thaiss's suggestion that "one way to measure the success of your WAC workshops is to see, over the years, how many other cross-curricular initiatives sprout up" (99). A compelling example of these predictions in action can be found in Steve Parks and Eli Goldblatt's description of the multiple "writing beyond the curriculum" efforts under way at Temple University.

Service-learning and community-based writing could be well served by capitalizing on WAC's institutional success (the benefits would run in the other direction, too, of course). After all, WAC and community action advocates share not only similar teaching values and a similar educational reform agenda, but also a combination of administrative savvy and scholarly capability needed to launch cross-curricular initiatives. Also, most service-learning academic projects, whatever the discipline, have writing at their center, whether in the form of text-based projects or of reflection on the service experience through journal, expressive, or analytical writing.

Some universities have active and exemplary service-learning writing programs up and running (and interest seems to be increasing). Yet, as Keith Morton reminds us, service-learning courses are still "counter-cultural," and "faculty seeking institutional permission and legitimacy or collegial and institutional support must acknowledge this in deciding whether to engage in service-learning" (279). Service-learning is still too young to be considered an institutional fixture of U.S. higher education; likewise, community-based writing instruction is still too young to be considered a fixture of rhetoric and composition.

Reflecting on the future of WAC, David Russell concludes that "disciplines must find or create places where student writing matters to the disciplinary community" (*Disciplines* 302). He adds, "Finding ways to harness the efforts of the disciplines—where the faculty's primary loyalty and interests lie—will perhaps achieve more in the long run than structurally separate programs, no matter how well intentioned and well financed" (304). Therein lies both the challenge and the opportunity for service-learning, as well. As Edward Zlotkowski suggests, despite the growing interest in service-learning, especially its civic and moral dimensions, its survival depends largely on "factors that shape faculty professional activity and faculty self-identity. Without these adjustments, the movement will either quickly exhaust its natural constituency (faculty already sympathetic) or lose many of its best practitioners through the failure of the academy to recognize and reward their work" (24; also see Morton, "Issues"; Holland; Rubin). Zlotkowski argues, much as Russell does with respect to WAC, that if service-learning is to "achieve that critical mass necessary to make its significance felt throughout higher education" then its advocates must "begin investing more intellectual capital" in moving from "one-size-fits-all service-learning" to "service-learning as a pedagogy carefully modulated to specific disciplinary and interdisciplinary goals" ("Linking" 25).

This approach is not without its own risks. Some in the WAC movement (e.g., Mahala) and in the service-learning movement

(Lisman; Mattson and Shea) warn that the move to accommodate disciplinary values and priorities represents a betrayal of the
original reformist ambitions of each movement. While I recognize this concern, I remain hopeful that service-learning can re-
tain its reformist spirit even as it pragmatically seeks a greater
voice and research presence in particular disciplines. Indeed, this
book is premised on that hope.

Composition has proven a relatively welcoming place for
service-learning because it gives top priority to matters of pedagogy. However, while service-learning is already starting to draw
upon and extend composition studies in meaningful ways, it still
needs further scholarly investigation informed by multiple research
perspectives. The significant literacy outcomes of the programs
studied here (as well as many others beyond the scope of this
book) are encouraging. Therefore, even as we must attend to the
precarious institutional position of service-learning, we should
be heartened by the prospects for community-based teaching and
research.

Higher education continues to grapple with how to articulate its relationship to the world beyond campus. Dewey offers a
compelling vision of education intertwined with public service,
one echoed by Ernest Boyer in the epigraph to this chapter, in
which he envisions a new kind of college that would take "special pride in its capacity to connect thought to action, theory to
practice," and would also "be committed to improving, in a very
intentional way, the human condition." In recent years, as is evident in debates over the purpose of the English curriculum and
over what it means to be a public intellectual, those in the humanities are having trouble even communicating to the public
the content and significance of what we do as teacher-scholars.[4]

Alone, service-learning cannot collapse the gap between our
work as academics and our responsibilities as citizens, but it does
represent a vital bridge between inquiry and action. By listening
to and collaborating with community partners, we will often,
much to our pleasure, find many claims of contemporary composition theory affirmed in practice. But we also risk having to

question some familiar assumptions about the teaching of writing. If we can see such risks as creative opportunities, then we might just be reminded, along with our students, that writing affords us a means not only to imagine a better world, but also to help bring it into being.

Appendix A: Course Materials and Student Samples from Writing in College and Community

The texts that follow are from Writing in College and Community, a service-learning course I taught at Kansas State University in 1998. Many students took this course because it fulfilled a communications requirement. Over the course of the semester students wrote an academic research essay, a popular audience version of that essay, a nonprofit agency profile (composed collaboratively by a project team), a community writing project (composed collaboratively by a project team), an individual log/dialogic journal, and a short capstone reflective essay. Working in teams, the class completed six service-learning projects: three students created a Web page for the local Big Brothers/Big Sisters chapter; four wrote and desktop-published a newsletter on breast-feeding for the local department of public health; three wrote and desktop-published a brochure for a local historical site; two composed a speech for the director of the local food bank for a holiday event; two wrote a press release for the Retired Senior and Volunteer Program (included below); and three conducted a survey on the sexual education curricula at local schools and then wrote a letter about sexual education to the state board of education (included below).

Expository Writing III:
Writing in College and Community

Welcome! This syllabus introduces you to the aims, requirements, and structures of Expository Writing III. The goal of this course is to help you better meet the writing challenges posed by college, workplace, and community settings. To be successful in these arenas, one must be an able and versatile writer, and becoming such a writer comes through practice and experience. Your experience this semester will center on exploring and analyzing a social concern of your choosing, and then collaborating with a local community partner (and your classmates) to address that concern pragmatically. Thus, you will write several kinds of documents, including an academic research essay, a reflective essay, a collaboratively composed report, a memo, and several other genres practiced in college and community settings.

Basic Expectations:
This course will work only if we are all actively engaged. This means that all need to participate in class discussions, ask questions, share work in progress, and respond thoughtfully to the drafts of others. Thus, you are expected to attend class regularly. All assignments must be on time (late drafts lose half their points, and coming to class without a draft when one is due results in an absence). Note, in particular, that you will be collaborating with classmates and community partners during much of the semester. Others will be relying on you and therefore it is vital that you demonstrate motivation, respect, and accountability during the community projects.

Required Text: Linda Flower, *Problem-Solving Strategies for Writing in College and Community* (Fort Worth, TX: Harcourt Brace, 1998)

Required Writings:
Academic Research Essay on a Social Concern
Popular Audience Version of that Research Essay
Report Profiling your Community Partner (collaboratively written)
Community Writing Project (collaboratively written)
Dialogic Journal (during the Community Writing Project)
End-of-Semester Reflective Essay
Several Short and In-Class Writings

Schedule of Assignments

Aug. 24 & 26   Introductions / Course Goals / Personal Goals
                & Concerns
Aug. 28   Orientation to the Course / First Short Writing Assignment Explained (Self as Writer)
Aug. 31   Exploring Writing and Community Concerns of Interest
Sept. 2   First Writing Assignment (Self as Writer) Due
Sept. 2 & 4   Exploring and Focusing Research Essay Topics
                Read: Flower, Chapters 1 and 2
Sept. 7   University Holiday

Sept. 9	Planning and Exploratory Writing for Research Essay
	Read: Flower, Chapters 4, 5, and 6
Sept. 11	Exploratory Draft Due
Sept. 14, 16, & 18	Researching and Drafting the Essay
	Read: Flower, Chapters 7 and 8
Sept. 21	Mid-Draft Due / Peer Response
Sept. 23 & 25	Revising and Editing
	Read: Flower, Chapters 9 and 10
Sept. 28	Final Draft Due
Sept. 30	Recasting the Essay for a Popular Audience
	Read: Flower, Chapters 9 and 10
Oct. 5	Mid-Draft Popular Essay Due / Peer Review
	Read: Flower, Chapters 11 and 12
Oct. 7	Final Draft Popular Essay Due
	In-Class: Report Assignment Introduction
Oct. 9	Getting to Know Community Partners
	Read: Flower, Chapter 14
Oct. 16 & 17	Collaborating, Planning, Interviewing
	Read: Flower, pp. 355–373
Oct. 19	Exploratory Writing for Collaborative Report Due
Oct. 21	Drafting and Revising the Report
Oct. 23	Community Partner Profile Report Due
Oct. 26, 27, & 28	Beginning the Community Writing Project / The Dialogic Journal / Meetings with Partners / Project Expectations / Memo
Nov. 2–23	Work on Projects [team deadlines arranged with instructor] / Continuation of Dialogic Journals / Small Group Conferences / Some Classes Canceled for Team Conferences
Dec. 2	Community Writing Projects Due / Thank-You Letters to Partners
Dec. 7 & 9	In-Class Work on Reflective Essays
Dec. 11	Last Day of Class / Portfolios due by 5 P.M.

Grading Sheet

Academic Research Essay on a Social Concern

Exploratory Draft	___ / 2
Mid-Draft	___ / 2
Quality of Peer Response	___ / 2
Final Draft	___ / 10

Popular Audience Version of That Research Essay

Mid-Draft	___ / 2

Quality of Peer Response   ___ / 2
Final Draft   ___ / 8

Report Profiling Your Community Partner
     Exploratory Writing (team grade)   ___ / 2
     Final Draft (team grade)   ___ / 8
     Individual Contribution +/-   ___ /

Community Writing Project (community partner
will participate in this evaluation)
     Final Draft (team grade)   ___ / 40
     Individual Contribution +/-   ___ /

Dialogic Journal   ___ / 6

End-of-Semester Reflective Essay   ___ / 8

Class Participation (Discussion, Readings,
Group Work, In-Class Writings)   ___ / 8

A=91–100 / B=81–90 / C=71–80 / D=65–70 / F=below 65

Shelly: Elderly Health Issues

At the time she took the course, Shelly was a junior nursing major. She also had experience working at nursing homes, which she drew upon in her research essay. This essay developed over several drafts and with the benefit of peer and teacher review.

Research Essay

How Restful are Rest Homes?

Victoria, who is 85 and has a dementia similar to Alzheimer's, resides in an area nursing home. Victoria's family decided several months ago, after a series of falls in her home, that she needed 24 hour nursing care. Her mental capacity is so severely limited that she is no longer able to perform any activities of daily living, such as eating and bathing, on her own.

Victoria had been a resident in the facility for nearly a year when her family began noticing a significant degeneration in her mental status. Her long and short term memories were rapidly failing; she was unable to recognize her children. Soon after, she could no longer walk and was confined to either her wheelchair or her bed. One morning, Victoria's daughter received a phone call from a nurse at the facility. Victoria had developed a pressure ulcer on her tailbone, caused by lying in the same position and not being turned while in bed. The opening had eaten through two layers of skin, exposing her tailbone.

Confused and concerned, Victoria's family decided to research pressure ulcers, also known as decubitus ulcers. Their findings were alarming. Decubitus ulcers are preventable and usually manifest when bedfast residents are not properly turned every two hours, relieving pressure on their skin. When patients are left longer than two hours in a particular position, the skin begins to break down rapidly. Apparently, the staff at Victoria's nursing facility had neglected to turn her while in bed.

Unfortunately, Victoria's scenario occurs often to nursing home residents. Nearly 1 in 6 residents will develop some type of pressure ulcer during a stay at a nursing facility (Vladek, 1990). With proper care by the nursing staff, these painful sores are preventable. So why was the nursing care Victoria received not adequate enough to prevent the pressure ulcer?

Questions such as this have been on the minds of many Americans. As the baby boomers pass age 65 in the next century and begin to need nursing care, these questions will demand a thorough answer. Currently, nearly 13% of the total United States population is over the age of 65 (Hobbs & Damon, 1996). Approximately 1.5 million of these people live in nursing homes, and Atkins contends that this number is expected to triple during the next thirty years (1994). Annual costs to this population exceeded $74 billion in 1993 and by 2003 are expected to reach $176 billion (Fairchild, Knebl, & Burgos, 1995). Nursing home care is the fastest growing component of major health care in the national budget; thus, efforts to improve its quality are especially important.

Over the past three years, I have worked nearly 2000 hours in a nursing home. In these years of my employment as a CNA, or nurse's aide, I have seen first hand the need for dramatic improvement in many areas of long term care. The quality of care residents receive is most in need of improvement. I have continually seen a poor quality of care provided to these residents. Basic activities of daily living, such as having their teeth brushed, are often neglected by staff. Some residents' teeth may go unbrushed for weeks. Further, many residents who have lost bladder control are forced to sit in wet clothes until the CNA's can change them because staff failed to take them to the bathroom.

Every nursing facility in the nation is subject to an annual survey, which is conducted by a state employee with a Registered Nurse license, or RN. In this audit the surveyors point out deficiencies in nursing care, violations of resident's rights, or potential health hazards. These examiners are allowed to reprimand the facility using a number of methods, including fines, temporary bans on new admissions, or revoking licenses of the facility. Once the survey is complete, the facility is required by law to post the results and their response to the findings in open view to the public.

I studied the survey results of the four nursing homes in the Manhattan area. The deficiencies reported ranged from "'severe" offenses, such as residents developing pressure ulcers (as was the case with Victoria), to "minor" offenses, such as a nurse having a soda pop in the room where medicine is stored. Unfortunately, the majority of the deficiencies cited, nearly 65%, were major offenses. These offenses included a nurse failing to call the doctor when a resident fell and complained of hip pain, overdosing a resident on blood thinners, and a CNA emptying a urinal into a resident's bathroom sink. This CNA then dropped the resident's dentures into the unsanitized sink and placed them in the resident's mouth.

In one nursing facility in Manhattan, the results of the survey were so atrocious that the state placed a ban on any new admissions until the facility was able to demonstrate that it had remedied the problems. Meanwhile, another facility had a deficiency free survey and was not cited for any violations. The other two facilities had "average" surveys, with several violations but none serious enough to warrant a fine or admissions ban. Although these two homes were not financially reprimanded by the state, they were held responsible for making sure the deficiencies were corrected in a timely manner.

In an interview with the administrator of a local facility, she explained that most of these deficiencies were due to staffing problems, meaning that most citations occurred when CNA's were in contact with the residents (B. Faust, personal communication, September 21, 1998). Of the 7 deficiencies found, 6 occurred while nursing staff was in direct contact with a resident. These citations included CNA's failing to toilet a resident every two hours, incorrectly transferring a resident from her wheelchair into bed, and not wearing gloves while providing personal care on an incontinent resident. The Institute of Medicine (IOM) found in a 1996 report that nearly 85% of all care in a nursing home is provided by nurse aides. Alarmingly, many of these CNA's providing the care have been, in my experience, and in the IOM's opinion, inadequate and unqualified.

Certification as a nurse aide is not difficult to attain. The class takes one week to complete, and only 20 hours of clinical, on-the-job training is required for passing. After passing the class, one must take a 20 question licensing exam to receive the certificate. Once a license is earned, there is no license renewal or continuing education which must be completed by the CNA. This has allowed many inadequately trained and underqualified staff members to continue working as aides.

Another staffing problem plaguing nursing facilities is a high turnover rate. In many nursing homes, CNA's are paid very little and are required to care for more residents than they can properly serve. Not surprisingly, the turnover rate among nurse's aides is usually very high--from 70% to over 100% (IOM, 1996). This factor causes stressed environments because often aides are forced to work with fewer colleagues and are often called upon to pick up the slack left by the aide who did not show up or quit.

According to Monro (1990), there is a strong correlation between nursing staff turnover rates and quality of care in long-term care facilities. The number of staff working in the facility on each shift also affects quality of care. A study by Johnson-Pawlson and Infeld (1996) found that long-term care facilities staffing at minimum legal levels provided a poorer quality of care than those facilities which exceeded the minimum requirement. This study also linked higher nursing staff levels with improvements in resident rehabilitation. In my experience, CNA's with larger assignments could not provide the same caliber of quality care as those with smaller assignments.

High turnover rates not only lower quality of care to residents; they are also costly to each facility. Marilee Nily, Director of Nursing at a local nursing home, stated that orientating one new CNA costs the facility nearly $500 (personal communication, September 21, 1998). This figure covers the wage paid to both the orientee and the CNA who is conducting the training, as well as the cost of new uniforms, inservices the new employee must attend, and the mandated Hepatitis B vaccine and Tuberculosis test. Last year, Nily reported, 23 new employees quit within one month of their hire date. Thus, this facility wasted nearly $12,000 training employees who worked less than a month. Nily further stated that over 83% of the CNA's her facility hires in a year will quit within six months. My personal experience has proven this statistic; out of nearly

45 CNA's, I am the only aide at my facility who has been employed there over a year and a half.

Poorly qualified CNA's, high turnover rates, and minimal staff continue to be problems which plague area and national nursing facilities. Nursing homes are institutions which fulfill an important need for a unique part of the population. Thus, the need to remedy the numerous problems which plague these institutions is great.

Staffing problems, in my opinion, need to be addressed before any changes can occur in the long term care setting. One method to combat turnover rates is to increase incentives and wages. Many CNA's leave the nursing home for higher paying jobs with appealing benefits. Increasing wages will increase the amount spent on staffing, but I contend this cost will be lower than training employees who will soon resign. If staff turnover is low, residents will benefit from the continuity of care they will receive.

Tightening the laws which regulate nursing home policies would also improve status quo. Kansas laws currently require one CNA for every 19 residents (M. Nily, personal communication, September 21, 1998). I feel this is extremely lenient. Residents receive a much greater quality of care when the ratio is closer to 1:10. CNA's are often forced to work alone with over 30 residents and do not have enough time to provide the high standard of care for which they were hired. Although this is illegal, I have regularly seen it occur. With a lower CNA to patient ratio, CNA's will have time to provide the quality of care expected by families, residents, and administration.

Once nursing staff pass the licensing exam, they are never tested again, unless they stop working for a number of years. This proves problematic because nurses are often forced to "'short-cut" procedures and assessments in order to save time. In my experience, the best nurses are generally new graduates because they complete tasks as they were taught in school. Once they work for a while, nurses often "cut corners" in order to complete each duty expected of their shift. Thus, once a nurse passes the board exam, techniques which were stressed during nursing school are often either forgotten or ignored. For this reason, states must mandate repeated testing of nursing staff.

These vital changes require substantial effort to revise regulatory laws and facility policies. However, improving the environment in most nursing facilities depends on these alterations. As the baby boomers creep toward age 65, and average life-expectancy increases, nursing home care is becoming an increasing concern among citizens and policymakers. Now is the time to remedy the numerous problems in long term care facilities, before Victoria's story becomes a reality in your family.

Works Cited

Atkins, G.L. (1994). *Old age in the 21st century: A report to the assistant secretary for aging.* U.S. Department of Health and Human Services. New York: National Academy on Aging, The Maxwell School, Syracuse University.

Fairchild, T., Knebl, J., & Burgos, D. (1995). *The complex long-term care service system.* In Z. Harel & R.E. Dunkle (Eds.), Matching people and services in long-term care (pp. 73–88). New York: Springer.

Hoobs, F.B. & Damon, B.L. (1996). *U.S. Bureau of the Census. Current population reports, special studies, sixty-five plus in America.* Washington, DC: U.S. Government Printing Office.

Institute of Medicine (1996). *Nursing Staff in Hospitals and Nursing Homes: Is it Adequate?* Washington, D.C.: National Academy Press.

Johnson-Pawlson, J., & Infeld, D.L.(1996). Nurse staffing and quality of care in nursing facilities. *Journal of Gerontological Nursing,* 18, 13–16.

Monro, D.J. (1990). The influence of registered nurse staffing on the quality of nursing home care. *Research in Nursing and Health,* 13, 263–270.

Vladeck. B. (1990). *Unloving Care.* New York: Basic Books.

Popular Version of the Research Essay

Shelly chose to recast her essay as an editorial for the *American Journal of Nursing.* After studying the conventions of editorials in that publication, she wrote her own.

How Restful are Rest Homes?

As the baby boomers pass age 65 in the next century and begin to need nursing care, much of the focus on health care reform will shift to long term care facilities. Nearly 13% of the total United States population is over 65 and this percentage is expected to triple in the next twenty years. Annual costs of caring for this population exceed $74 billion and are projected to reach $176 billion by 2003. Nursing home care is the fastest growing component of major health care in the national budget; thus, efforts to improve its quality will greatly affect those of us working in such a setting. As nurses we must take action toward improving status quo in our nation's nursing homes.

My first job in the health care field was in a long term care facility. I remember, as many of you surely do also, how difficult it was to complete my assigned duties while providing quality care. There simply was not enough time in the day to care for the residents as I would have liked. The enormous pressure I felt from administrators, family members, coworkers, and residents to perform was often overwhelming. Coupled with low pay and hard labor, this pressure drives many nursing staff to quit. As we all know, high turnover rates only hurt the residents of the facility because they miss out on continuity of care. We must utilize our leadership skills as licensed nurses to facilitate a positive atmosphere where our staff feels appreciated and needed. We are responsible for creating teamwork and alliances between our staff, as well as for raising morale.

Another problem which plagues long-term care facilities is a largely poorly-educated staff. The CNA's, who provide more direct patient care than we nurses do, are often undertrained, underpaid, and overstressed. Our job as charge and floor nurses is to make certain that new nursing employees are properly orientated to the facility and to each resident's requirements. The administration of these facilities must assist these reforms by offering higher wages, increasing benefits, and providing support to nurses as we strive to change our working environment.

While most states do not require us to retake licensing exams once we initially pass, this proves problematic to nursing homes because many staff either forget or disregard the principles taught to us in nursing school. In many facilities, I have witnessed licensed nursing staff using either unsanitary or incorrect procedures. Cutting corners in order to save time only jeopardizes the patient's health and well being. We must not compromise our teachings for simple time convenience. Thus, it is our responsibility to make sure we complete tasks fully and in the interest of the patient, not our own schedules. If we do not take the initiative to police ourselves, the state will be forced to toughen nursing regulations.

Along with using proper procedure, we must also take responsibility for furthering our medical knowledge with every chance. Continuing education is often the only exposure we will have to variations in nursing theory and practice, as well as to new medicines, treatments and procedures.

Nursing homes can be one of the toughest settings in which to work. As citizens become more aware of the situations in these homes, pressure is mounting to fix their problems. We must take the initiative to monitor and correct our own behavior. If we choose not to mend our attitudes and practices, our jobs will become more stressful as we will be more tightly governed by both internal and external regulators. Preserving and reintroducing quality care in long term care facilities is key. The autonomy of our profession depends on it.

Agency Profile

Shelly was paired with another student, Ken, to work with the local chapter of the Retired and Senior Volunteer Program. They collaboratively wrote the following agency profile report, which underwent peer and instructor review.

Retired & Senior Volunteer Program

The Retired and Senior Volunteer Program (RSVP) pairs volunteers 55 and older with service opportunities in their communities. RSVP incorporates the skills of these seniors with public and non-profit organizations ranging from educational institutions to health care clinics. This nation-wide program matches seniors' skills, life experiences, and interests with community needs.

RSVP was founded in 1971 with an appropriation of $500,000 from the Administration on Aging. That summer eleven projects were launched; this number has grown to over 750 annually. This non-profit service agency is supported by a fiscal budget of over $30 million in federal funding from the Corporation for National Service. The 450,000 volunteers who comprise RSVP today have worked over 80 million hours in the community on projects ranging from human needs services to health and nutrition clinics.

Locally, the Manhattan RSVP was established in 1974 with few volunteers and minimal recognition. Manhattan's program has grown to include over 580 volunteers, ranging in age from 55 to 100, with the average volunteer being 76 years of age. Today, the local chapter of RSVP has two paid employees, a director, Lori Bishop, and her administrative assistant. Lori has worked with RSVP for over 13 years. In that time she has affiliated with roughly 98 service sites, including local elementary schools, nursing homes, and the Riley County Senior Center.

Although RSVP responds to a broad range of community needs, currently their main focus is the Leadership in Literacy program. This service is a collaboration among RSVP of Riley County, Bluemont and Woodrow Wilson Schools, and trained volunteers to aid the reading development of kindergarten through third grade students. Leadership in Literacy pairs struggling students with caring adults who are committed to aiding their reading success. The desired outcome of this program is to intercept "at risk" students before they develop negative attitudes about school, learning, and themselves.

Other major projects of Riley County RSVP entail intergenerational activities. In these projects, students and the senior volunteer work together to complete objectives such as creating arts and crafts. Volunteers also enter classrooms and read literature. Children benefit greatly from this because they are more attentive when someone other than their teacher is instructing them. RSVP participants also educate students by relating living history, such as recalling war stories, describing events of the Depression, and growing up without a Nintendo.

Another major focus of RSVP within the school system is an annual "Santa City," which is a major fundraiser. This "no parents allowed" holiday store allows Kindergarten through 6th grade students to purchase items made by Santa's elves (senior volunteers). Children gain experience with the use of money and counting, as well as autonomy in choosing gifts of their liking without parental influence.

Retired and Senior Volunteer Program not only serves the needs of the community with senior volunteers, but also enriches the quality of lives touched. Children and the elderly are among the many who benefit from this program.

Community Writing Project

Shelly and Ken were asked by RSVP to write a press release about a local intergenerational tutoring program. This involved gathering information from the director, visiting the site, interviewing some RSVP members, and working through several drafts with the director. The press release was sent to the local media, and although not picked up by local papers, it was published by RSVP as part of a mass mailing announcing its 25th anniversary events.

Retired Seniors Provide Learning Tools
for Manhattan's School Children
Retirement is often thought of as a time to relax, move to Arizona or Florida, and play bridge and shuffleboard. To oth-

ers, retirement can be a productive time to share a lifetime's collection of experience and knowledge. Such is the attitude with the Retired and Senior Volunteer Program (RSVP) and its participants.

RSVP incorporates the skills of seniors age 55 and older with service opportunities in their communities. These volunteers pair with non-profit agencies which address social needs and concerns. Nationally, the 450,000 volunteers who comprise RSVP have donated over 80 million hours in the community on projects such as manning information desks at hospitals, delivering meals to shut-ins, and acting as foster grandparents to underprivileged children.

Riley County's RSVP began in 1974, three years after the national program, with few volunteers and even less recognition. Today, over 580 of Manhattan's seniors volunteer in more than 98 service locations, including Mercy Health Center, nursing homes, and local elementary schools.

At Bluemont Elementary, RSVP has enacted a program, Leadership in Literacy, that matches "at risk" students with senior volunteers. Currently, the program is being piloted with kindergarten students, while future plans will include 1st through 3rd graders. This service, which resembles no other in the country, was created to combat Manhattan's alarming illiteracy rate. Recognizing that 54% of Bluemont's school children read below grade level, RSVP volunteers provide struggling students with the tools for reading success. On staff at Bluemont are specially trained teachers devoted to not only strengthening literacy skills, but also facilitating different learning styles. The goal of this intergenerational program is not only to improve literacy skills, but also to enhance relationships, conversational abilities, and other life skills. In addition, the volunteers broaden and encourage self-esteem, the lifeblood of a successful student.

RSVP also conducts an annual activity with a seasonal theme. "Santa City," a major fundraiser for RSVP, began as an outlet for grade-school children to purchase inexpensive presents for Christmas. These gifts made by "Santa's senior elves," RSVP volunteers, are selected by the children without their parents present. The shopper's money, counting, and decision-making skills are enhanced through a visit to "Santa City". The popularity of this event has grown so dramatically that RSVP has created a parent's shop, which also allows them to purchase hand-made gifts.

Continuing their work with children, Riley County's RSVP provides "real life" accounts and experiences for young students through intergenerational activities. In local schools, volunteers share real history lessons by recalling life during World War II and before Nintendo. Such reports interest students because history is removed from books and presented first hand.

Other simple, yet effective, activities pairing students and volunteers include creating arts and crafts and acting out popular children's stories. Carolyn Baugh, one of the teachers in the Leadership and Literacy program, feels role-playing provides many educational benefits. "Children are allowed to add a personal touch as they interpret stories with their own expression and creativity." Baugh stated that these activities not only increase self-esteem, but also allow teachers to gauge the child's sequencing skills and learning style. Lori Bishop, the director of Riley County's RSVP, encourages those young and old to become involved with the program. "We need more participants to allow for one-on-one relationships between child and volunteer. These are important to RSVP's mission as well as to schools." Parental support for its educational projects, as well as support from corporate sponsors and other community organizations, is vital. In addition, donations are appreciated for "Santa City" and other RSVP projects. To learn more about the Retired and Senior Volunteer Program and its 98 local projects, contact the Manhattan office at [phone number was listed here].

Log/Dialogic Journal

Log 10/23/98—Ken and I met to discuss progress thus far
Log 10/26/98—Finally got hold of Lori and set up a meeting
Journal Entry: 10/28/98
Before Interview: I am anxious to get started! Playing phone tag with Lori was nerve-racking. So far, I feel Ken and I are working together fine. I volunteered to contact Lori initially so it was on my shoulder to get a hold of her. When Ken and I initially discussed this project, we decided to work closely together. I know he has strong writing skills, so I feel confident in our ability to produce quality work. We both are pretty relaxed so far and don't foresee any problems. I am nervous about our meeting today because we are meeting at Bluemont School and not RSVP. Will she have the information we will need for our agency profile?

Journal Entry: 10/28/98
After Interview: I am a little frustrated at this point. Lori did not provide us with any literature for our agency profile. She told Ken and I in our meeting that she would leave informa-

tion for us at her office. When I went to pick it up Friday evening, she hadn't even been there all day. I am learning from this though—things don't always go as planned.

Ken and I met last night to finish our profile. It was difficult at first to combine our two writing styles. We both had ideas we thought would work. Eventually we got it figured out.

I am fairly intrigued by RSVP. I like the idea of keeping the older citizens involved. It makes me think of Freud's stagnation vs. generativity. RSVP is keeping the volunteers from becoming stagnant. I like the idea of bridging the intergenerational gap.

Log 10/28/98—1:30pm, first meeting with Lori at Bluemont School
Log 10/30/98—Ken and I corresponded by phone
Log 11/1/98—Ken and I met to do the profile
Log 11/2/98—met with Tom to discuss progress
Log 11/4/98—second meeting with Lori at Bluemont

Professor Deans: 11/5/98
Shelly: It seems to me like you and Ken are on track. Full steam ahead. Show me a draft of the article before submitting it to RSVP, please.

I'm intrigued by your Freud reference. Could you reflect a bit more on the stagnation vs. generativity concept?

I also would like you to reflect on how this work with RSVP relates to your chosen profession, and/or with the research you did for your social concern essay. Where are the connections? The conflicts? The questions you have?

Journal Entry: 11/4/98—late entry after 2nd meeting
We met with Lori on this date at Bluemont again. She seemed excited for us to write our article. As we were leaving the meeting Ken and I noticed the article hanging on the door that was in the Mercury a month ago. It was very similar to what Lori had asked us for. Lovely! Even the volunteers she suggested we contact for quotes were the same! (Back to square one!) Ken contacted Ned Seaton, the feature editor at the Mercury, as Lori had suggested. Mr. Seaton told Ken that he wasn't interested "in that crap and frankly that is not news." Okay then! Luckily, Tom straightened us out and gave us some direction for this article. Oh! Ned said we could write the article as a letter to the editor. However, Lori has written several lately that have not been printed. Thus, we have decided to write a press release. Even if it does not make the Mercury, hopefully Lori can use it to send to RSVP nationals.

Log 11/6/98—Tom straightened us out in class about our project
Log 11/9/98—met with Ken to work on article

Journal Entry 11/9/98 [In response to an in-class prompt asking students to consider the larger social problems related to
their projects]
Why is RSVP connected to literacy?
I was floored when Lori told us at our last meeting that
54% of Manhattan kids read below their grade level! That
number is very alarming. RSVP recognized this statistic and is
trying to make a change.
Why do we have this literacy problem?
The only explanation I can provide for this is that children
are not getting the attention and teaching they need and deserve at home. I remember how shocked I was when my niece
could read well before kindergarten. My sister-in-law worked
with Kodie every day on reading and vocabulary. I am not claim-
ing that all parents must spend 2/3 of their day teaching their
kids, but they must devote at least a few hours a day to their
child's learning. Home is the only place where kids get one-on-
one help and stimulation! Those who are exposed to an environment condusive to learning only prosper.

[In response to instructor prompt in earlier entry]
How does RSVP address the issue of stagnation vs.
generativity?
Freud's stagnation vs. generativity describes the stage in
psychosocial development when older adults either become stagnant and "go out to pasture" or they become involved in the
generations (younger). When we stereotype the elderly, we see
them as being stagnant. I like that RSVP breaks around this by
keeping these retirees from becoming stagnant and apathetic.
Involving retirees in intergenerational activities is a prime example of Freud's generativity. These RSVP volunteers are investing in future generations by furthering their development.

Journal Entry: 11/12/98—after 3rd meeting
After our meeting with Lori today, I felt better about our
project. Lori . . . liked our article. There were a few places that
needed corrections. For example, Ken and I understood that
54% of Manhattan's school children read below grade level.
Lori pointed out that this number applies only to Bluemont's
school children.
The other lady who was at the meeting was wanting us to
write some vignettes for the paper. Ken saved us on that one

when Lori asked us how long she "had us." She thought that she had us next semester! When she learned that our project was due December 2nd she said the article was ample work. They will be using it to promote RSVP for its upcoming 25th anniversary.

Log 11/10/98—met with Ken to work on press release.
Log 11/11/98—met with Ken to revise; met with Tom to revise; met with Lori to revise.

Journal Entry: 11/13/98—My reflections
    How does RSVP connect with my chosen profession?
    One aspect I noticed about RSVP is the level of caring possessed by the volunteers. These elders donate hours and hours of their "leisure time" to further the intellectual and emotional development of the kids. If it were not for the caring and compassion of these volunteers, RSVP would not exist. This quality is parallel to my nursing future. The reason I will be a good nurse practitioner is that I enjoy helping people and I like to contribute all that I can to see that my patients thrive. I, like the RSVP volunteers, take an interest in each person that I take care of. Also, the goal of RSVP is to intercept "at-risk" kids (before they fall too far behind), help develop their skills, and "graduate" them from the program. As a nurse, I want to fix my patient and never see them in the same condition again. I hope to come into their lives, leave a lasting impression, and exit quickly.

Professor Deans: 11/13/98
Shelly: The project seems on track. Steady on. You've reflected on those things about RSVP that you find particularly appealing—and indeed, I think those aspects of the organization are outstanding, as well. But I also wonder . . . If you were in charge of RSVP, would you do anything differently? If so, which things? How?

Journal Entry: Wow! I would change several aspects of RSVP. First, I would put more time and energy into PR and advertisement. I have lived here for 3 years and did not know RSVP even existed before this project. I have recently seen some adds in the Mercury.
    I also would promote RSVP to KSU students. Even though students are generally not 55 or over, RSVP could use these students on several projects (Leadership in Literacy, Santa City, etc.). I announced RSVP's need for volunteers at my sorority's

chapter meeting on Wednesday. After the meeting, over 10 people asked for the phone number and were interested. Nearly all of KSU's majors require volunteer work—RSVP needs to tap into this population!!

Another change I would make would be to redo all of the brochures about Leadership and Literacy and RSVP. The literature I was given by Lori was not very informative or sophisticated. Lori said they were "thrown together". (I could tell. Maybe your next class could help them!)

Log 11/16/98—met with Ken to revise Lori's comments
Log 11/18/98—met with Lori with final draft

Journal Entry: 11/18/98 [In response to an in-class prompt]

Academic Compared to Community Writing

Same	Different
Need for proper usage of punctuation	Academic seems more formal
	Goals usually differ
I enjoy both types of writing!	Audience
Both require revision	Must work with an outsider to complete community writing process—can be frustrating
Organization must still be logical	
Initial Research	I find community writing easier to get motivated for, but more difficult to put together
Process	Communication is much more important in community writing

One of the major things I see from this list is how important it is to effectively switch between the two styles. I had difficulty with writing for my community partner because I was still in the "academic mode". This proved problematic because the audience is so different for community and academic writings. I need to work on being more flexible. I feel more comfortable writing academic essays—straying from this "comfort zone" gets hairy!!

Professor Deans: 11/23/98
Shelly: I spoke to Lori today and she was very happy with both your work as well as you and Ken personally. She said that she would be sure to credit you both when she uses the press release.

Your reflections above are thoughtful and perceptive. As the project comes to a close, so will your journal. Take the last entry to write on a topic of your own choosing.

Journal Entry: 12/2/98 Wow! This semester has flown by! It's hard to believe that I have been at KSU for two and a half years now. I am going to miss all of the action. But, I am excited to start nursing school and accomplish one of my goals. At times, however, it is difficult for me to not get sad about leaving KSU—I have had an amazing time here. At least Topeka isn't too far for visitors to travel!

Tom, thanks for helping me realize my strengths (and weaknesses) as a writer. I have realized the need for flexibility in my writing. I was pretty scared about this class . . . thanks for not making it too painful.

Best of luck, Shelly

Professor Deans:
And best to you too! I've enjoyed your journal.

Reflective Essay

At the very end of the semester, students were asked to write a short reflective essay on themselves as writers and/or citizens.

Moving Beyond the Green Ink
English and writing have always been an enjoyable aspect of school for me. I feet confident in my ability to effectively communicate, both orally and in writing, and I take pleasure from completing writing assignments. As I was reflecting on my writing experience while in college, I realized a weakness in my writing abilities: I feel great anxiety when required to write for informal audiences.

I vividly remember the event which lead to this distress. As a junior in high school, I took senior English (Composition 1) in the Spring of 1996. Because I was the only student who had ever skipped a grade, I had a lot to prove both to myself and others. Thus, I put enormous pressure on myself to excel in the class. Our first assignment was to outline our expectations of the class and our future plans. As Mrs. Reed [not her real name] handed the first paper back, I can remember sweating. When I received mine, my mouth dropped open and my eyes welled up with tears. My paper was so marked in Mrs. Reed's green ink that it looked like St. Patrick had gotten sick. Looming at the top of the page was my grade. 22/50. Ouch.

Thoughts ran through my head like a marathon runner saying, "You'll never make it in senior English. Go back to your own grade." After regaining my composure and drumming up courage, I inquired about my 'rade. She replied that the grade was not concrete and coulc improve with corrections. She went on to explain her policy about not using "to be" verbs and only using third person. I also was required to use justified margins and Times New Roman 10 point font, as well as not use the same word to start a sentence in the entire piece. Either I had to quickly adapt my writing or I would not succeed in the class. That evening I promised myself that I would do everything in my power to avoid receiving such an embarrassing grade again.

At least one paper was assigned every week in that class. With each task, I slaved at the word processor to conform to her standards. I have never struggled with writing so extensively in my life. By the time I wrote my fourth or fifth paper, I had developed a skill for appeasing the beast in Mrs. Reed. Needless to say, at the end of the semester I took my "A" in that class and ran.

That semester's experience had more of an effect on me than I realized at the time. In fact, I did not realize the root of my anxiety toward writing in other styles than academic until late in this semester. I breezed through the academic essay and popular version of that draft with ease and enjoyment. However, the community writing project proved more problematic.

Luckily, Ken was a clever partner and in the press release for RSVP he often kept me focused when I became frustrated. When drafting versions of the piece, I continually wrote too lengthy of paragraphs and added excessive detail and vocabulary. Ken had to remind me that the release was going to be read by people with a sixth-grade education. I struggled throughout the project to keep the composition on that level; I did not feel comfortable turning in such informal work.

This uncomfortable feeling can be attributed to my schooling experience. Every paper I have written, aside from the community writing project, has been completed in an academic format. As I was working on the RSVP project, I remember envisioning Mrs. Reed and her green pen and feeling nervous.

Because of this response, I have thought extensively about the expectations on students to write papers of the finest academic quality.

While I feel academic writing is crucial in both the university and business world, I would like to see more English Composition teachers develop the ability to write informally with their students. Unless the student is a journalism or mass communications major, chances are that he or she has never been required to draw on these skills. I am amazed that I am in my third year of college and I am just now utilizing and developing the skill to write to informal audiences! I propose that more teachers, not of just English Composition, should require at least one essay for an informal audience per semester. I am confident I will be asked to write either a literature review or a press release at some point in my medical career. Students need to feel comfortable doing so in their field.

Although my memory of Mrs. Reed and her dreaded green ink remains fresh, I know after completing the RSVP press release with Ken that I have the ability to write successfully to informal audiences.

Sarah: Sex Education in High Schools

At the time she took the course, Sarah was a sophomore majoring in business but she was also developing an interest in women's studies.

Research Essay

Sexual Education: Who's Accountable?

The first thing my high school principal said when I asked him about sexual education at Mankato Jr/Sr High School was, "Our kids don't do that kind of stuff anyway." I know that in some respects Mr. Terpening was just teasing me. However, I also know that in many ways he was serious. He may not actually believe that teenagers in Mankato are sexually inactive, but he is consciously trying to avoid the situation. I was born and raised in Mankato, Kansas, a rural community with a population of fewer than one thousand people. The high school that I graduated from always averages fewer than one hundred students. In a school this small, people know each other rather well. They know each individual's personality, and often his or her thoughts and actions. This is why I can say, with quite certainty, that Mr. Terpening is denying the fact that his students are sexually active.

There is no form of sexual education at Mankato Jr/Sr High School. According to Mr. Terpening, "We are not in tune to this issue because we don't feel it does any good, at least I don't. Although we are mandated to have something, and we do that in our health class that is held in freshmen P.E. That way we get everyone at least one time in their high school career." However, I began kindergarten at the Mankato Elementary School and graduated from Mankato Jr/Sr High School without ever having any form of sexual education.

Mankato is not the only smaller school system, with less than 100 students, that doesn't have any form of sexual education. According to Mr. Terpening, "We have it [sexual education] covered as well as anyone else does in our district." A friend of mine who went to high school in Gridley, Kansas, a town with a population of only 400, informed me that there was no sexual education in that school system. However, while attending junior high in Burlington, Kansas, population 4,000, she received sexual education.

Manhattan High School, which constitutes a larger school system with a population of 1,859 students, has a well defined sexual education program. At Manhattan High, all ninth graders have to take nine weeks of health, with three to four weeks dedicated to sexual education. According to Jan Wickman, the head of the health department at Manhattan High, "It is a pretty comprehensive course. Students are taught about birth control, dating, biological aspects of the course and attitudes. We also take a 'Just Say No' stand with our course. We teach that no is a contraceptive, we teach abstinence."

In *Sexuality and the Curriculum,* James T. Sears states, "The reemergence of political and religious conservatism in the United States combined with the abortion controversy and the twin crises of AIDS and teenage pregnancy have catapulted sexuality education into tens of thousand of classrooms. Twenty-two states and the District of Columbia now mandate the teaching of sexuality in the public schools; only three states did in 1980" (Sears 8). Sexual education is mandated in all public schools in Kansas. Elementary and Secondary Schools Accreditation Regulation 91-31-3 for the state of Kansas states, "Effective September 1, 1988, each board of education shall provide a comprehensive education program in human sexuality, including information about sexually transmitted diseases, especially acquired immune deficiency syndrome (AIDS)" (Regulation). However, many school systems, particularly

smaller schools systems like Mankato, are not providing sufficient education in this area. By realizing the importance of
sexual education and that many smaller public school systems,
like Mankato Jr/Sr High School, are not sufficiently providing
the required sexual education, it becomes evident that some
form of accountability is necessary in order to successfully educate Kansas students in human sexuality.

First of all, you may be asking yourself, "How does this
topic affect me?" "Our children are our future," a common
theme in the United States, may answer that question. Today,
the average American teenager deals with many dangers. For
instance, sexually transmitted diseases and teenage pregnancy
weigh heavily on a teenager's mind when he or she decides to
become sexually active. Lack of education on the dangers of
sexual activity only increases the problems affecting teenagers.
Thus, the problems of our future are bound to increase.

Furthermore, according to *Fatal Advice*, "By 1990, 6,233
cases of AIDS were reported in persons aged 20-25, with an
additional 19,568 cases reported in people aged 25-29. . . Since
scientists put the average time from infection to diagnosable
symptoms at ten years, the bulk of the 25, 701 young men and
women diagnosed with AIDS by 1990 had been infected as
teenagers" (Patton 35). This is the age group that most of you
are sexually involved with. If an individual contracts HIV as a
17 year old, he or she may not discover the disease until age
27. Even if an individual you are sexually involved with shows
no symptoms of HIV, it is possible that the disease just hasn't
developed and without the knowledge to know this, they may
be putting you at risk.

According to the Alan Guttmacher Institute website,
"Among sexually experienced teens, about 8% of 14-year-olds,
18% of 15-17-year-olds and 22% of 18-19-year-olds become
pregnant each year" (Guttmacher). Educating teens on forms
of contraception decreases the number of teen pregnancies.
According to Sherry Snyder, the school nurse and sexual educator at Beloit High School, "when I came here [Beloit High]
we had way too many pregnancies, but since I started teaching, our pregnancy rate has cut in half." By decreasing the number of teenage pregnancies, the amount of money that we must
all spend supporting important programs such as Planned Parenthood, will hopefully decrease.

Also, just because you have had sexual education, you cannot assume that everyone has. A friend, from Mankato, did
not find out until she was almost twenty years old that diseases
could be contracted from oral sex. When you ask an individual
about his or her sexual history and possible STD's, the reply

most likely will be that he or she does not have any diseases. However, if the individual does not have the education to know the symptoms, or how to contract these diseases, you many be putting yourself in danger.

Secondly, to comprehend why it is necessary, it is important to understand sexual education in the public schools. What should be taught in a sexual education course: abstinence, contraception or both? At which grade level should sexual education begin? What controversies surround sexual education in public schools?

Consider the first question: Which topics should be covered in a human sexuality course in a Kansas public high school? The Junction City High School curriculum for Human Sexuality states that by ages 14-18 years old, the adolescent should: be informed about human sexuality; be aware of social pressures; be informed about personal relationships; and be educated for parenthood. Michelle, a friend from Junction City, had sexual education in her ninth grade health class. She states, "They basically just touched on a little bit of everything. They talked about abstinence, STDs, and birth control. They showed us how to put a condom on a banana and how you get STDs. They really didn't talk about teenage pregnancy much, they told us that it was easy to get pregnant and told us how you get pregnant, but they didn't give us statistics like how often you get pregnant when you have sex. They just taught us the basics."

Lisa Kinderknecht has been teaching P.E. and Health to freshmen at Manhattan High since 1990. According to her, sexual education, which is taught mainly to ninth graders, consists of three weeks dealing with: Sexual Harassment; Date Rape/Rape; The Reproductive System; Dating and Relationships; Sexually Transmitted Diseases; AIDS; Pregnancy; Prevention/Birth Control/Contraception; and Abstinence. According to Sherrie Snyder, the sexual education course at Beloit High, with a student body of approximately 500 students, consists of: Day 1: Healthy Sexuality; Day 2: AIDS; Day 3: AIDS; Day 4: Date Rape; Day 5: Violence in Relationships; Day 6: Sexually Transmitted Diseases; Day 7: Sexually Transmitted Diseases; Day 8: Birth Control; Day 9: Birth Control and Abortion; Day 10: Sexual Lifestyles. Because it is mandated in the state of Kansas, there must be a curriculum for Human Sexuality at Mankato Jr/Sr High School. However, it was not made available to me.

The second concern is: at what age should sexual education take place? As suggested in *Sex Education and the Public Schools*, "The sex education of the small child should begin in kindergarten and continue into college" (Haims 51). My friend Katie, who is from Ark City, Kansas, a town similar in size to Manhattan, began her sexual education in third grade and was continually taught through her freshmen year of high school. She states, "They taught us really basic stuff first, but then in junior high and my freshmen year we got really specific, talking about STDs, oral sex and contraceptives."

The state mandate claims that, "The program shall include instruction at the elementary and secondary level" (Regulation). However, the typical sexual education course in Kansas seems to occur in ninth grade health classes. According to *Sexuality and the Curriculum,* "a study of 758 eighth-grade students from three rural counties found that nearly two thirds of the boys and 4 out of 10 girls had engaged in sexual intercourse" (Sear 9). When I was in the eighth grade, a friend of mine came crying to me because she thought she was pregnant. She had gotten drunk at a party and woke up in bed with another classmate, not remembering what the two of them had done. I can remember trying to come up with an excuse to get out of the house so I could illegally drive one hour to Hastings, Nebraska, so she could buy a home pregnancy test. The typical American child experiences some form of sexual activity by the time he or she reaches the ninth grade. Therefore, as the mandate states, sexual education needs to start in elementary school and proceed throughout high school.

The third question of sexual education in the public high school concentrates on what debates still surround the courses? Sexual education is going to occur whether it is taught by parents, taught in school, learned from stories or gained through experience. The main controversy about sexual education stems from the debate over where and by whom it should be taught.

Although published in 1973, the four arguments for and three arguments against sexual education listed in *Sex Education and the Public Schools* still apply today. First, "One of the strongest arguments for sex education in the public schools is that most parents are not doing an adequate job of educating their children about sex" (Haims 29). According to Betsy Bergen, an Associate Professor of the College of Family Studies and Human Services at K-State, "Parents say they want to teach sexual education, but from my experience, from asking students, many parents don't teach." Most often parents are either too uncomfortable to discuss this topic with their children, or they do not feel it is necessary to educate their children until they reach high school. Betsy Bergen also states, "Parents are not aware of their children's sexual activity, of how young students are when they begin. Parents are not willing to understand that sixth, seventh, and eighth graders are experiencing sexuality. They either don't know or don't want to believe it."

This summer, my younger brother, a freshmen in high school, asked me if he could get AIDS by kissing someone. I told him no, that HIV was mostly transmitted through unprotected vaginal intercourse. However, when I informed him that the risk of contracting HIV from oral sex was low, but that there were other diseases that he could contract from oral sex, his reply was, "What other diseases?" My brother, a freshmen in high school, someone who will probably soon become somewhat sexually active, did not know that there were other sexually transmitted diseases that he could contract. This is why this topic is extremely important to me. The thought that my baby brother is out there without the knowledge to protect himself scares me. After he asked me this question, we had a big discussion about sex. We covered just about everything that there is to talk about: STDs, contraception, oral sex, vaginal intercourse, slang terms, menstruation, and I answered every question that he had. If every parent would do this, sexual education in public schools would not be necessary. However, obviously not every parent does, because my parents (who educated me in almost every area other than sexual education) never discussed sexual education with either my brother or I.

The second argument for sex education in the public schools "is the need to correct much of the misinformation about sexual matters learned within the peer group" (Haims 31). Students talk about sex with each other. Most likely, if students are educated in classes, they talk about what they have learned. However, if teenagers have no formal sexual education, they are only going to discuss rumors they have heard, without the knowledge to understand that many of these rumors are completely false. Betsy Bergen stated that when she taught a human sexuality course to a high school in Western Kansas, she discovered a myth at that school that "if you smoke marijuana before sex, you won't get pregnant." One girl that I went to high school with honestly believed, until we were juniors in high school, that you could not get pregnant if you had sex in water because that was what her older brother, who "had sex all the time," had told her.

Next, "It is hoped that through good programs in sex education, some of this defenselessness about sex among our young people may be abated" (Haims 31). As I stated before, a very close friend from Mankato, who was sexually active in high school, did not find out until she came to college that STDs could be contracted through oral sex. When I chose this topic for my essay, I called a twenty year old friend from Mankato and asked her, what are the symptoms of Chlymydia, Gonorrhea and Syphilis? She had no idea. By educating students of the numerous sexually transmitted diseases, the symptoms of each and the ways that one can contract the diseases, hopefully the risks students take decrease. *Fatal Advice* states, "Studies published as early as 1988 clearly showed that young people were knowledgeable about routes of transmission, but still lacked information about prevention. . . Thirty-two percent of the sexually active teens reported sometimes using condoms, while 37 percent reported never using condoms, with 20 percent of this latter group having unprotected intercourse with multiple partners" (Patton 39). However, "Sexual Activity Falls Among Teens," an article from *The Salina Journal,* claims that, "The 1997 survey of 16,262 students nationwide showed that a lower proportion of high schoolers are engaging in risky sexual behavior than in 1991, when the CDC [Centers for Disease Control and Prevention] began giving teen-agers anonymous questionnaires every two years about their sex lives" (The Associated Press A5). This information suggests that sexual education is working.

The final argument for sexual education suggests that, "The greatest support for sex education is provided by our youth" (Haims 33). According to *Sex Education and The Public Schools*, "A Harris Poll (March 1970) indicated that 93 percent of American school children want factual information about sexual conduct" (Haims 33). Although this information is out-dated, it would be very unlikely that many students receiving sexual education would say it is unnecessary. When asked if she thought her students took their human sexuality course seriously, Lisa Kinderknecht replied, "Yes! We try to make it so it relates to everyone." Also, I know many students from Mankato who wish we had sexual education. I wish I would have had a sexual education class. When I asked my friend who didn't know about STD's if she wished we had sex education at Mankato, her reaction was, "Oh my God, yes! There is so much I feel like I don't know and it scares me when I see extremely dangerous things going on in Mankato, and it is because the kids don't know it is dangerous."

In contrast, the first argument against sexual education is that "it is a threat to the family as the primary source of information about sex" (Haims 34). As stated earlier, many families do not educate their children on sexual education. However, if a parent firmly objects to his or her child receiving sexual education in his or her school, there is an opt-out clause. The Kansas mandate states that a human sexuality course must, "include procedures whereby any pupil, whose parent or guardian so requests, shall be excused from any or all portions of the program without any penalty resulting from such action" (Regulation). According to Eric Jensen, a graduate teaching assistant in the College of Family Studies and Human Services, "If a kid is opted-out, the teacher must develop a curriculum, which the parents agree to, that the student does outside of class." Thus, if the parents of a child oppose sexual education in the high school, they may just remove their child from the program, leaving sexual education available to those students whose parents are comfortable with the subject being taught in the classroom.

The second argument claims that, "It has also been suggested that if sex education is offered in the schools, it will lead children to engage in undesirable sexual behavior" (Haims 35). However, according to "Sexual Activity Falls Among Teens," an article in *The Salina Journal,* "Asked if they had ever had sexual intercourse, 53 percent of those surveyed in 1997 said no, compared with 46 percent in 1991. Asked if they used a condom the last time they had sex, 57 percent of students said yes, compared with 46 percent in 1991. Dr. Lloyd Kolbe, director of the CDCs Division of Adolescent and School Health, said that the findings give further evidence that teaching teen-agers about safe sex hasn't resulted in more promiscuity" (The Associated Press A5). Mankato Jr/Sr High School is a perfect example that avoiding sexual education doesn't stop students' sexual activity. Last year, the community of Mankato went through a big upheaval when they found out one of Mankato's "good girls," a sophomore in high school, thought she might be pregnant. To add to that, she did not know who the father was. She knew it was either a certain freshmen or a certain eighth grader, but she wasn't sure which one was the father. Since 1995 there have been three teenage pregnancies, and rumors of terminated pregnancies in Mankato. This may not sound like a large number, but the size of Mankato must be considered in this statistic.

Finally, "Perhaps the most significant argument against the inclusion of sex education in our schools is the lack of qualified teachers" (Haims 36). Sexual education is probably, for many instructors, one of the most difficult subjects to teach. Some instructors may not have had the proper education. The Kansas mandate states, "The program shall: (B) require that teachers and building administrators have appropriate academic preparation or inservice training designed to develop a basic knowledge of and a sensitivity to the area of human sexuality; and (C) require that all teachers who teach courses in human sexuality hold appropriate certification to provide such instruction" (Regulation). All physical education instructors must take college health courses, where sexual education is taught. However, according to Eric Jensen, "Many districts do what they are legally required to do, but many of the inservices dealing with human sexuality lack substance or quality."

Furthermore, some instructors may be uncomfortable with the subject. Human sexuality is a very sensitive subject, and it takes a special person to make students comfortable in this setting. Just because an instructor has had the training on what to teach in a human sexuality course, doesn't mean that he or she will be good at it. According to Betsy Bergen, "Whoever the teacher is, there must be a level of trust." This could be a huge problem in smaller school systems. Most teachers are coaches and involved with their students outside of school. For example, my English teacher in high school also taught me dance lessons on Saturday mornings at her home. My P.E. teacher, the one who supposedly is teaching Health/Sexual Education, is a friend of my father. It would be very hard for a student to be open and honest about sexual matters with his or her father's friend, even if they are an educator. This is a common occurrence in smaller schools. According to Sherrie Snyder, "What I found by observing other school systems, is that a school might write up a beautiful curriculum, but the teacher doesn't necessarily teach it. At Cawker City [a school in Mankato's district] the superintendent took over the sexual education because the teacher was not teaching, it was too uncomfortable."

Understanding the arguments for and against sexual education hopefully helps explain why human sexuality education is mandated in the state of Kansas. The examples given above should demonstrate the variety of sexual education that Kansas students are receiving. Junction City High School, Manhattan High and Beloit High are three examples of larger school systems. Mankato is the main example of a smaller school. The differences between the two programs are obvious. There are some problems with the sexual education programs in larger schools. For example, Lisa Kinderknecht's main complaint about the Manhattan program was, "I wish it was longer. I am trying to get a lot of information covered in a short time, but some information is better than none at all, so I'm not being picky." That is the main point. At least these larger schools get some education. In many smaller schools, little or no sexual education is being taught. However, the state mandates that human sexuality be taught in public high schools. How is this problem occurring?

There is no form of accountability for the sexual education programs in Kansas high schools. At this point, all a public high school has to do is write a curriculum, which is determined by each school, and turn it into the Kansas Board of Education. It is just assumed that the course is being taught. There is no check system to guarantee that the curriculum is being followed. The result is that many schools, especially smaller schools, are not teaching sufficient sexual education or, in Mankato's case, no sexual education at all.

How is this problem to be solved? It is not a simple task. However, I believe there is a solution that is reasonable and possible.

How is it determined that classes such as Math, History and English are being taught? Each year students are given a series of tests called the SAT, that evaluate what students are learning. Why is sexual education not included in this test, or perhaps a separate test?

Working with Fred Prindaville, a psychologist at the Pawnee Mental Health Clinic in Concordia, Kansas, I have devised a sample test that could be distributed to evaluate each school's human sexuality program. [Sarah attached the test, which in fact was a combined test and survey, to her essay in an appendix.] Many sexual education courses give tests within the high school. For example, Katie, a graduate of Ark City High School states, "In my class we took a pre-test and a final. Everyone flunked the pre-test, but we all got A's and B's on the final because we learned everything that was covered on that test." The test that I have created could be distributed once a year, by the state, to a selected grade level in each high school. Yet the objective would be the same, to test what students are learning.

I feel that since most sexual education in Kansas occurs in freshmen health classes, the test should be given to Sophomores towards the beginning of each new school year. This would not only evaluate each high school's sexual education program, but help discover what information most students are retaining.

The test would be divided into three sections. The first part would be an analysis of how the course is taught. The second would test students on subjects that should have been covered in each course. The final part would gather information on each student's perception of the sexual education they received.

There are a few problems that could arise with this solution. First of all, funding is certain to be a problem. The funding for this test would come from the Kansas Board of

Education, which means that the tax payers of Kansas would pay for the test. However, the costs of these tests would be minimal compared to the costs of programs that help with teenage pregnancy. The funding of the tests would outweigh the funding of teenage pregnancy programs, such as Planned Parenthood, because successful sexual education programs should decrease teen pregnancy.

Secondly, the mandate states that each school is responsible for creating its own curriculum. This could cause problems with some of the questions in the second section, the comprehensive section, of the test. However, by comparing the curriculums of Junction City High School, Manhattan High and Beloit High, it is evident that most curriculums cover the same topics. Yet, if a certain school has a problem with a particular question, the instructor could cross that question off and give reasons why that question was excluded.

The Kansas Board of Education took the first step by mandating human sexuality. However, the process cannot stop there. A form of accountability must be developed. Many larger school systems are not teaching the entire curriculum, and even more dangerous, many smaller school systems are teaching nothing at all. Furthermore, the Kansas Board of Education, the body responsible for educating adolescents in the State of Kansas, is unaware of this fact.

There is no easy solution. Nothing is going to make sexually transmitted diseases, teen pregnancy and misinformation disappear. However, the statistics and examples in this paper prove that sexual education is a necessary and potentially successful program. Over time, and with increased education, the rate of unwanted pregnancies and avoidable diseases could decrease—in order to do this, though, required sexual education must be taught.

When I started this essay, I set out to prove that sexual education should be required in all high schools. I was unaware that human sexuality had been mandated in the state of Kansas since 1988, because I never received sexual education in high school. By understanding that some smaller school systems are not teaching required sexual education courses, the dangers that stem from this, and the need for sexual education, it becomes evident that some form of accountability must be developed in order to guarantee a complete education for Kansas high school students. The test I have devised is a possible solution to the accountability problem. This is definitely not the only solution, and it may not be the best, but it is a way to see what schools are following the guidelines and what the students of Kansas are learning in Human Sexuality.

Works Cited

Bergen, Betsy. Personal interview. 24 Sept. 1998.

Elementary and Secondary Schools Accreditation Regulation 91-31-3, (g).

Guttmacher, Alan. "Teen-Pregnancy." *Website.* http://www.agi-usa. org/pre-birth. 19 Sept. 1998.

Haims, Lawrence J. *Sex Education and the Public Schools.* Lexington: Lexington Books, 1973.

Jensen, Eric. Personal interview. 25 Sept. 1998.

Kinderknecht, Lisa. Personal interview. 25 Sept. 1998.

Patton, Cindy. *Fatal Advice: How Safe-Sex Education Went Wrong.* Durham, NC: Duke University Press, 1996.

Prindaville, Fred. Telephone interview. 24 Sept. 1998.

Sears, James T. *Sexuality and the Curriculum: The Politics and Practices of Sexuality Education.* New York: Teachers College Press, 1992.

Snyder, Sherrie. Telephone interview. 24 Sept. 1998.

Terpening, Harold. Telephone interview. 10 Sept. 1998.

The Associated Press. "Sexual Activity Falls Among Teens." *The Salina Journal.* 18 Sept. 1998: A5.

Wickman, Jan. Telephone interview. 10 Sept. 1998.

Agency Profile

Sarah was teamed with Chad and Kelly, who had also chosen youth and education issues for their research essays (although neither had investigated sex education). They opted to extend Sarah's project into some form of grounded social action. Since no local non-profit agency was working on this issue, we decided that they should write a letter directly to the body that has power over statewide secondary education, the Kansas Board of Education. However, they would need more information on Kansas schools in order to compose a compelling letter. Instead of composing an Agency Profile, they wrote a proposal for a survey that they would conduct to help further investigate their topic.

Community Project Proposal

Hypothesis: We suspect that the majority of Kansas secondary schools are not fulfilling the required curriculum for sexual education classes, particularly smaller schools.

This is the hypothesis we intend to test and either prove or dismiss. We will conduct a survey of approximately three small schools (1A, 2A, and 3A) and three large schools (4A, 5A), with the target class being sophomores. We hope to survey 30-50 students per school, except in the cases where there are fewer than 30 in the school. The schools we will contact are Manhattan High School, Rock Creek High School, Mankato High School, Frankfurt High School, Freestate and Lawrence High Schools, Beloit High School, Riley High School, and one of the Topeka schools. Our plan is to contact schools until we find six, three large and three small, that will agree to allow us to administer the survey.

The people we will initially try to contact at the schools are the principals. We will explain to them that we are Kansas State University students and our assignment is to do a community profile project. Our specific project is composing a letter to the Kansas Board of Education about sexual education curriculums in Kansas schools. We will explain that our main objective is to compare between large and small schools the curriculums and the knowledge students have gained from sex ed. classes. One thing we will stress is that the schools we survey will remain anonymous, as well as the students, and that the point is not to report how each school is teaching but how schools as a whole are doing. We will also provide them with a copy so that they can review the questions.

After getting permission from the principal we will get the name of the sexual education teacher in the school (if there is one). We plan to get in contact with him/her so that the teacher can help select two classes of twenty-five students or less to give the survey to. Once again, we want to target the sophomore level because most school's sexual education classes occur during the Freshman year. Also, we need to make sure that we get a copy of each school's curriculum from the teacher or principal so that we can compare results with the tests.

After we have gotten back all the surveys, we plan to review the data and, based on it, compose a letter to the Kansas Board of Education. Some issues we want to cover in the letter are whether sexual education is being taught in all schools, how effectively it is being taught, and when and how long the courses are. Some of the problems we foresee with sexual education in Kansas are insufficient education because the suggested curriculum was not taught and also funding issues for future evaluations of education.

Our main concern in our project is developing some form of accountability. By this we mean that each Kansas High School sexual education program should be evaluated. We propose that the schools should be required to not only teach a specified sexual education curriculum but also administer a standardized test that will provide evidence of student comprehension.

Community Writing Project

After consulting with a psychology professor to insure fair survey questions, and overcoming quite a few hurdles with school administrators about the surveying, the team crafted a letter, which then went through several revisions.

Sarah ____, Chad ____, Kelly _____
Kansas State University
___ West Hall
Manhattan, KS 66506

December 1, 1998

The Kansas Department of Education
120 SE 10th
Topeka, KS 66612

Dear Kansas Board of Education:

In 1988 the Kansas Board of Education mandated sexual education in all high schools, which in our opinion was an important and courageous decision. We, three students attending Kansas State University, admire the fact that because of this mandate, many school systems throughout the state of Kansas realize the importance of sexual education. However, through research, we have discovered that improvements are still needed. Our project focuses on creating a form of accountability for sexual education courses in Kansas high schools. Our main goal is to suggest that a standardized survey could solve the problem of inconsistent, and in some cases non-existent, sexual education instruction in our public schools.

Through our research, which consisted of surveying approximately 150 Kansas high school freshmen and sophomores, we discovered a lack of accountability for sexual education in our public schools. The mandate makes each high school responsible for creating its own curriculum for sexual education; however, nothing guarantees that the high school teaches that curriculum. Therefore, as a possible solution to the problem, we have created a sexual education survey. Our survey determines whether developing a standardized survey for sexual education solves the accountability problem.

The survey contains three sections (see attachment). The first part analyses how the course was taught; the second tests students on subjects that should have been covered in each course; and the final part gathers information on each student's perception of the sexual education they received. We feel that the test would be most effective if it were distributed, once a year, to sophomores in every Kansas high school. The survey not only evaluates sexual education, but also solicits student input.

The best way to determine whether a standardized sexual education test is necessary would be to do a study with the survey. Therefore, we contacted high schools throughout the state of Kansas. We chose nine schools, ranging from size 1A-6A, in which to implement our survey. However, we discovered some problems during this process. Only four of the nine high schools allowed us to distribute the surveys. Why wouldn't the high schools allow us to survey their students? One reason given by administrators was that they wanted to protect their students. What are they trying to protect them from? The students should be receiving sexual education in high school and therefore need no protection from this subject.

Furthermore, since the mandate allows each high school to create its own curriculum, we discovered difficulty in creating one test for every school. Each school had something different that it wanted eliminated from the survey. For example, one school eliminated questions referring to sexual lifestyles (homosexuality/heterosexuality); another school would not allow us to include questions concerning forms of contraception.

Even though we ran into problems, we gathered some interesting results from the schools that did participate:

* 35% of students stated that they have not received any form of sexual education thus far.

* 20–30% of students, when asked to rate the areas of sexual education taught (such as forms of contraception, sexually transmitted diseases, and abstinence), rated all areas as "bad" or "not at all".

* 49% of students surveyed could not name 4 forms of contraception.

* 36 % of students, when asked what they would change about their sexual education, said that either sexual education courses should be offered or increased.

These statistics suggest that high school students want and need sexual education, and that even among those who received information, many feel that they could benefit from additional courses.

The conflicts we experienced prove that sexual education is a very sensitive topic. However, it is a mandated course and often not taught efficiently. Our results prove that approximately 30% of the high school students surveyed report either not being offered a sexual education course, or not feeling that they receive adequate sexual education.

We realize that our sample size was rather small; however, we think it is important to not only note what results we gathered from this survey, but also ask ourselves why we were not allowed to survey more schools. How are we to know the effectiveness of a curriculum if we are not allowed to evaluate the course? Any course—whether math, science, English or sexual education—needs evaluation to guarantee success. Therefore, we ask you to conduct a larger scale survey across the state of Kansas.

Our project suggests needed improvements in Kansas high school sexual education courses. We feel the need to bring these results to your attention. We have enclosed the survey we created with the assistance of faculty at Kansas State University. We simply used this survey for our research, but we received positive feedback from the teachers and students to whom it was administered. Therefore, if you do choose to implement a similar survey, we foresee cooperation between Kansas public high schools and the Kansas Board of Education because it addresses the needs of students. Due to our shared interests in the well-being of Kansas high school students, we ask you to consider our proposal.

Sincerely,

Chad _____   Sarah _____   Kelly _____

Log/Dialogic Journal

Journal Entry: 10/21/98

I am excited about this report. I am very glad that I am able to continue my research/investigation of this topic. It is very important to me and I am very dedicated to it.

I am looking forward to working with my partners; however, this is going to be challenging for me. All the research that I have done on this topic makes me feel like this is my paper/topic. Yet, it is now my group's topic. It is going to require a lot of work on my part (this is very important) to relax and accept Kelly and Chad's perspectives. After all, this is just as much their paper/topic, as mine, now.

It is kind of hard to listen to their suggestions that go in different directions than I had planned. However, these suggestions are very important and have been extremely useful. It is just very important for me to remember that this is now a group project and we must move in the direction that the group wants to.

Otherwise, I think that we will work very well as a team. We all three basically have the same vision for the paper.

Log Entry: 10/21/98

* We discussed the fact that our first assignment would be a Proposal rather than a Profile report.

* We made a brief outline of the final project and the Proposal.

* We also composed a list of all schools/individuals that we plan to contact. We felt that it would be best to call 4-5 larger schools and smaller schools, so that hopefully two out of those would definitely allow us to distribute the survey. (Suggested by Kelly)

* We decided that we did not need to meet again until Monday (I guess our paper will not be done until Wednesday.)

Journal Entry: 10/26/98

The hardest part of working on a group project is allowing others to do the work. I am one of those people that often likes to do everything myself (this is a very bad habit) but it is extremely important that each of us does work. It was very hard for me to let Kelly write the Proposal. Not because I think she will do a bad job, just because I like to do everything myself. I am very glad she offered to write it, however. Our group seems to be working well together.

I think it is very important for us to decide a possible thesis and basically what we want to accomplish/prove/present with this project, (the next time we meet).

Log 10/26/98

* We met during class today and wrote our hypothesis for the paper/proposal.

* I suggested that we write our report to the Board under 4-5 different headings:

    * Problem

    * Solution

    * Funding/Complications

    * Implementation

    * Results

    We all agreed that this was a plan to work towards.

* As a group we briefly worked on the proposal and then Kelly suggested she take it and put our outline into paper form and then we should meet to revise/edit.

* We discussed the fact that we need to be contacting schools, soon.

* We decided that I should write thank you letters to those people I interviewed for my paper and inform them of what my group is now doing. I will then follow up with a phone call.

* We decided to meet Tuesday night, 10/27, at 7:30, to review the proposal and divide duties (who's calling who).

Journal Entry: 10/27/98

Working in groups is much harder than I thought it would be. My group just met tonight to review/write the proposal that Kelly was working on. It is hard to turn in an assignment that is written in a different style from your own. Kelly wrote a very good Proposal, but it was very different (in style) from something that I would have written. It was kind of hard for me to relax about this, but I think that this is a very good lesson for me to learn.

On a whole, though, our project is going well. We are all three moving in the same direction and very involved in the topic.

Log 10/27/98

* We met tonight at 7:30 to work on the Proposal and other things.

* Chad and I read through the Proposal and made some suggestions and then Kelly said she would get it typed up.

* We then revised and narrowed the test and I am going to retype it.

* We also split up people to contact.

Kelly: Manhattan High, Lawrence/Freemont, Bob Yunk
Chad: Rock Creek, Frankfurt, Topeka
Me: Mankato, Beloit High, Beloit St. Johns and Eric Jensen

Journal Entry: 10/28/98

I have written quite a bit on this subject already. On the whole, I think our project is going rather well. Our group is working together and everyone is pitching in.

I am a little nervous about time. A month seems like a lot of time to work on this, but if we have any problems with schools allowing us to distribute the surveys, we may be pressed for time. I think it is very important for us to start contacting schools as soon as possible. However, I would like to get thank you notes to those individuals who I interviewed in my paper before I contact them again. I should get those notes out by tomorrow and then begin calling on Monday of next week.

Professor Deans:

Sarah: I can sympathize with your initial feeling of "ownership" over this topic—after all, you put in a great deal of time and effort for the research essay, and that forms the foundation for the community project. As you realize, it is now a group thing, and this means sharing control. I often, when working in a group, want to take control, and find myself working hard to hold back, be patient, work collaboratively. I especially feel the urge to do it all myself when I know the topic well, when I feel like an "expert." Such tensions are a natural part of group work.

I'd like you to reflect here on why this topic is so important for you. In the journal you repeat several times how important the project is to you, and I sense your dedication. Where is it coming from?

Journal Entry: Undated

Why is this topic so important to me? I am not completely sure. I think sexual education is a very important subject. High Schools educate children on math, history, English, etc., which are important topics, but they rarely affect a student's life. However, sexual education is a topic that most likely affects all students' lives. I think it is very important that in education, we also learn something about our lives. In college, I have taken many courses that have caused me to reflect on my life and the choices I make; however, in high school, I never took a class like this. Sexual education is a class that attempts to teach students how to make educated choices in their sexual lives. But this doesn't really tell you why the topic is important to me.

I really don't think it is a vengeance against my high school. I am disappointed in the education that I received, but I think sexual education needs to be altered (a form of accountability) for all schools. I do think sex ed. is an extremely important course—but I think the main thing that upsets me is that schools can get away without teaching it or teaching their curriculum. Nobody would let a school get away with not teaching math, and in my opinion, sex ed. is just as important.

Also, the thought of my brother not being educated on this subject scares me to death. When he began asking me questions about sex, I realized how uneducated he was (I was the same way at his age). It really makes me mad to think that my brother could unknowingly put himself in danger just because he was not taught a course that he is supposed to receive in high school.

Also, part of my passion for this topic stems from my desire to be an attorney. I want to be a lawyer so that I can help people. After law school, I want to work in a woman/family center helping rape and assault victims. However, I would also love to work on getting something passed to make schools accountable for sex ed.

Log 11/3/98—Contacted my three schools. Each sounded interested, but wanted to see the survey first.
Log 11/4/98—Met Chad to go over the tests.
Log 11/5/98—Mailed the tests to each school.

Journal Entry: 11/9/98 [In response to in-class prompt]

Field Issues

How does society's view on sexuality affect sexual education?
- Society as a whole views sex as something that shouldn't be discussed/taught.

How does community involvement affect a school's sex ed. program?

How does the Kansas Board of Education's views on sex ed. affect how it is taught?

Should administrators (for each school) be allowed to determine what is and what isn't allowed to be taught in their school's sex ed. program?

I have never discussed this question, but this is one of the main problems/concerns with sex ed. By allowing administrators to determine sex ed., we basically allow the community to determine what is being taught. Do administrators eliminate areas of sex ed. because they don't think it is important to education, or because they do not think the community would agree with it? Do administrators ever eliminate areas because of their personal beliefs and values?

If the Kansas Board of Education created a set curriculum and then distributed standardized tests to each school to evaluate sex ed. programs would this problem decrease?

Professor Deans:

Sarah: Your reflections remind me that one of the most important legal decisions ever—Brown vs. Board of Education, that integrated schools—shares some of the issues you're dealing with here: the roles of activist law, and the question of whether local school administrators and communities should be able to set their own policies (even if they seem unjust). In that case, much of the community opposed integration; but the federal government demanded compliance with federal law. Certainly your project is smaller in scale, but it does raise some of the same issues.

Today many people—particularly conservatives—say that the government should stay out of people's lives. How activist a role do you think the government and legal profession should play in society?

Log 11/13/98: Contacted all three schools.
Beloit High said that they would definitely distribute the sur-

veys—there was a few changes that they wanted made; I said that would not be a problem.

Mankato had decided not to distribute the surveys, but we talked for a while and Mr. Terpening decided that it would be possible to give the surveys to the Freshmen PE class.

The instructor at St. Johns said that she would like me to come distribute the tests, and to explain what it is for and why I am doing it. We decided that Friday at 11:30 would be the best time. She also had a few changes to be made.

Log 11/16/98: I made copies of all the tests and mailed the surveys to Beloit High and Mankato.

Log 11/17/99: Kelly, Chad and I met at Java to discuss the problems with Kelly's schools and what we were going to do. Then we worked on our outline and rough draft.

Log 11/18/99: I called both Beloit High and Mankato to make sure that they received the tests and were still planning to distribute them (both said yes). I let them know that if it was O.K., I would pick up the tests on Friday.

Journal Entry: 11/18/99 [In-class journal entry]

Academic Writing Compared to Community Writing

Same	Different
Use of resources	More use of community as a resource in this class.
Writing Techniques	
Written for a Grade	Audiences
	More independent
Process	
Essays for my Women's Studies and Lit. Studies have dealt only with literature	Because most of our research is based on the community we have discovered many more complications and problems than with a typical writing assignment

Journal Entry: 11/19/98

I talked to my brother last night. He informed me that the surveys were distributed to his Freshmen P.E. class yesterday.

When I asked him what he thought of the test, he told me that he had to leave some of the answers blank. In a way, this made me feel kind of good—it scares me to death that he didn't know all of the answers—but it proves that there is a purpose to all of the work that I have put into this project.

I also asked Scott what the reactions of this classmates were. His reply was that most people didn't say anything—but some student made comments about how stupid the surveys were. However, after he told me this, Scott said, "They only thought they were stupid because they didn't know anything."

As I was talking with Scott, I felt scared—for what the student's did not know—but it also felt pretty good to have some solid proof to support my claim.

I just hope that someone in that school will look at the surveys and realize how ignorant their students are, regarding sexual education. I'm sure nothing will change (without someone aggressively pushing the issue), however I will feel that I have done some good, if I make just one person in that school think about the lack of sexual education.

I must admit that I do feel somewhat proud. I expected problems—I am just ecstatic that four schools are allowing us to distribute the surveys. I wish we could have gotten some larger schools, but I honestly don't know whether we would have had time to get everything passed through the larger schools even if we had started as soon as we began the project. We definitely procrastinated too long, but we may not have gotten them anyway.

In all honesty, I expected more problems than we actually ran into. I was afraid that we wouldn't get any schools.

I did think that it was going to be harder to get it passed in the smaller schools than in the larger schools—but it sound as though the larger schools were somewhat opposed to the survey. It definitely makes me wonder why they were so against it.

Professor Deans:
Interesting—perhaps because larger schools have larger and less responsive bureaucracies.

Log 11/20/98: I distributed the survey's at St. John's High School and also picked up the complete surveys at Beloit High and Mankato.

Log 11/22/98: Chad, Kelly and I met at the Library to write the rough draft. We looked through the surveys and decided what evidence we were going to use. Then Chad and I wrote some brief ideas and sentences down and then I went home to put all our thoughts into a letter.

Log 11/23/98: Chad, Kelly and I met at the library to revise and edit our rough draft.

Journal Entry: 11/24/98

Referring to your question on how active the government and legal profession should be in society; I think it depends on the issue. It is hard to draw the line. When it comes to a topic such as sexual education, I would like to be able to say that the government should stay out of it and actually the schools should just stay out of it, and that all parents should teach their children sexual education. (This would eliminate many problems with accountability and opposition to sex ed., etc.) Unfortunately, this is never going to happen. Therefore, the government and schools must become involved.

How involved do I think the government should become in schools' decisions about sex ed.? In some ways, I think the government should make most, if not all of the major decisions. For example, I think there should be a set curriculum for all high schools in Kansas. However, there are definite drawbacks to this. As conservative as Kansas is, it would definitely be possible that the curriculum the Board would create, might cover fewer topics than the curriculum a school personally creates.

Also, I do think administrators and parents should have a voice in what their children are learning. However, sexual education is such a controversial topic and very few individuals agree on every part of it. Therefore, a third party should be introduced to be objective (government).

From my experience, some administrators (especially in smaller school systems) are easily persuaded by a few out-spoken/powerful members of the community. If this is true, should these administrators have the power to make crucial decisions, such as what is going to be taught?

I guess in certain instances, the government and legal services act as a third and objective party. Therefore, there are definitely areas of society where the government should be allowed to make some decisions. However, there are many different areas where I think the government is way too involved in society—areas where they have no right to make decisions. So, I guess I don't really have a yes or no answer on involvement; I think it depends on the topic. But who gets to decide which topics are O.K. for the government to be involved in? — Hard question to answer —

Journal Entry: 11/24/98

I just wanted to state that I am very pleased with how well our group is working together. We are all contributing in some way or another. Each of us have found our strength within the group. I was worried about how the writing process was going to go, but in my opinion it was rather painless. We came up with most of the ideas as a group and then I just put them into sentence form. I think this was much easier than trying to write each sentence as a group.

Professor Deans:

Sarah: Your reflection on the role of government attended to the importance of reviewing the context for each particular case—something I think is very important. They also reveal the conflicts and tough calls that go along with public policy. Well done.

As you begin to wrap up your community project, so too will this journal end. Perhaps you should finish with one more entry on a topic of your choosing.

Journal Entry: 11/30/98

The main experience I have gained from this project is working with a group. I was a little hesitant at the beginning of the project, but on the whole, I thought our group worked rather well together. It was interesting that as the process went along, we realized each other's strengths and contributed in that way. I think I will definitely use this experience in future group projects. Not everyone has the same strengths, but each individual excels at something and the key to successful group work is discovering those strengths and using them.

I have also learned the importance of a narrow topic. As I wrote my first paper, the problems with my topic and directions that my paper could go in just kept increasing. The opposite happened here. We started out way too big and then narrowed our topic. At first we wanted to discuss funding and curriculum and etc., which are all topics that need to be dealt with, but not in one month and a two page letter.

Log 12/1/98: Chad, Kelly and I met at my place to finalize the revisions on our project.

Journal Entry: 12/1/98

I am somewhat upset to see that this project is ending. Don't get me wrong, I am very glad to have the letter finished; but I spent most of this semester working on this topic of accountability for sex ed. and I am sad to see that end. It is hard to leave this topic unfinished. Although the projects were for class, I felt that I was doing something, trying to make changes. Now, I sort of feel like I am abandoning this topic, but I don't know what else to do.

I am very pleased with the outcome of the project, though. I think the revisions that we made on the letter make it very persuasive. Most of all, though, I am impressed with the fact that we got four schools to participate in the survey. I think with more time and more work on our part, we could have gotten more schools (even larger schools) to participate. It wasn't easy convincing the schools to do it. It took some work, cooperation and persuasion—but it happened. After all that we have done, I still believe some form of accountability needs to be developed to assure successful sexual education in all Kansas High Schools. However, I am afraid that a standardized curriculum would have to be set—and I don't think that will ever happen. It would be interesting to see how similar/ different the curriculums are throughout Kansas—but that is an entire project itself.

Thank you for allowing me to continue my work on this topic throughout this semester. I have enjoyed it and hopefully, some day, I will be able to continue it and do something substantial.

Professor Deans:

Hopefully the Board of Education will respond to your letter. That seems to me a fruitful next step.

I've enjoyed seeing your active and probing mind at work in this journal.

Appendix B: Community Writing Course and Program Descriptions

While the following annotated list of courses and programs is not comprehensive, it suggests the scope and diversity of service-learning initiatives nationwide. More information on particular programs can be gathered from the people and Web sites listed in the *Contact* portion at the end of each entry. The list will be updated on the *NCTE/CCCC Service-Learning in Composition Web Site* at http://www.ncte.org/service.

Arizona State University

The Service-Learning Project links three different composition courses to a three-credit-hour, upper-division service internship. After a series of training workshops, each student tutors two children, three times a week for thirteen weeks. In first-year composition, students use their tutoring experiences as a "subject bank" for their critical thinking, reading, researching, and writing assignments. The information they gain through their research informs and guides their work as tutors. Next, in Writing Reflective Essays, students synthesize critical readings of essays, their own lives and their tutoring experiences to write reflective essays that explore issues such as class, educational opportunity, ethnicity, and culture. Finally, in Language in a Social Setting, students learn theories of how culture influences language acquisition, and then test and apply that knowledge as they tutor in the community. The Service-Learning Project also places and supervises students as America Reads tutors in community centers and schools. For more details, see Brack and Hall, "Combining."

    Contact: Jan Kelly, Program Coordinator, Arizona State University, Main Campus, PO Box 873801, Tempe, AZ 85287-3801, ph 602/ 727-6382, Jan.Kelly@asu.edu; and Gay W. Brack, Project Director, Arizona State University, Main Campus, PO Box 873801, Tempe, AZ 85287-3801, ph 602/965-8232, Gay.Brack@asu.edu

University of Arizona

Three courses—Advanced Composition, Technical Writing, and Business Writing—integrate service-learning into the curriculum. In Advanced Writing, students write about their work with nonprofit agencies which they selected, and in Technical Writing students produce Web pages for a local agency. Business Writing has students produce grant proposals that are submitted for funding by a local agency.

Contact: http://w3.arizona.edu/~guide/sl/

Augsburg College

Service-learning is an integral part of the journalism curriculum. In the traditional day program, students select a ten-hour service assignment in literacy, inner-city schools, homeless shelters, food banks, transitional housing, AIDS programs, or women's and children's shelters. Students work at the site and then define an "urban issue beat" such as housing, immigration, health issues, or education. Students in the Weekend College, for working adults, participate in an ongoing study of the portrayal of people on television news. Each member of the class is assigned a news broadcast and then completes a survey form, making a sight count of how people of color and European Americans are portrayed in each news story. All members of the class have media-related beats to cover, such as TV news, media ethics, crime coverage, the media, and the law. In both day and weekend settings, students write journal entries about their community service experiences as well as three assignments related to their beats—simple news, a meeting or speech, and a feature interview. Students also participate in interdepartmental community service-learning seminars with students and faculty from other courses and departments.

Contact: Cass Dalglish, Associate Professor of English, Augsburg College, PO Box 1, 2211 Riverside Ave., Minneapolis, MN 55454, ph 612/330-1009, dalglish@augsburg.edu

Azusa Pacific University

In one course, Freshman Writing Seminar: Service Learning Mini-Course at a Local School, students complete multiple drafts of essays in narrative, explanatory, and argumentative modes. As a final project, students observe a class at a local elementary or middle school, receive training, and then, based on what they have already learned in their writing, lead and design a five-lesson mini-course appropriate for younger students.

In addition, students increase the value of their writing and service experience by reflecting upon it through journals and other creative acts.

Contact: Andrea Ivanov-Craig, Department of English, Azusa Pacific University, 901 E. Alosta Ave., Azusa, CA 91702, ph 626/815-6000, Ext. 3491, ivacraig@apu.edu

Belmont University

Two service-learning sections of first-year composition pair Belmont students with at-risk students from a partnering elementary school in a literacy tutoring program. Reading and writing assignments for the course tap the tutoring experiences in direct and indirect ways. Other composition sections are sometimes given an optional service-learning assignment. One such project involved researching a neighborhood undergoing revitalization, interviewing residents and associations in the area, and developing profiles for a neighborhood newsletter and Web site. Also, Victorian Literature, a class with a Web component, considered how today's technology revolution mirrors the Industrial Revolution, creating similar inequities between classes, inequities especially apparent in literacy patterns and in our understanding of the community. Students tutored children in a neighborhood community center's tutoring program and later made advocacy presentations for audiences that could contribute to the tutoring program or service-learning at Belmont.

Contact: Marcia McDonald, Director of the Teaching Center, Belmont University, 1900 Belmont Blvd., Nashville, TN 37212, ph 615/460-5423, mcdonaldm@mail.belmont.edu

Bentley College

In addition to the courses discussed in Chapter 4, several other composition and cultural studies service-learning courses are offered.

Contact: For details, see the Bentley College Service-Learning Center Web site at http://bnet.bentley.edu/dept/bslc/index.html

Brown University

One course, Literacy and Writing, asks the question: What is literacy and what is its relationship to writing? Literacy, usually taken for granted, is explored in depth through readings in autobiography, history, fiction, education, theory, and sociology. Throughout this writing-intensive course, students work in a literacy program affiliated with the Swearer Center for Public Service. A number of other Brown University service-learning courses are literature based.

Contact: A description of this course and others can be found at http://www.brown.edu/Departments/Swearer_Center/index.html

University of California, Berkeley

The Coronado After-School Program, "Writing Communities," unites children, teens, and adults from Richmond schools, the East Bay YMCA and UC Berkeley during after-school hours to create an education space through reading, writing, and computer activities. Undergraduates draw upon theories of literacy, technology, and ethnography as they partici-pate in and come to understand the language and learning of youths in the Coronado Elementary School and Coronado YMCA. Teens from Kennedy High School also act as mentors for the elementary school children. With the guidance of UC Berkeley faculty, the teens and un-dergraduates collaborate on an ethnographic research project to ex-plore the culture of the program and the community that sustain it. Through writing, photography, and computer technology, the children and teens of Richmond work together with Berkeley undergraduates to document and represent their lives, their community, and their views on a variety of issues of local importance. Berkeley also hosts a Service-Learning Research and Development Center (http://www-gse.berkeley. edu/research/slc/servicelearning.html).

Contacts: Jane Hammons, Senior Lecturer, College Writing Pro-grams, 216 Dwinelle Annex, UC Berkeley, Berkeley, CA 94720, ph 510/ 642-5570, jhammons@cwp60.berkeley.edu; and Chalon Emmons, Graduate Student, Graduate School of Education, LL&C, 5th Floor, Tolman Hall, Berkeley, CA 94720, 510/642-5570, cemmons@ uclink4.berkeley.edu

Carnegie Mellon University

For more recent activities at the Community Literacy Center (beyond those discussed in Chapter 5), see their Web site. Projects on the culture of work and on intercultural inquiry are also underway through the Center for Community Outreach.

Contacts: Community Literacy Center (http://english.hss.cmu.edu/ clc), Center for Community Outreach (http://outreach.mac.cc.cmu.edu).

Chandler-Gilbert Community College

Service-learning has been incorporated into all sections of First-Year Composition, which is a requirement for all students. The reading and writing curriculum of First-Year Composition is designed around the theme "Creating Community in a Changing World." Faculty have edited their own multicultural reader to go along with the writing assignments which ask students to observe, research, and write abut community issues. Students are asked to serve at various nonprofit agencies in the community in conjunction with the various topics and issues that they choose to write about. Students are also encouraged to serve at agencies that relate to their career interests. For example, a student who is a nutrition major may be writing about health care issues of the elderly and serve at a nursing home in order to better understand the issues related to her or his career and writing topic.

Contact: Duane Oakes, Director of Student Life and Service Learning, Chandler-Gilbert Community College, 2626 E. Pecos Road, Chandler, AZ 85225, ph 408/732-7146, oakes@cgc.maricopa.edu, http://www.cgc.maricopa.edu/stserv/slife/sl_index.html

University of Cincinnati

Three sections of English composition contain service-learning which develops throughout the courses. The first course introduces the community themes, community service, service-learning, and the various academic goals of the writing sequence (such as making accurate and insightful observations, evaluating the strengths and weaknesses of written materials, working successfully in groups to build skills in language and teamwork, and increasing a sense of social responsibility). Students do not perform community service during this course. The second course continues the development of the goals of the writing sequence, placing special emphasis upon reflection, synthesis, and research skills. Although students do not perform community service, they receive orientation and training in preparation for service in the third course (listening and talking to representatives from community agencies and making visits to appropriate agencies). In the third course, students perform meaningful service in appropriate community agencies. Their service is the basis of a major capstone project (e.g., an essay) in which they demonstrate competence in course goals. For further details, see Ogburn and Wallace, "Freshman."

Contacts: Floyd Ogburn, #205 University College, University of

Cincinnati, Cincinnati, OH 45221, ph 513/556-1690, ogburnfk @ucollege.uc.edu; and Barbara Wallace, #205 University College, University of Cincinnati, Cincinnati, OH 45221, ph 513/556-2021, wallaceb@ucollege.uc.edu; http://www.ucollege.uc.edu/service/ index.html

Colby College

Each semester, between three and eight sections of composition integrate service into their curriculum. The placements have included the homeless shelter, the town senior citizen center, and many school placements from kindergarten through junior high. Recently some placements have engaged students in writing projects—following the model of service-learning at Stanford. Texts have included *Writing for Change* by Ann Watters and Marjorie Ford and *Writing Lives* by Sara Garnes, David Humphries, and Vic Mortimer. Journals and reflective essays on the experiences are required.

Contact: Peter B. Harris, Professor of English, Colby College, Waterville, ME 04901, ph 207/873-5587, pbharris@colby.edu

Colorado State University

Some teachers in composition courses offer students the option of writing for a community group in place of one of the essay assignments. In English education and ESL courses, students offer tutoring as literacy volunteers in a variety of community settings in order both to contribute to the community in support of CSU's land-grant mission, and, as Professor Gerald Delahunty notes, to improve classroom learning by making discussions "more focused and less abstract because students have real experience upon which to base their points."

Contact: Nick Carbone, Writing Center Director, English Department, 310 Eddy Hall, Colorado State University, Fort Collins, CO 80523-1773, ph 970/491-0222, ncarbone@lamar.colostate.edu, http:// www.colostate.edu/Depts/WritingCenter/wcenter/csl/csl.htm

University of Colorado

The service-learning practicum pairs first-year students with young readers from the Reading Buddies component of the Boulder County Learning to Read Program. Following training, the students meet for one and a half hours a week with their buddies and spend another half hour per week preparing for these sessions. The instructor meets with the students and their buddies on a weekly basis to facilitate lesson preparation and to model teacher–student interaction. Each student writes a "language experience story" that records autobiographical experiences from his or her buddy's life. Students also compile a portfolio of work completed with their buddies which is used to evaluate their service-learning participation. To connect the practicum with the writing course, the students discuss readings about literacy, child development, and pedagogy. Through teaching writing, students become better writers, and, by sharing successes and frustrations, they become teachers together.

Contact: Kayann Short, Farrand Academic Program, CB 180, University of Colorado, Boulder, CO 80310-0180, ph 303/492-1267, shortk@spot.colorado.edu

Denison University

The special version of a first-year composition course, Words and Ideas, uses service-learning pedagogy and focuses on issues of literacy and education in America. First-year students not only investigate, read, and write about urgent issues in contemporary American society—educational theory and social class, for example—but also, as literacy tutors active in the community, they have the opportunity to engage with those issues. Students work in one of several venues: after-school tutoring programs in under-funded elementary and middle schools; adult basic education tutoring at a drug rehabilitation halfway house; individual tutoring situations at two local teen centers or in the homes of community members. Students thus experience firsthand the theories and dilemmas contemplated in the classroom. As involved community activists, they also find themselves in a position to test those theories and, potentially, do something about those dilemmas.

Contacts: Kirk Combe, Department of English, Denison University, Granville, OH 43023, ph 740/587-6247, combe@denison.edu; and Richard Hood, Department of English, Denison University, Granville, OH 43023, ph 740/587-6460, hood@denison.edu

DePaul University

Every other year at DePaul, an upper-division, writing-intensive, service-learning course is taught. A group of twenty to thirty undergraduates and the instructor spend six hours learning how to conduct writing tutorials and run writing groups. Then a writing center is set up, in a single Chicago Public High School, in the classes of teachers who have requested assistance. In addition to tutoring and writing reflectively about it, students read about issues of literacy acquisition in urban settings (Keith Gilyard's *Voices of the Self* and Bill Ayers and Patricia Ford's *City Kids, City Teachers*) and write a four-part research project, using a method the instructor devised called the inquiry contract, about an issue deeply imbedded in the high school students' lives as learners. The final product of the contract is a "working document," a text that deals with the issue for an audience beyond the university.

Contact: David Jolliffe, Professor, Department of English, DePaul University, 802 West Belden Avenue, Chicago, IL 60614, ph 773/325-1783, djolliff@condor.depaul.edu

Foothill College

Several sections of Basic Writing Skills include a community service writing focus and optional service-learning projects. Although students are trained in a variety of reflection activities and are asked to address their service experiences in their essays, much of the writing in Foothill's program is analytical and text-based, and community service experiences are seen as another development resource. For details, see Arca, "Systems."

    Contact: Rosemary L. Arca, Language Arts Division, Foothill College, 12345 El Monte Road, Los Altos Hills, CA 94022, ph 415/949-0543, arca@admin.fhda.edu

Gardner-Webb University

In special honors sections of English 102, Composition II (which is part of Gardner-Webb's core curriculum), students select and explore social issues in which they are interested. Under instructor guidance they plan service-learning projects which give them firsthand experience with the problems, controversies, and questions associated with these issues. Through a semester-long process of examining their experiences in journals while studying and practicing various techniques of argument, as well as doing extensive research on their designated issue, they develop and learn to speak their own authority. A key course goal is that students develop ethos, which Aristotle defined as "moral character." As one initially skeptical student concluded in his journal, "This project was a very good way for me to actually experience things instead of just writing about them. Research is all right; however, . . . one finds it very hard to argue an opposing viewpoint with someone who has not only researched the topic but has spent time doing it as well."

Contact: Gayle Bolt Price, Campus Box 7265, Gardner-Webb University, Boiling Springs, NC 28017, ph 704/ 434-4414, gprice@gardner-webb.edu

Gateway Community College

Service-learning is an important element of the English curriculum. In most of the English 101 classes, students write one essay based on a service experience in the community, which is connected to readings and discussions on issues related to the individual, family, and natural environment. In about half of the English 102 sections, students write an essay for which they have completed primary research on a career or social problem in the community, consisting of twenty hours of a service internship. Other English 102 sections complete an international (or global) awareness research project as an alternative to the service.

Contact: http://www.cgc.maricopa.edu/instruction/langhum/english/english_101_and_102.html

George Mason University

A technical writing course and a community service course offer service-learning. In the technical course students spend the first half of the semester learning fundamentals of technical and report writing. During the second half, they form teams and contact organizations in the D.C. area for which they could conduct writing projects. Projects include a manual detailing job scope and duties for an administrative position in a professional association; a citizen's guide to waterfront development on the Chesapeake Bay; a user's guide for constructing and maintaining riparian paths in northern Virginia; and a Web site for a homeless shelter in Arlington, Virginia. Coursework includes regular status reports on projects and group meetings, interim drafts of projects, final projects, and presentations of them to the class. The Community Service Link is a grouping of three courses: English Composition; Introductory Sociology; and Freshman Seminar. Student community service consists of nine two-hour sessions helping in classrooms in an elementary magnet school in a lower socioeconomic (primarily Hispanic and African American) neighborhood. Through weekly field notes, students record their observations of the day's experiences, reflect on them in light of sociological concepts, and pose questions that lead to topics for research projects.

Contact: Jim Henry, Associate Professor of English, George Mason University, MSN 3E4, Fairfax, VA 22030, ph 703/993-2762, jhenry@osf1.gmu.edu, http://mason.gmu.edu/~jhenry/eng410.html

(Technical Writing course); and Ruth Overman Fischer, George Mason University, Department of English MSN 3E4, 4400 University Drive, Fairfax, VA 22030-4444, ph 703/993-2772, rfischer@gmu.edu (Community Service Link course)

Georgia State University

Service-learning has been incorporated into two courses, Rhetoric and Composition and Professional Writing. Students choose partners (largely nonprofits) and complete work that benefits the partners in ways they define and find meaningful. Through the service-learning, students hopefully gain the understanding that all writing is an action that affects people's lives and helps determine relations between people. Service-learning gives students a chance to serve others and to see the effects of their actions.

Contact: http://www.gsu.edu/~engjtg/service.htm

Gonzaga University

A service-learning project in English Composition enables students to understand why service is an opportunity for growth. The project essentially has three parts: (1) a weekly journal; (2) a minimum of ten hours of service-learning time at an agency of the student's choice that offers services to others; and (3) a persuasive research paper and presentation about the social issue the student chose to address. The paper contains reflections on experience as well as research from the library, from the Internet, and from interviews with patrons and volunteers; the presentation will be a short, ten-minute depiction of the students' experiences and knowledge.

Contact: http://www.gonzaga.edu/service/gvs/service_learning/courses/ENGL101.htm

University of Hawaii

Advanced Expository Writing attempts to stimulate real-world writing environments for most of the assignments. The course follows the writing process through prewriting, writing, revising, editing, and publication. Students develop additional critical reading skills, analyze various types and styles of nonfiction, and practice different writing styles for various purposes. Much of the work for this class also involves the use of the Internet for research, communication, production, and access to

class assignments. The course also contains a service-learning component. This is optional but recommended. After gaining instructor approval, students design and write a document (letter, brochure, news
release, Web page, etc.) for a nonprofit agency.
  Contact: http://leahi.kcc.hawaii.edu/~cook/eng215w/215syl.html

Hocking College

The course description of a communication service-learning option reads:
"Participating in actual community service work, students will have a
unique and valuable opportunity to use their own experiences as a basis
of observation and analysis in this hands-on writing course. Students
pursue individualized learning goals through weekly service experiences
within an instructor-approved organization or agency." These, plus classroom assignments, are documented in journal work, two essays, and a
research report. Texts include: *Writing for Change: A Community Reader*
by Ann Watters and Marjorie Ford and *Keys for Writers* by Ann Raimes.
  Contact: Ruth Reilly, Hocking College, Nelsonville, Ohio 45764,
ph 740/753-3591, Ext. 2384, reilly_r@hocking.edu

Indiana University

Once a year, an advanced writing course named Community Service
Writing is offered. Also, there are occasional first-year writing courses
that integrate the practice of service-learning. Efforts are ongoing to
create a Writing in the Community project that will provide graduate
students with the necessary orientation to conduct writing workshops
at various community locations.
  Contact: Joan Pong Linton, Department of English, Ballantine Hall
442, Indiana University, 1020 E. Kirkwood Avenue, Bloomington, IN
47405-7103, ph 812/855-2285, jlinton@indiana.edu, http://
www.indiana.edu/~iss/newsletter/nlapr97service.html

Johnson County Community College

The English faculty are free to include service-learning within any of
their courses and programs, so long as the required exit competencies
continue to be met, and to make service-learning either optional or
mandatory for their students. The college guideline is that service-learning students will complete at least twenty hours of community service,
but faculty are free to specify shorter assignments. The exception is that

all students enrolled in an honors program must complete twenty hours of service-learning in conjunction with one or more of their courses. The college has a service-learning coordinator who advises, places, and enrolls students in a community service activity once the faculty have identified and referred the students. The community agencies verify student volunteer hours and provide feedback on the nature and quality of student service. Students bring community reports to their faculty and prepare reflective journals, papers, and perhaps oral presentations on their service-learning experience.

Contact: Chris Jensen, Faculty Liaison f(˜ Service Learning, Johnson County Community College, 12345 College at Quivira, Overland Park, KS 66210-1299, ph 913/469-8500, cjensen@johnco.cc.ks.us

Kansas State University

Upper-division courses such as Professional Writing and Advanced Expository Writing have included writing-about-the-community research essays and writing-for-the-community projects with local nonprofit agencies and community organizations (see Chapter 6). Also, a first-year composition course has collaborated with the local Living Wage Campaign advocacy group to explore and write about work, class, and wage topics.

Contact: Thomas Deans, Department of English, Denison Hall, Kansas State University, Manhattan, KS 66506-0701, tdeans@ksu.edu, http://www-personal.ksu.edu/~tdeans/

Lafayette College

A First Year Seminar course entitled Challenging Differences: Building Community in a Diverse Society involves service-learning. As part of the College's Comprehensive Writing Program, the course entails six writing assignments based on experiential learning through group discussion, self-reflection, and weekly volunteer hours. The course is divided into five sections which discuss specific questions dealing with the community and analyze the student's role in that community. As the course syllabus states, "The course is intended to provide an opportunity for students to examine a topic from the perspective of a variety of disciplines to develop their writing skills and learn how to use library resources in their research."

Contact: Gary Miller, Chaplain, Lafayette College, Easton, PA 18042, ph 610/250-5320, miller@lafayette.edu, http://www.lafayette.edu/millerg/fys/syll.html

Loyola College in Maryland

See Ilona McGuiness, "Educating for Participation and Democracy," for a description of her writing course.

Marquette University

Service-learning is frequently an option in upper-division writing courses but rarely in the required first-year program. Placements are coordinated through a campuswide Service-Learning Program, which works with agencies, conducts cultural sensitivity programs, and organizes both orientations and reflections (programwide and site-specific). In Advanced Composition and Writing for the Professions classes, students prepare documents for nonprofit agencies—for example, manuals, program brochures, or an oral history narrative. Some students also write for community agencies through an individually supervised writing internship. In each case, the community-based writing is a means for applying the rhetorical and stylistic principles of the course.

> *Contact:* Bobbi Timberlake, Administrator, Service Learning Program, Brooks 100, Marquette University, Box 1881, Milwaukee, WI 53201-1881, ph 414/288-3261, TimberlakeB@Marquette.edu

University of Michigan

For a sampling of English courses, literacy initiatives, and research, see articles by Minter, Gere, and Keller-Cohen; Schultz and Gere; Gere and Sinor; Stock and Swenson; and Crawford.

> *Contact:* http://www.umich.edu/~ocsl/

Michigan State University

The Service Learning Writing Project (SLWP) is a multidisciplinary program of service-learning, writing instruction, and public culture studies. It is a joint effort of the College of Arts and Letters, the Department of American Thought and Language, the Service Learning Center, and the Writing Center. Contact the Writing Center at Michigan State University (The Writing Center, 300 Bessey Hall, Michigan State University, East Lansing, MI 48824-1033) to request a free copy of *Writing in the Public Interest: Service-Learning in the Writing Classroom*, edited by David Cooper and Laura Julier. This eighty-five-page curriculum development guide includes a student resource packet, sample syllabi, a portfolio of student writing projects, and a bibliography.

Contacts: David Cooper and Laura Julier, Department of American Thought and Language, 229 Ernst Bessey Hall, Michigan State University, East Lansing, MI 48824-1033, cooperd@pilot.msu.edu, julier@pilot.msu.edu, http://writing.msu.edu/atl/community.html

Michigan Technological University

Students in Writing for Community: First-Year English explore and expand various perceptions and definitions of "community" and the social services that support communities. Students create two final products: (1) Web pages describing volunteer opportunities at local non-profit and grassroots organizations, and (2) research papers in which students deliberate about the social issues of these local agencies. The students' Web pages become a part of a volunteer opportunity Web site for campus and community people. Students interact with the community by interviewing the directors of the agencies and may volunteer (but are not required to). Students write deliberative research papers that might be used by the agencies for grant writing or other public communication purposes. Other goals of the course include students' consideration of how resources are distributed within society and local communities; who is listened to, who gets silenced, and why; how people take action, organize, and change the status quo; and how to become rhetorically skilled, ethically sensitive, and civic-minded in all aspects of their lives—not just personal, but also, as relevant for each individual, business, church, school, and community.

Contact: Sarah Cheney, Humanities Department, Michigan Technological University, sacheney@mtu.edu

Millikin University

The Millikin University Honors Program requires community service of its students each year. Founded on literacy-based community service work connected to cohorted first-year writing and University Seminar courses, the service-learning sequence introduces students to multiple notions of community. In the first year, students tutor GED, ESL, and lower-level adult readers through Project READ. In the second year, Honors students consider the university itself as a community of learners who must understand one another's needs and respond to those needs as they are able, mentoring and tutoring incoming students through a variety of university centers and programs. In the third year, students refocus on the broader social community in which the university exists, mentoring gifted students in the Decatur school system and learning what it means to develop and complete projects addressing those students' individual interests and learning goals. In the fourth year, students concentrate on understanding what it means to be contributing members of their professional communities, completing a senior Honors project and coming to understand what constitutes service in their disciplines. Taken as a sequence, this approach is both integrated (focusing on learning goals specific to each year of the Honors curriculum) and participatory (teaching students how to think about and contribute to a variety of communities).

Contact: Nancy C. DeJoy, Professor of Excellence in Teaching, Department of English, Millikin University, 1184 W. Main St., Decatur, IL 62522, ph 217/362-6413, ndejoy@mail.millikin.edu

Mills College

A service-learning course entitled Social Action and the Academic Essay contains equal numbers of local high school students and college juniors and seniors. The students are put into partnerships, which meet once a week outside of class, to write shared journals and work on classwork together. The high school students give each college student a new audience and perspective for his or her writing, and, in return, each college student helps a high school student discover what writing in college is like. All high school students are enrolled in Upward Bound, a federal college-preparatory program for students who are potential first-generation college students and/or who are part of low-income families. The entire class discusses readings and reviews essays, and each week a group (college students, high schoolers, or the entire group) reflects on how this course makes them feel about education and working with different people.

Contact: Cynthia Scheinberg, Associate Professor, Department of English, 5000 Macarthur Blvd., Mills College, Oakland, CA, 94613, ph 510/430-2213, cyns@ella.mills.edu

University of Nebraska–Lincoln

Students can develop their own internships for credit, or they can take courses which have service-learning components. The Literacy and Community Issues course invites students to examine current literacy theories and issues in the context of a literacy internship within a community or workplace site. Students' projects have included tutoring elementary children, developing a Web site for the literacy council, tutoring women refugees, designing a brochure for a pediatric clinic, leading a book club for middle school students, and writing an employee handbook for a business. In the Literature of Women Writers course, students participate in service-learning projects which directly affect the lives of women. Students have tutored women in prison, written materials for the Rape/Spouse Abuse Crisis Center, worked on the help line for PFLAG (Parents and Friends of Lesbians and Gays); organized workshops for Planned Parenthood; and worked in the early childhood program for a women's halfway house. Within some first-year composition courses, students have worked as writing partners with local elementary students.

Contact: Amy M. Goodburn, 139 Andrews Hall, University of Nebraska–Lincoln, Lincoln, NE 68588-0333, ph 402/472-1831, agoodburn1@unl.edu, http://www.unl.edu/english/index.htm

University of North Carolina–Charlotte

In Citizenship & Service Practicum students meet twice a week to hold conversations on issues of community, citizenship, and social justice as they discuss readings and interact with guest speakers from the community. Beyond the classroom, each student completes forty hours of volunteer work and keeps a reflective journal.

Contact: Glenn Hutchinson, Department of English, UNC–Greensboro, Greensboro, NC 27402, ph 704/544-2272, gchutchi@uncg.edu; and Denny Fernald, Associate Professor of Psychology, Department of Psychology, UNC–Charlotte, Charlotte, NC 28223, 704/547-4741, cdfernal@email.uncc.edu

University of North Carolina–Greensboro

Writing Community: Reflection in Action is a special theme for the second semester of first-year English. Students discuss readings about community, interact with guest speakers from the community, and volunteer at a project of their choice. The instructor is currently planning a writing class at a nearby homeless shelter in which college students and shelter residents will collaborate through writing.

Contact: Glenn Hutchinson, Department of English, UNC–Greensboro, Greensboro, NC 27402, ph 704/544-2272, gchutchi@uncg.edu

North Idaho College

Six faculty members in the English department incorporate service-learning into their first-year writing courses. Each student who chooses the service option works for twenty hours over the course of a semester at one of sixty community agencies. In English 101, service-learning provides the focus for essays based on students' personal experience. In English 102, service-learning serves as research for argumentative essays. In addition, students write brochures, Web sites, research reports, fundraising materials, and letters to the editor when asked to do so by their supervisors. Students write about, for, and with their community agencies.

Contact: Laurie Olson-Horswill, English Professor and Service-Learning Faculty Coordinator, North Idaho College, 1000 West Garden Avenue, Coeur d'Alene, Idaho 83814, ph 208/769-7827, ljolsonh@nic.edu

Oberlin College

A monthlong project, Grassroots Grant-Writing Winter Term Project, is jointly sponsored by a community group, Lorain County's Grassroots Development Program, Oberlin College's Center for Service and Learning, and Oberlin's Expository Writing Program. Twelve students are selected to work with six nonprofit organizations. Working in pairs, the students meet with representatives from the organizations and draft grant proposals for them. Orientation sessions on grant writing and funding research are followed by writing workshops and individual conferences in which students discuss each other's drafts. Past grant proposals from this project have been funded for up to $150,000.

Contacts: Daniel Gardner, Assistant to the President for Community Affairs, Center for Service and Learning, Oberlin College, Oberlin, OH 44074, ph 440/775-8055, Daniel.Gardner@oberlin.edu; and Anne Trubek, Assistant Professor of Expository Writing, Oberlin College, Oberlin, OH 44074, ph 440/775-8615, Anne.Trubek@oberlin.edu

Pace University

English Composition enables students to engage in authentic reading and writing activities, enhance their computer skills, pursue an inquiry-based research project, and forge meaningful links with senior citizen community members. Students establish a partnership with senior citizens who wish to share their life stories as well as learn some computer skills. The students, through interviewing at the local community center and e-mail correspondence with the older adults, identify some research-able topics. Then the seniors learn more about computing from their student mentors, collaborate with the students on a Web-based research project, and get to write their brief memoir sketches. We have created a class Web site to feature some of the life stories and research projects.

Contact: Linda Anstendig, Department of Literature, Communica-tions, and Journalism, Pace University, Pleasantville, N.Y. 10570, ph 914/773-3956, Lanstendig@pace.edu, http://webpage.pace.edu/lanstendig; and Dr. Eugene Richie, Director of Writing, English Depart-ment, Pace University, 1 Pace Plaza, New York, NY 10038, ph 212/346-1414, ERichie@pace.edu

Pacific Lutheran University

Hard Times and Our Times links first-year seminars in writing and critical conversation to provide the opportunity for in-depth inquiry related to "hard times" in the past and the present. Those enrolled in both courses also participate in a service-learning project in which they tutor at a local alternative high school. This allows students to share their skills with others and, in turn, learn others' perspectives on contemporary social issues. In Inquiry Seminar: Writing for Discovery, students read fiction and nonfiction that talks about "hard times." Through journal entries, reflective essays, and inquiry papers, this seminar offers stu-dents an opportunity to practice and develop a variety of study and writing skills that should help them throughout their college experi-ence. In Inquiry Seminar: Critical Conversation, students debate, dis-cuss, and present understandings of these issues while exploring "hard times." Texts include essays, nonfiction, drama, literature, and films—as well as the firsthand experience in a service project. This seminar offers students an opportunity to practice and develop skills in critical analysis, which should serve to guide their future private and civic ac-tions. Students complete oral presentations relating to such themes as homelessness, AIDS, and doctor-assisted suicide.

Contact: C. Douglas Lamoreaux, Director of Graduate Studies, School of Education, Pacific Lutheran University, Tacoma, WA 98447-0003, ph 253/535-8342, lamorecd@plu.edu

Pepperdine University

A course titled The Call of Service-Learning links academic exploration of complex social issues (e.g., homelessness, poverty, education, racism)

with service opportunities in diverse Los Angeles communities. Students actively participate in a site visit to the Museum of Tolerance, a supervised weekend in a downtown mission, and weekly service in an L.A.-area literacy project. For details, see Novak and Goodman, "Contact Zones."

    Contact: http://arachnid.pepperdine.edu/loriegoodman/GSHU_frames.htm

Portland State University

One English composition section requires two hours a week off-campus, in place of some regularly scheduled class time. Students in this course tutor in reading and writing at a local elementary school. They must make a firm commitment to these tutoring hours as both the elementary school students and the staff depend on them. Because of the extra demands of the course, students may also enroll in a practicum and receive one hour credit in addition to the three credits typical of English composition. Class hours combine lecture, discussion, and small group work. Writing assignments relate to the community service experience and include an ongoing personal/reflective journal, a personal narrative, a critical or analytical paper, and a final documented research paper.

    Contact: Mary Seitz, Senior Instructor–English, Portland State University, P.O. Box 751, Portland, OR 97207, ph 503/725-3567, Seitzm@pdx.edu

Raritan Valley Community College

See the article "Service-Learning and First-Year Composition" by Brock Haussamen for a description of a course that connects college writers to senior citizens in long-term care facilities.

Rensselaer Polytechnic Institute

Rhetoric and Writing is a required 200-level writing course for many undergraduate students. For their final projects, students are asked to work with local clients on projects which range from brochures and newsletters to Web sites and posters. Many of the students choose on-campus clients, but some choose clients from local community organizations. At midsemester, students meet with their clients to discuss potential projects and then write proposals describing their proposed final project. The remainder of the semester is spent creating the communication piece and meeting with their clients to gather feedback. Also offered at Rensselaer is a course entitled Web Design for Community Networking, in which students research topics, consult with clients in the community, and design and build Web pages promoting the community's economic and social assets (http://troynet.llc.rpi.edu).

Contact: Christina L. Prell, Language, Literature and Communication Department, Rensselaer Polytechnic Institute, Sage Building, Troy, New York 12180, ph 518/270-5924, prellc@rpi.edu, http://www.rpi.edu/ ~prellc

San Francisco State University

Literacy and the Writing Process is an upper-division composition course in which students work as mentors with low-income elementary school children in an after-school care setting. Their work with children then becomes material for their writing in terms of development and analysis, as well as a way to learn about electronic publishing and other aspects of print production. Children in the program write and perform poetry, plays, stories, and sometimes songs, which are collected into an anthology and produced in performances.

Contact: Michael John Martin, Lecturer in English, College of Humanities, San Francisco State University, San Francisco, CA 94132, ph 415/338-3089, mmartin@sfsu.edu, http://userwww.sfsu.edu/~mmartin/ vilhome.htm

University of South Florida

The approach for this year-long service-learning course is problem-based instruction, meaning that students must recognize a problem/issue, apply knowledge to develop a response to the problem/issue, and, through experience, find new and personal ways of understanding the problem/ issue. Students participate in group field trips during the fall semester. Following the trips, each group presents information to the class, describing, summarizing, and analyzing their observations. Students then work in groups to identify social conditions/issues observed during their field trips. In the late fall/early spring, the student or group researches information on the social issue and the agencies or organizations who act on the issue. Then, the student or group acts on the plan of action by volunteering in one of the agencies or organizations acting locally. Finally in the late spring, the student or group prepares a reflective paper on the experience to be published on the Web.

Contacts: Charla Bauer and Susan Fernandez, http://www.usf. edu/~lc/

Southwestern College

First-year composition courses and a community literacy project through AmeriCorps and America Reads contain service-learning components. In most first-year composition courses, the student has the option of putting in fifteen hours of community service. The students write about their experiences in a reflective journal, write a paper about the experience, and use it as a springboard for their required research paper. The students research the issues that they are dealing with in their service; this research includes interviewing people at the agency they are working with and using their own experience at the agency. The AmeriCorps Program supports America Reads, a national initiative that mobilizes volunteers to help children learn to read independently by the end of the third grade. Forty students are trained and placed as literacy tutors in area elementary schools. Each AmeriCorps student commits to nine hundred hours of service per year, including initial training, enrollment in a service-learning course and child development courses, weekly AmeriCorps team meetings/workshops, academic/career counseling sessions, participation in three to six community service projects, and approximately fifteen hours of tutoring each week. After completing hours, the AmeriCorps students receive an educational award and college transcript recognition.

Contacts: Kathy Parrish, Professor of Language Arts, Southwestern College, 900 Otay Lakes Road, Chula Vista, CA 91910, ph 619/ 421-6700, Ext. 5548, kparrish@SWC.CC.CA.US (first-year composition courses) and Silvia Cornejo-Darcy, Southwestern College, 900 Otay Lakes Road, Chula Vista, CA 91910, ph 619/421-6700, Ext. 5812, scornejo@swc.cc.ca.us (AmeriCorps project)

Southwest Missouri State University

See "A Service-Learning Approach to Business and Technical Writing Instruction," an article in which Leigh Henson and Kristene Sutliff draw on ten years of using service-learning in technical writing courses.

Stanford University

Community Service Writing is a project of Stanford University's Program in Writing and Critical Thinking. Students involved in the project are assigned, as part of their coursework for a first-year writing class, to write for a community service agency. Students write a wide variety of documents, such as news releases, grant proposals, brochures, editorials, letters to legislators, and researched reports. Other courses, such as Feminist Studies Senior Seminar, also incorporate service-learning.

Contact: Ardell Thomas, ardelita@leland.stanford.edu; or Leslie H. Townsend, Program in Writing and Critical Thinking, Mail Code 2087, Stanford University, Stanford, CA 94305, ph 415/723-2631, townsend@leland.stanford.edu, http://haas.stanford.edu

St. Joseph's University

Literature and Medicine, a literature-based introduction to medical humanities intended for those entering the health-care professions, asks students to read a variety of texts and work in hospital, hospice, or long-term health care settings. The course intends that classroom experience will inform service, since what students read in texts, as well as how they read those texts, can assist in reading the people they meet and the circumstances in which they find themselves.

Contact: Mary Schmelzer, Assistant Professor of English, St. Joseph's University, Philadelphia, PA 19131, ph. 610/660-1857, schmelze @mailhost.sju.edu

Susquehanna University

Literature, Writing, and Practice includes literary and composition study applied to social issues and practices. The course focuses on the challenges of literacy, language, and communication in national and global contexts. Problems and topics in information technology may also be included. Another aspect of the course is a required service component in the form of a practicum to be done off-campus.

Contact: http://www.susqu.edu/facstaff/m/mura/service/writing.htm

Syracuse University

Working closely with the Syracuse University Center for Public and Community Service, the Writing Program has offered lower- and upper-division writing courses with a strong service-learning component since 1997. By engaging students in critical thinking through community involvement, increasing pedagogical collaboration within and across academic units, and promoting civic responsibility within the larger community, the Writing Program aims to improve literacy skills of students by teaching them to evaluate and compose effective texts for a variety of audiences and contexts, both academic and civic. Students write *about* the community (narrating, analyzing, representing, and reflecting on their service experiences and on the critical role literacy plays in citizenship); *in* the community (tutoring at local high schools and middle schools, community centers, and other literacy volunteer sites); and *for* the community (performing such writing tasks as Web site design, Web maintenance, grant applications, volunteer manuals, and case studies, as needed by nonprofit agencies).

    Contacts: Tobi Jacobi and Tracy Hamler Carrick, thcarric@ mailbox.syr.edu

Temple University

The University Writing Program is committed to an approach called Writing Beyond the Curriculum, which contextualizes academic writing instruction in community/school collaborations. Undergraduates in some beginning and advanced writing courses, as well as our literacy track, tutor in immigrant communities and basic education programs. The Institute for the Study of Literature, Literacy, and Culture supports graduate and undergraduate courses in many disciplines with service-learning components, and the Institute sponsors New City Press, which publishes texts produced by neighborhood writing groups for neighborhood audiences. Urban Rhythms (http://www.temple.edu/ur/), a Temple undergraduate Webzine, publishes college and school writers and places college tutors in middle school classrooms to encourage writing. The John S. and James L. Knight Foundation has recently given the Writing Program a grant to further our work in community literacy.

Contact: Eli Goldblatt (egoldbla@nimbus.temple.edu, ph 215/204-1868), University Writing Director, and Steve Parks (sparkss@astro.temple.edu, ph 215/204-1795), Director of the Institute for the Study of Literature, Literacy, and Culture, Temple University Writing Program, Department of English, 1011 Anderson Hall, 1114 W. Berks St., Temple University, Philadelphia, PA 19122, http://www.temple.edu/english/uwp.html

Texas Christian University

Writing Partners is coordinated by Write to Succeed, a nonprofit corporation founded by writing instructors at Texas Christian University to promote community service writing collaboratives in local and virtual communities. Writing Partners brings college and K–12 classes together for semester-length collaboration on writing projects. The students form one-to-one and small group partnerships in which they exchange correspondence and later drafts of individual papers and group projects. Most of the collaboration is conducted through writing; however, once each term a class (of either age group) will host a face-to-face writing workshop.

Contacts: Brooke Hessler (hbhessler@delta.is.tcu.edu) and Amy Rupiper (alrupiper@delta.is.tcu.edu), Department of English, Texas Christian University, TCU Box 297270, Fort Worth, TX 76129, ph 817/257-7240

University of Utah

Some technical and professional writing courses use service-learning projects with community agencies, thus allowing students to put the writing principles learned in the first half of the quarter into practice in a real situation. The students are split into groups which are each given the name of a person to contact in a local nonprofit organization which has expressed interest in having technical writing done. The first four or five weeks of the quarter are set aside for preliminary experience in writing reports and résumés, and the service-learning project involves the last six weeks of the quarter. For details, see Huckin, "Technical."

Contact: http://www.hum.utah.edu/uwp/3400/intro.htm or http://www.hum.utah.edu/uwp/wrtg301/service.html.

Virginia Tech

Students in Advanced Composition: "Real World" Writing and Writing Technologies work as staff writers for local nonprofit organizations, using advanced writing technologies to create a series of "real world" texts that will actually be used by these organizations. Students learn to compose sophisticated and effective hard-copy brochures using PageMaker desktop publishing software, multimedia electronic "slide shows" using PowerPoint presentation software, and World Wide Web pages using Adobe PhotoShop and Claris HomePage HTML software. For more details, see Heilker, "Rhetoric."

Contact: Paul Heilker, Director of the First-Year Writing Program, English Department, Virginia Tech, Blacksburg, VA 24061-0112, ph 540/231-8444, Paul.Heilker@vt.edu, http://www.english.vt.edu/~heilker/heilker.html

Washington State University

Many sections of Introduction to Writing have incorporated service-learning. The classes have combined reading and writing inquiries regarding environmental issues while engaging in community cleanup and tree-planting initiatives. The success of these projects has led to other composition faculty bringing service-learning into their writing courses, such as Writing and Research, and Technical and Professional Writing. In both of these programs, individual faculty have explored ways in which their students can engage in writing and researching as service through contributing to programs on campus and in the community. For example, some students have helped regional American Indian tribes research and write proposals for state and federal programs, and other students have contributed to the design and publishing of brochures for community programs. One course, Composition and Rhetoric for Teaching, is an upper-division course for English education majors. The students tutor high school seniors in their process of researching, drafting, and revising their senior projects. WSU students are trained through the university writing center and volunteer approximately six hours of service that is supported by the WSU Community Service Learning Center.

Contact: Anne Maxham-Kastrinos, Assistant Director of Composition, Department of English, Washington State University, Pullman, WA 99164-5020, ph 509/335-2740, maxham@mail.wsu.edu

University of Washington

The Community Literacy Program was created in 1992 by the University of Washington's Interdisciplinary Writing Program and Carlson Center for Leadership and Public Service. This program combines a five-credit reading and writing course, focused on issues of literacy and public education, with a three-credit placement in public elementary schools or in one of various literacy-based programs for young children. Writing assignments ask students to reflect on their own experience and to create a dialogue between their experiential research in the community and their library-based research on campus. The program also seeks to foster the development of community, both through students' engagement in the schools, and through a collaborative workshop-based classroom on campus.

Contact: Elizabeth Simmons-O'Neill, Senior Lecturer, Interdisciplinary Writing Program Coordinator, Community Literacy Program, Interdisciplinary Writing/English, Box 354-330, University of Washington, Seattle, WA 98195, ph 206/685-3804, esoneill@u.washington.edu

Winona State University

In Advanced Expository Writing, a service-learning writing project accounts for 40 percent of the final grade. Based on their own interests, needs, and majors, student choose a public service organization and negotiate a workable writing project—camera-ready copy, a Web page, a recorded public service announcement, or some other document needed by the agency. Students are encouraged, but not required, to collaborate in pairs or small groups. The instructor provides an introduction letter, guidance on public discourse, instruction in several genres of public documents, editorial support, and group mediation (as needed). Students are empowered to schedule, design, write, and implement the project in consultation with the service organization. For details, see Eddy and Carducci, "Service."

Contact: Gary Eddy, Department of English, Winona State University, Winona, MN 55987-5838, ph 507/457-5633, geddy@VAX2. WINONA.MSUS.EDU, and Jane Carducci, ph 507/457-2376, jcarducci@vax2.winona.msus.edu

Appendix C: Service-Learning Resources and Contacts

Organizations and Networks

Several organizations support service-learning at the college level. In English, a Special Interest Group on Service-Learning and Community Literacy meets each spring at the Conference on College Composition and Communication. A new periodical devoted to service-learning in composition, *Reflections on Community-Based Writing*, has also been launched (to request copies, see http://www.ncte.org/service/listserv.html).

National organizations that support service-learning across the curriculum include:

Campus Compact (http://www.compact.org/). Supports both volunteerism and service-learning in higher education through networking, publications, conferences, workshops, and grants. Campus Compact also has several state and regional affiliates.

The National Society for Experiential Education (http://www.nsee.org/). Includes service-learning in its publications, conferences, and workshops.

The American Association for Higher Education (http://www.aahe.org/). Publishes series of books on discipline-specific service-learning (including one on composition) and hosts conferences.

The Invisible College (http://www.selu.edu/Academics/ArtsSciences/IC/index.htm). An interdisciplinary faculty organization that hosts a listserv and an annual conference.

American Association of Community Colleges (http://
www.aacc.nche.edu/initiatives/SERVICE/SERVICE.HTM).
Web page includes information on resources, program development, and workshops.

The Corporation for National Service (http://www.cns.gov/).
The federal government agency that supports and funds many
service-learning initiatives, K–college.

The National Service-Learning Clearinghouse (http://
www.nicsl.coled.umn.edu/). This database focuses more on K–
12 than on college service-learning, although it includes links
to many university service-learning centers.

Web Pages

In cooperation with Campus Compact, NCTE has sponsored the
"Service-Learning in Composition" Web site (http://www.ncte.
org/service), which includes teaching resources, research resources,
and links. For Web pages on particular service-learning writing
initiatives, see Appendix B.

The Service Learning Homepage at the University of Colorado (http://csf.colorado.edu/sl/) is a comprehensive site with
many links and resources.

Listservs

NCTE hosts a listserv to share information, exchange ideas, and
promote dialogue about service-learning in composition. To join,
visit the NCTE homepage (http://www.ncte.org), follow the "Conversations" link, and scroll down to "Service-Learning."

The Service-Learning Homepage at the University of Colorado (http://csf.colorado.edu/sl/) hosts a general listserv for faculty, administrators, program organizers, and community
organizations.

The Invisible College listserv (http://www.selu.edu/Academ-
ics/ArtsSciences/IC/index.htm) includes faculty from a variety of
disciplines.

Service-Learning Research and Curriculum Materials

For further information on service-learning in composition, a good place to start is *Writing the Community: Concepts and Models for Service-Learning in Composition* (Adler-Kassner, Crooks, and Watters). Also see the "Research" section of the "Service-Learning in Composition" Web site (http://www.ncte.org/service). As for service-learning in general, Jossey-Bass (http://www.josseybass.com/) seems committed to publishing scholarly books in this area.

Pedagogical materials and sample syllabi are available from a number of the organizations listed above, including the University of Colorado's "Service-Learning Homepage" and Campus Compact's homepage. The Edward Ginsberg Center for Community Service and Learning at the University of Michigan also has available for sale the Praxis series of books on developing service-learning courses and programs (1024 Hill Street, Ann Arbor, MI 48109-3310, phone (734) 647-7402; mjcsl@umich. edu; http://www.umich.edu/~mserve/).

In composition, two mass-marketed student texts have appeared: Linda Flower's textbook *Problem-Solving Strategies for Writing in College and Community* (1997) and Ann Watters and Marjorie Ford's *Writing for Change* (1995), a reader that comes with a curriculum guide titled *A Guide for Change*. If asked, the Writing Center at Michigan State will send a curriculum development guide, *Writing in the Public Interest: Service-Learning in the Writing Classroom*, edited by Laura Julier and David D. Cooper (The Writing Center, 300 Bessey Hall, Michigan State University, East Lansing, MI 48824-1033). Many syllabi from various service-learning courses are posted in the "Teaching Resources" section of the "Service-Learning in Composition" Web site (http://www.ncte.org/service) and on Web pages listed in the "Contact" sections of Appendix B.

Academic Journals

The Michigan Journal of Community Service Learning is a peer-reviewed scholarly journal that publishes service-learning research as well as reflections on teaching (Edward Ginsberg Center for Community Service and Learning, University of Michigan, 1024 Hill Street, Ann Arbor, MI 48109-3310, phone (734) 647-7402; mjcsl@umich.edu; http://www.umich.edu/~ocsl/MJCSL/). Several journals have also run special issues on service-learning, including *The Writing Instructor* (winter 1997), *Educational Record* (summer/fall 1997), *New Directions in Teaching and Learning* 73 (April 1998), *Academic Exchange Quarterly* (both the winter 2000 and the spring 2000 issues), and *The Journal of Language and Learning Across the Disciplines* (coming in fall 2000).

NOTES

Chapter One

1. For a more complete discussion of the results of this study, see Eyler and Giles's *Where's the Learning in Service-Learning?*

2. One further notable finding from the UCLA study: students who participate in service as undergraduates are more likely to donate money as alumni (a fact that may pique the interest of college administrators).

3. These findings are summarized in Sax and Astin. The studies on which the article is based can be found in Sax, Astin, and Astin, and, for the longitudinal study, in Astin, Sax, and Avalos.

4. For a more detailed overview of this program, see Cooper and Julier, *Writing in the Public Interest.*

Chapter Two

1. While service-learning practices in general invite a range of genres, one cannot include them all in a one-semester course. Different courses will focus on different genres and discourses. Furthermore, many service-learning approaches to writing instruction resonate with the goals of activity theory, since community writing projects generally do not aim for the "generalizable skills" goals of composition, but instead are engaged with larger activity systems that give writing meaning and motive, whether those activity systems be specific academic disciplines or particular nonacademic organizations (like nonprofit agencies). See Russell, "Activity Theory."

2. For a similar argument (but one not attached to service-learning), see Lovitt and Young.

3. For a definition of pragmatism, see Blackburn. For explanations and interpretations of Deweyan philosophy, see Campbell, *Understanding*;

Westbrook; Ryan; Peters; West, *American Evasion*; Robertson; Fishman and McCarthy, *Challenge*.

4. See Kolb, as well as commentary on Kolb in McEwen.

5. Ryan's remarks also might point to one reason behind the current revival of pragmatic philosophy in the academy at large. See, for example, Morris Dickstein(editor), *The Revival of Pragmatism*. See also Rorty; Orrill. A compelling argument for reviving pragmatism in composition studies is articulated by Roskelly and Ronald.

6. In their book *John Dewey and the Challenge of Classroom Practice*, Stephen Fishman and Lucille McCarthy also emphasize Dewey's preoccupation with reconciling dualisms. Fishman identifies four primary Deweyan dualisms: concerning morality, individual/group; concerning art, creativity/appreciation; concerning day-to-day practice, impulse/reflection; and concerning education, student/curriculum. Fishman then further investigates four more dualisms "nested" within the student/curriculum category: individual/group; continuity/interaction; construction/criticism; and interest/effort (16). The individual/society dynamic on which I focus matches Fishman's individual/group dualism; yet I conflate the others into one: action/reflection. In part, I do this for purposes of economy; but the choice also reveals a difference of emphasis in interpreting Dewey's educational theory. Fishman and McCarthy keep their eyes trained almost exclusively on Deweyan teaching and learning *within* the classroom, while I underscore elements of Deweyan theory that suggest a greater emphasis on the relation of classroom teaching and learning to the community *beyond* the school. For a review of Fishman and McCarthy and related works, see Deans, "Toward Hopeful."

7. Nora Bacon discusses issues pertinent to selecting high-quality service-learning writing projects in "Community Service Writing: Problems, Challenges, Questions." While she does not invoke Dewey, her criteria overlap with Dewey's criteria for educative experience. She states that most successful projects share key characteristics: "The writing was meaningful because it had a 'real' purpose; the assignment exposed students to new people and environments; the project gave students valuable information about or insight into social issues; students took pride in their final products; . . . the writing made a genuine contribution to the community organization; and students working with agencies were highly motivated and thoroughly engaged in their writing" (41).

8. See Jones for an in-depth discussion of Dewey's thought as it relates to debates about individual agency and socially geared antifoundational theories in composition studies.

9. For further discussion of Dewey's understanding of democracy, see Westbrook; Campbell, *Understanding* 140–265; Kloppenberg; and Bernstein.

10. Richard Rorty's *Achieving Our Country* also revisits this Deweyan approach to democracy with vigor, asserting that academics need to muster a more pragmatic "social hope" if we are to effectively address pressing national problems. This stands in contrast to much of Rorty's earlier work, which underplays the democratic and political implications of pragmatic philosophy in favor of a linguistic approach to pragmatism.

11. Fish's understanding of pragmatism, however, is devoid of the explicit democratic political aspirations evident in Dewey's work. Fish insists that nothing definite or substantial—or even democratic—necessarily flows from a pragmatist philosophical stance.

12. In "Teaching for Change," Fishman and McCarthy extrapolate what such philosophical distinctions between Deweyan and radical pedagogies mean for actual classroom practice and student learning. See also Diggins, who finds Dewey "more moderate than radical as a political thinker" (213).

13. In his discussion of service-learning, C. David Lisman expresses a related critique of liberatory pedagogy: "Unfortunately, the neo-Marxist approach, in my opinion, focuses too much on teaching as the medium of social transformation. This is an overly intellectualized approach" (82).

14. There is some disagreement over how to characterize Freire's work and its evolution since the early 1960s. Torres notes that Freire first started his literacy campaign in Brazil with a *reformist* rather than a revolutionary approach; then his pedagogical theory became more revolutionary after the military takeover and Freire's exile ("From"). Aronowitz notes a more recent pendulum-like "shift from revolutionary to democratic discourse" ("Paulo" 20) due to global changes during the 1980s and 1990s.

15. For details on the particularly Brazilian political context of Freire's work, see Silva and McLaren, "Knowledge"; Torres, "From"; and Torres, *Politics*.

16. Foremost on the research agenda for service-learning should be more empirical studies that account for the complexity of student responses to community-based pedagogies in action. Two such excellent studies are Bacon, *Transition*, and Long, *Rhetoric*.

Chapter Three

1. For discussions of both the problems and potentials of collaborative writing as students enter into a client relationship with nonprofits, see Crawford, as well as Henson and Sutliff.

2. For a practical overview of writing for government and nonprofit social service agencies, see Turnbull.

3. In "Taking Control of the Page" Sullivan emphasizes the "verbal-visual integration" needed in generating documents. Addressing various components including graphics, desktop publishing, and printing, she insists that "we must develop a rhetoric of the page that includes visual dimensions of meaning" (58). This emphasis on verbal-visual integration appears now, of course, everywhere in professional communication studies.

4. For a favorable assessment of client-based group projects, see Wickliff. See also Cooper, "Client-Centered."

5. Zan Goncalves and I also have found it necessary to teach our students the social dimensions of writing for the community. First we coach students in reading the culture of the agency (and then ask them to write an essay on it). We also role-play initial phone calls and meetings with agency staff and instruct students on protocol for following up with their contacts. For details see Deans and Meyer-Goncalves. For another example, see Gorelick.

6. Students are not the only ones whose motivation can be renewed by service-learning—teachers also regularly report a boost in energy and engagement, as did Gullion in a memo she wrote to the Provost at the end of the semester: "The service component re-energized me as a teacher, because it required a different style of teaching (predominantly a problem-solving approach that involved more coaching)."

7. Park's conclusions resonate with those of Russell ("Activity Theory") and Heilker ("Rhetoric").

8. Similarly, Peter Elbow reflects on the need to be cognizant of multiple audiences: "When I write something for publication, it must be right for readers, but it won't be published unless it is also right for editors—and if it's a book it won't be much read unless it's right for reviewers. Children's stories won't be bought unless they are right for editors and reviewers and parents" ("Closing" 67).

9. While even well-planned "writing *for*" programs will result in some projects of questionable quality, those which are not carefully organized run the grave risk of being not only unfruitful for students but also ethically suspect in their unreciprocated draw on the time and resources of community partners.

10. In our interview, Gullion spoke of planning to do one large "writing *for*" project for the entire class, which would limit her work to one community partner, rather than the seven attended to by her teaching assistant during the spring of 1997. In 1998, Gullion left UMass to take a position at a community college.

Chapter Four

1. For further comment on differences between "critical thinking" and "critical consciousness," see Aronowitz, "Introduction."

2. Of course, this has been a long-standing concern of many composition scholars, from Moffett and Britton onward. For a recent perspective, see Petraglia.

3. Haussaman makes a final point: "[W]hile many four-year institutions have service-learning programs, service-learning has a special impact at community colleges, where students come from the local community and, to a large extent, will remain in it. Community service is integral to the notion of the community college" (197). For more on service-learning in community colleges, see Franco, and Parsons and Lisman.

Chapter Five

1. Flower and Long are careful to distinguish between the rhetoric of conversation and the rhetoric of negotiation. While they value both, they maintain that literate social action should move beyond conversation (sharing multiple perspectives) to negotiation (navigating multiple discourses and priorities, making choices, and forging hybrids in collaboratively moving toward solutions). Dewey conflates the two in the term "dialogue."

2. In their article "Teaching for Change: A Deweyan Alternative to Radical Pedagogy," Steven Fishman and Lucille McCarthy mark a similar

contrast between radical and Deweyan modes of teaching and inquiry. Like Flower, Fishman and McCarthy are drawn to the progressive liberalism of Dewey, which puts stock in individual agency and the possibility of incremental change from within a system (both often undervalued in the radical pedagogy tradition). Like Flower, Fishman and McCarthy are critical of the confrontational and adversarial stance on which much radical pedagogy is predicated. They prefer Deweyan cooperation and piecemeal (but meaningful and traceable) change. This preference is evident in phrases which, according to Elenore Long, Wayne Peck often uses to describe CLC goals, such as "broadening the intersections of interest" among community constituencies, and seeking (to echo Cornel West) "opportunities for transformational praxis."

3. While the curfew project dealt with responding to a timely political circumstance, the previous series of CLC projects, on "Risk, Stress, and Respect," entailed exploration of and action on broader issues of teen life, public policy, and the public perceptions of teens—not just one particular city issue.

4. Whether the "home discourse" of the college student is in fact standard academic discourse is dependent on the particular student and the college or university. I suspect that most upper-division and graduate Carnegie Mellon students mentoring at the CLC, like most students at elite universities, are quite at home in academic discourse.

Chapter Six

1. Kevin Mattson traces parallels between service-learning and the extension movement of the Progressive Era. His article suggests that many institutional forces are aligned *against* such movements. For an oral history of the relationship of service-learning to 1960s activism, see Stanton, Giles, and Cruz.

2. See Russell, *Disciplines*, esp. 261–70, on initiatives at Colgate and Berkeley.

3. See Fulwiler and Young, *Programs;* Fulwiler, "Showing"; Fulwiler, "How Well"; Herrington, "Writing to Learn"; and McLeod, *Strengthening.*

4. See Mortensen. See also Deans, "Response to Mortensen"; Cushman, "Public"; Ervin; Bérubé; and R. Jacoby.

WORKS CITED

Note: John Dewey's writings are often cited from the multivolume collections published by the Southern Illinois University Press, edited by Jo Ann Boydston: The Early Works, 1882–1898; The Middle Works, 1899–1924; and The Later Works, 1925–1953. The abbreviation EW is used for the Early Works series, MW is used for the Middle Works series, and LW for the Later Works series, followed by the volume number, a colon, then page numbers.

Ackerman, John M. "The Promise of Writing to Learn." *Written Communication* 10 (1993): 334–70.

Adler-Kassner, Linda. "Digging a Groundwork for Writing: Underprepared Students and Community Service Courses." *College Composition and Communication* 46 (1995): 552–555.

———. "Ownership Revisited: An Exploration in Progressive Era and Expressivist Composition Scholarship." *College Composition and Communication* 49 (1998): 208–33.

Adler-Kassner, Linda, Robert Crooks, and Ann Watters, eds. *Writing the Community: Concepts and Models for Service-Learning in Composition*. Washington: American Association for Higher Education and NCTE, 1997.

Adler-Kassner, Linda, Robert Crooks, and Ann Watters. "Service-Learning and Composition at the Crossroads." *Writing the Community: Concepts and Models for Service-Learning in Composition*. Washington: American Association for Higher Education and NCTE, 1997. 1–18.

Anson, Chris M. "On Reflection: The Role of Logs and Journals in Service-Learning Courses." *Writing the Community: Concepts and Models for Service-Learning in Composition*. Ed. Linda Adler-Kassner, Robert Crooks, and Ann Watters. Washington: American Association for Higher Education and NCTE, 1997. 167–180.

Works Cited

Anson, Chris M., and L. Lee Forsberg. "Moving Beyond the Academic Community: Transitional Stages in Professional Writing." *Written Communication* 7 (1990): 200–231.

Applewhite, Eric, and Daryl Davis. *Responses to Uncertainty in Mentoring at the CLC.* Unpublished Student Inquiry Project. Carnegie Mellon U, 1995.

Arca, Rosemary L. "Systems Thinking, Symbiosis, and Service: The Road to Authority for Basic Writers." *Writing the Community: Concepts and Models for Service-Learning in Composition.* Ed. Linda Adler-Kassner, Robert Crooks, and Ann Watters. Washington: American Association for Higher Education and NCTE, 1997. 133–142.

Aronowitz, Stanley. "Introduction." *Pedagogy of Freedom: Ethics, Democracy and Civic Courage,* by Paulo Freire. Lanham, MD: Rowman, 1998. 1–19.

———. "Paulo Freire's Radical Democratic Humanism." *Paulo Freire: A Critical Encounter.* Ed. Peter McLaren and Peter Leonard. New York: Routledge, 1993. 8–24.

Astin, Alexander W., Linda J. Sax, and Juan Avalos. "Long-Term Effects of Volunteerism During the Undergraduate Years." *The Review of Higher Education* 22.2 (1999): 187–202.

Ayoob, Michael. *"Nigger"—As Bad as it Sounds?* Unpublished Student Inquiry Project. Carnegie Mellon U, 1995.

Bacon, Nora. "Community Service and Writing Instruction." *National Society for Experiential Education Quarterly* 14 (spring 1994): 14–27.

———. "Community Service Writing: Problems, Challenges, Questions." *Writing the Community: Concepts and Models for Service-Learning in Composition.* Ed. Linda Adler-Kassner, Robert Crooks, and Ann Watters. Washington: American Association for Higher Education and NCTE, 1997. 39–56.

———. "Service-Learning and Critical Consciousness." Re-Imagining Theoretical, Pedagogical, and Institutional Practices in Composition Studies Panel. Conference on College Composition and Communication. Minneapolis Convention Center. 13 Apr. 2000.

———. "The Transition from Classroom to Community Contexts for Writing (Service-Learning)." Diss. University of California, Berkeley, 1997.

Barber, Benjamin R., and Richard M. Battistoni, eds. *Education for Democracy: Citizenship, Community, Service : A Sourcebook for Students and Teachers.* Dubuque: Kendall, 1993.

Bazerman, Charles, and James G. Paradis, eds. *Textual Dynamics of the Professions: Historical and Contemporary Studies of Writing in Professional Communities.* Madison: U of Wisconsin P, 1991.

Bazerman, Charles, and David R. Russell, eds. *Landmark Essays on Writing Across the Curriculum.* Davis, CA: Hermagoras, 1994.

Bentley College Service-Learning Project Overview. Bentley College Service-Learning Project. Waltham, MA: Bentley College.

Berlin, James. "Freirean Pedagogy in the U.S.: A Response." *(Inter)views: Cross-Disciplinary Perspectives on Rhetoric and Literacy.* Ed. Gary A. Olson and Irene Gale. Carbondale: Southern Illinois UP, 1991. 169–76.

———. *Rhetorics, Poetics, and Culture.* Urbana, IL: NCTE, 1996.

Bernstein, Richard J. "Community in the Pragmatic Tradition." *The Revival of Pragmatism: New Essays on Social Thought, Law, and Culture.* Ed. Morris Dickstein. Durham: Duke UP, 1998. 141–56.

Berthoff, Ann E. "'Reading the Word . . . Reading the World': Paulo Freire's Pedagogy of Knowing." *Only Connect: Uniting Reading and Writing.* Ed. Thomas Newkirk. Upper Montclair, NJ: Boynton, 1986. 119–30.

Bérubé, Michael. *Public Access: Literary Theory and American Cultural Politics.* London: Verso, 1994.

Bizzell, Patricia. *Academic Discourse and Critical Consciousness.* Pittsburgh: U of Pittsburgh P, 1992.

Bizzell, Patricia, and Bruce Herzberg. "Writing Across the Curriculum: A Review Essay." *The Territory of Language: Linguistics, Stylistics, and the Teaching of Composition.* Ed. Donald McQuade. Carbondale: Southern Illinois UP, 1986. 340–54.

Blackburn, Simon, ed. *Oxford Dictionary of Philosophy.* Oxford: Oxford UP, 1994.

Blyler, Nancy Roundy, and Charlotte Thralls, eds. *Professional Communication: The Social Perspective.* Newbury Park, CA: Sage, 1993.

Bok, Derek Curtis. *Universities and the Future of America.* Durham: Duke UP, 1990.

Booth, Wayne. "The Rhetorical Stance." *College Composition and Communication* 14 (1963): 139–45.

Bouldin, Tyler, and Lee Odell. "Surveying the Field and Looking Ahead: A Systems Theory Perspective on Writing in the Workplace." *Writing in the Workplace: New Research Perspectives.* Ed. Rachel Spilka. Carbondale, IL: Southern Illinois UP, 1993. 268–81.

Boyer, Ernest. "Creating the New American College." *Chronicle of Higher Education* 9 March 1994: 48.

———. *Scholarship Reconsidered: Priorities of the Professoriate.* Princeton, NJ: Carnegie Foundation for the Advancement of Teaching, 1990.

Brack, Gay, and Leanna Hall. "Combining the Classroom and the Community: Service-Learning in Composition at Arizona State University." *Writing the Community: Concepts and Models for Service-Learning in Composition.* Ed. Linda Adler-Kassner, Robert Crooks, and Ann Watters. Washington: American Association for Higher Education and NCTE, 1997. 143–52.

Britton, James N. *Language and Learning.* London: Allen Lane, 1970.

Campbell, James. *Understanding John Dewey: Nature and Cooperative Intelligence.* Chicago: Open Court, 1995.

Campbell, JoAnn. "'A Real Vexation': Student Writing in Mount Holyoke's Culture of Service, 1837–1865." *College English* 59 (1997): 767–88.

Childress, Alice. *A Hero Ain't Nothin' but a Sandwich.* New York: Coward, 1973.

Coles, Robert. *The Call of Service: A Witness to Idealism.* Boston: Houghton, 1993.

———. "Putting Head and Heart on the Line." *The Council Chronicle* (April 1995): 24.

Community Literacy Center. *Raising the Curtain on Curfew.* Pittsburgh, PA, 1996.

Community Literacy Center. *Working Partners: An Urban Youth Report on Risk, Stress, and Respect.* Pittsburgh, PA, 1996.

Comstock, Cathy. "Literature and Service Learning: Not Strange Bedfellows." *Building Community: Service Learning in the Academic*

Disciplines. Ed. Richard J. Kraft and Marc Swadener. Denver: Colorado Campus Compact, 1994.

Conniff, Brian, and Betty Rogers Youngkin. "The Literacy Paradox: Service-Learning and the Traditional English Department." *Michigan Journal of Community Service Learning* 2 (fall 1995): 86–94.

Cooper, David D., and Laura Julier, eds. *Writing in the Public Interest: Service-Learning in the Writing Classroom. A Curriculum Development and Resource Guide.* East Lansing: The Writing Center at Michigan State University, 1995.

Cooper, David D., and Laura Julier. "Democratic Conversations: Civic Literacy and Service-Learning in the American Grains." *Writing the Community: Concepts and Models for Service-Learning in Composition.* Ed. Linda Adler-Kassner, Robert Crooks, and Ann Watters. Washington: American Association for Higher Education and NCTE, 1997. 79–94.

Cooper, Jennie C. "Writing for Real People: A Client-Centered Approach." *College Composition and Communication* 44 (1993): 386–88.

Crawford, Karis. "Community Service Writing in Advanced Composition Class." *Praxis I: A Faculty Casebook on Community Service Learning.* Ed. Jeffrey Howard. Ann Arbor: Office of Community Service Learning, University of Michigan, 1993. 75–83.

Crowley, Sharon. "Composition's Ethic of Service, the Universal Requirement, and the Discourse of Student Need." *JAC: A Journal of Composition Theory* 15.2 (1995): 227–39.

Cushman, Ellen. "The Public Intellectual, Service Learning, and Activist Research." *College English* 63 (1999): 328–336.

———. "Rhetorician as an Agent of Social Change." *College Composition and Communication* 47 (1996): 7–28.

Deans, Thomas. "'Going Public' through Service-Learning: A Response to Peter Mortensen." Online posting. 8 Feb. 1999. *CCC Online* ("Letters/Interchanges"): http://www.ncte.org/ccc/ex.html

———. "Toward Hopeful Action: On Recovering Romanticism and Pragmatism." *JAC: A Journal of Composition Theory* 19.2 (1999): 299–304.

———. "Writing Across the Curriculum and Community Service Learning: Correspondences, Cautions, and Futures." *Writing the Com-*

munity: Concepts and Models for Service-Learning in Composition. Ed. Linda Adler-Kassner, Robert Crooks, and Ann Watters. Washington: American Association for Higher Education and NCTE, 1997. 29–38.

Deans, Thomas, and Zan Meyer-Goncalves. "Writing out of Bounds: Service-Learning Projects in Composition and Beyond." *College Teaching* 46.1 (1998): 12–15.

Delve, Cecelia I., Suzanne D. Mintz, and Greig M. Stewart, eds. *Community Service as Values Education.* San Francisco: Jossey, 1990.

Dewey, John. *Democracy and Education: An Introduction to the Philosophy of Education.* New York: Macmillan, 1944.

———. "Ethical Principles Underlying Education." *John Dewey on Education: Selected Writings.* Ed. Reginald D. Archambault. New York: Random, 1964. 108–40.

———. *Experience and Education.* New York: Macmillan, 1938.

———. *John Dewey on Education: Selected Writings.* Ed. Reginald D. Archambault. NY: Random, 1964.

———. *John Dewey: The Later Works, 1925–1953.* Ed. Jo Ann Boydston. 17 vols. Carbondale: Southern Illinois UP, 1976–1991. (Referred to as *LW* Vol.#: page#.)

———. *John Dewey: The Middle Works, 1899–1924.* Ed. Jo Ann Boydston. 15 vols. Carbondale: Southern Illinois UP, 1976–1991. (Referred to as *MW* Vol.#: page#.)

———. "Need for a Philosophy of Education." *John Dewey on Education: Selected Writings.* Ed. Reginald D. Archambault. New York: Random, 1964. 3–14.

———. *The Public and Its Problems: An Essay in Political Inquiry.* 1927. Chicago: Gateway, 1946.

———. *The School and Society.* 1915. Chicago: U of Chicago P, 1967.

———. "The Way Out of Educational Confusion." *John Dewey on Education: Selected Writings.* Ed. Reginald D. Archambault. New York: Random, 1964. 422–26.

Dickstein, Morris., ed *The Revival of Pragmatism: New Essays on Social Thought, Law, and Culture.* Durham; Duke UP, 1998.

Works Cited

Diggins, John Patrick. "Pragmatism and Its Limits." *The Revival of Pragmatism: New Essays on Social Thought, Law, and Culture.* Ed. Morris Dickstein. Durham: Duke UP, 1998. 207–31.

Doheny-Farina, Stephen. "The Individual, the Organization, and Kairos: Making Transitions from College to Careers." *A Rhetoric of Doing: Essays on Written Discourse in Honor of James L. Kinneavy.* Ed. Stephen P. Witte, Neil Nakadate, and Roger Dennis Cherry. Carbondale: Southern Illinois UP, 1992. 293–309.

Dorman, Wade, and Susan Dorman. "Service-Learning: Bridging the Gap Between the Real World and the Composition Classroom." *Writing the Community: Concepts and Models for Service-Learning in Composition.* Ed. Linda Adler-Kassner, Robert Crooks, and Ann Watters. American Association for Higher Education and NCTE, 1997. 119–32.

Duin, Ann Hill, and Craig J. Hansen, eds. *Nonacademic Writing: Social Theory and Technology.* Mahwah: Erlbaum, 1996.

Eddy, Gary, and Jane Carducci. "Service with a Smile: Class and Community in Advanced Composition." *The Writing Instructor* 16.2 (1997): 78–90.

Ede, Lisa. "Audience: An Introduction to Research." *College Composition and Communication* 35 (1984): 140–53.

Ede, Lisa, and Andrea Lunsford. "Audience Addressed/Audience Invoked: The Role of Audience in Composition Theory." *College Composition and Communication* 35 (1984): 155–71.

Elbow, Peter. "Closing My Eyes As I Speak: An Argument for Ignoring Audience." *College English* 49 (1987): 50–69.

———. "Reflections on Academic Discourse: How It Relates to Freshmen and Colleagues." *College English* 53 (1991): 135–55.

Emig, Janet. "The Tacit Tradition: The Inevitability of a Multi-Disciplinary Approach to Writing Research." *The Web of Meaning: Essays on Writing, Teaching, Learning, and Thinking.* Ed. Dixie Goswami and Maureen Butler. Upper Montclair, NJ: Boynton, 1983. 145–56.

———. "Writing as a Mode of Learning." *College Composition and Communication* 28 (1977): 122–28.

Ervin, Elizabeth. "Academics and the Negotiation of Local Knowledge." *College English* 61 (1999): 448–69.

Eyler, Janet, and Dwight E. Giles, Jr. *Where's the Learning in Service-Learning?* San Francisco: Jossey, 1999.

Eyler, Janet, Dwight E. Giles, Jr., and John Braxton. "The Impact of Service-Learning on College Students." *Michigan Journal of Community Service Learning* 4 (fall 1997): 5–15.

Eyler, Janet, Dwight E. Giles, Jr., and Angela Schmiede. *A Practitioner's Guide to Reflection in Service-Learning: Student Voices and Reflections.* A Technical Assistance Project Funded by the Corporation for National Service. Nashville: Vanderbilt U, 1996.

Faigley, Lester. "Nonacademic Writing: The Social Perspective." *Writing in Nonacademic Settings.* Ed. Lee Odell and Dixie Goswami. New York: Guilford, 1985. 231–48.

Fish, Stanley. "Truth and Toilets: Pragmatism and the Practices of Life." *The Revival of Pragmatism: New Essays on Social Thought, Law, and Culture.* Ed. Morris Dickstein. Durham: Duke UP, 1998. 418–33.

Fishman, Stephen M., and Lucille McCarthy. *John Dewey and the Challenge of Classroom Practice.* Practitioner Inquiry Series. New York: Teachers College P; and Urbana, IL: NCTE, 1998.

Fishman, Stephen M., and Lucille Parkinson McCarthy. "Teaching for Change: A Deweyan Alternative to Radical Pedagogy." *College Composition and Communication* 47 (1996): 342–66.

Flach, Jennifer. Personal Interview. 14 November 1996.

Flower, Linda. *The Construction of Negotiated Meaning: A Social Cognitive Theory of Writing.* Carbondale: Southern Illinois UP, 1994.

———. "Literate Social Action." *Composition in the Twenty-First Century: Crisis and Change.* Ed. Lynn Z. Bloom, Donald A. Daiker, and Edward M. White. Carbondale: Southern Illinois UP, 1996. 249–60.

———. "Observation-Based Theory-Building." *Publishing in Rhetoric and Composition.* Ed. Gary A. Olson and Todd W. Taylor. Albany: State U of New York P, 1997. 163–85.

———. "Partners in Inquiry: A Logic for Community Outreach." *Writing the Community: Concepts and Models for Service-Learning in Composition,* Ed. Linda Adler-Kassner, Robert Crooks, and Ann Watters. Washington: American Association for Higher Education and NCTE, 1997. 95–118.

———. Personal Interview. 15 November 1996.

——. *Problem-Solving Strategies for Writing*. 4th ed. Fort Worth: Harcourt, 1993.

——. *Problem-Solving Strategies for Writing in College and Community*. Fort Worth: Harcourt, 1998.

Flower, Linda, and John R. Hayes. "A Cognitive Process Theory of Writing." *College Composition and Communication* 32 (1981): 365–87.

Foos, Catherine Ludlum. "The 'Different Voice' of Service." *Michigan Journal of Community Service Learning* 5 (fall 1998): 14–21.

Franco, Robert W. "Integrating Service into a Multicultural Writing Curriculum." *New Directions for Community Colleges* 93 (spring 1996): 83–90.

Freire, Paulo. "Education and Community Involvement." *Critical Education in the New Information Age*. Manuel Castells, Ramon Flecha, Paulo Freire, Henry A. Giroux, Donaldo Macedo, and Paul Willis. Lanham, MD: Rowman, 1999. 83–91.

——. *Education for Critical Consciousness*. New York: Seabury, 1973.

——. *Letters to Christina*. London: Routledge, 1996.

——. *Pedagogy of Freedom: Ethics, Democracy and Civic Courage*. Lanham, MD: Rowman, 1998.

——. *Pedagogy of Hope: Reliving Pedagogy of the Oppressed*. New York: Continuum, 1994.

——. *Pedagogy of the Oppressed*. 1970. Trans. Myra Bergman Ramos. New York: Continuum, 1985.

——. *The Politics of Education: Culture, Power, and Liberation*. South Hadley, MA: Bergin, 1985.

Freire, Paulo, and Donaldo P. Macedo. *Literacy: Reading the Word and the World*. New York: Bergin, 1987.

Freire, Paulo, and Miguel Escobar, Alfredo Fernandez, Gilberto Guevara-Niebla. *Paulo Freire on Higher Education: A Dialogue at the National University of Mexico*. Albany: State U of New York P, 1994.

Fulwiler, Toby. "How Well Does Writing Across the Curriculum Work?" *College English* 46 (1984): 113–25.

——. "Showing, Not Telling, in a Writing Workshop." *College English* 43 (1981): 55–63.

Works Cited

Fulwiler, Toby, and Art Young. *Programs that Work: Models and Methods for Writing Across the Curriculum*. Portsmouth, NH: Boynton, 1990.

Gadotti, Moacir. *Reading Paulo Freire: His Life and Work*. Trans. John Milton. Albany: State U of New York P, 1994.

Gere, Anne Ruggles, and Jennifer Sinor. "Composing Service Learning." *The Writing Instructor* 16:2 (1997): 53–64.

Giles, Dwight E., Jr., and Janet Eyler. "The Theoretical Roots of Service-Learning in John Dewey: Toward a Theory of Service-Learning." *Michigan Journal of Community Service Learning* 1 (fall 1994): 77–85.

Gilligan, Carol. *In a Different Voice: Psychological Theory and Women's Development*. Cambridge, MA: Harvard UP, 1982.

Gilyard, Keith. *Voices of the Self: A Study of Language Competence*. Detroit: Wayne State UP, 1991.

Giroux, Henry A. "Educational Reform and Teacher Empowerment." *Education and the American Dream: Conservatives, Liberals, and Radicals Debate the Future of Education*. Ed. Harvey Holtz. South Hadley, MA: Bergin, 1989. 173–86.

———. "Introduction." *The Politics of Education*. Paulo Freire. South Hadley, MA: Bergin, 1985. i–xxvii.

———. "Paulo Freire and the Politics of Postcolonialism." *Composition Theory for the Postmodern Classroom*. Ed. Gary A. Olson and Sidney I. Dobrin. Albany: State U of New York P, 1994: 193–204.

Goodman, Lorie J. "Just Serving/Just Writing: Writing the Community." *Composition Studies* 26.1 (1998): 59–71.

Gorelick, Risa. "Writing for Social Change: Connecting Composition, Cooking, and Community. *Louisiana English Journal* 3:1 (1996): 76–82.

Gray, Maryann J., Elizabeth H. Ondaatje, and Laura Zakaras. *Combining Service and Learning in Higher Education: Summary Report*. Santa Monica: RAND, 1999.

Greco, Norma. "Critical Literacy and Community Service: Reading and Writing the World." *English Journal* 81.5 (1992): 83–85.

Gross, Alan G. "Review: Theory, Method, Practice." *College English* 56 (1994): 828–40.

Gullion, Laurie. Personal Interview. 4 December 1996.

Hall, Leanna R. "Transforming the 'Empty Assignment Syndrome': A Study of Rhetorical Contexts for Service-Learning Composition Students." Diss. Arizona State U, 1996.

Harris, Joseph. "The Rhetoric of Theory." *Writing Theory and Critical Theory.* Ed. John Clifford and John Schilb. New York: MLA, 1994: 141–47.

Hatcher, Julie A. "The Moral Dimensions of John Dewey's Philosophy: Implications for Undergraduate Education." *Michigan Journal of Community Service-Learning* 4 (1997): 22–29.

Haussaman, Brock. "Service Learning and First-Year Composition." *Teaching English in the Two-Year College* 24 (1997): 192–98.

Heath, Shirley Brice. "Rethinking our Sense of the Past: The Essay as Legacy of the Epigram." *Theory and Practice in the Teaching of Writing: Rethinking the Discipline.* Ed. Lee Odell. Carbondale: Southern Illinois UP, 1993. 105–31.

———. "Work, Class, and Categories: Dilemmas of Identity." *Composition in the Twenty-First Century: Crisis and Change.* Ed. Lynn Z. Bloom, Donald A. Daiker, and Edward M. White. Carbondale: Southern Illinois UP, 1996. 226–42.

Heilker, Paul. "Rhetoric Made Real: Civic Discourse and Writing Beyond the Curriculum." *Writing the Community: Concepts and Models for Service-Learning in Composition.* Ed. Linda Adler-Kassner, Robert Crooks, and Ann Watters. Washington: American Association for Higher Education and NCTE, 1997. 71–78.

Henson, Leigh, and Kristene Sutliff. "A Service Learning Approach to Business and Technical Writing Instruction." *Journal of Technical Writing and Communication* 28:2 (1998): 189–205.

Herrington, Anne J. "Writing in Academic Settings: A Study of the Contexts for Writing in Two Chemical Engineering Courses." *Research in the Teaching of English* 19 (1985): 331–61.

———. "Writing to Learn: Writing Across the Disciplines." *College English* 43 (1981): 379–87.

Herrington, Anne, and Charles Moran, eds. *Writing, Teaching, and Learning in the Disciplines.* New York: MLA, 1992.

Herrington, Anne, and Charles Moran. "Writing in the Disciplines: A Prospect." *Writing, Teaching, and Learning in the Disciplines.* New York: MLA, 1992. 231–44.

Herzberg, Bruce. "Composition and the Politics of the Curriculum." *The Politics of Writing Instruction: Postsecondary.* Ed. Richard H. Bullock, John Trimbur, and Charles I. Schuster. Portsmouth, NH: Boynton, 1991. 97–118.

———. "Community Service and Critical Teaching." *College Composition and Communication* 45 (1994): 307–19.

———. Personal e-mail correspondence. 7 November 1997.

———. Personal Interview. 2 December 1996.

———. "Rhetoric Unbound: Discourse, Community, and Knowledge." *Professional Communication: The Social Perspective.* Ed. Nancy Blyler and Charlotte Thralls. Newbury Park, CA: Sage, 1993. 35–49.

———. "Service Learning and Public Discourse." Public Teaching, Public Writing Panel. MLA Convention. Sheraton Washington, Washington DC. 29 Dec. 1996.

Hirsh, E. D. *Cultural Literacy.* NY: Random, 1988.

Holland, Barbara. "Analyzing Institutional Commitment to Service: A Model of Key Organizational Factors." *Michigan Journal of Community Service-Learning* 4 (fall 1997): 30–41.

Honnet, Ellen Porter, and Susan J. Poulsen, eds. *Wingspread Special Report: Principles of Good Practice for Combining Service and Learning.* Racine: Johnson Foundation, 1989.

Huckin, Thomas N. "Technical Writing and Community Service." *Journal of Business and Technical Communication* 11:1 (1997): 49–59.

Jacoby, Barbara, ed. *Service-Learning in Higher Education: Concepts and Practices.* San Francisco: Jossey, 1996.

Jacoby, Russell. *The Last Intellectuals: American Culture in the Age of Academe.* NY: Noonday, 1987.

James, William. *Pragmatism.* Cambridge: Harvard UP, 1975.

Jones, Donald C. "Beyond the Postmodern Impasse of Agency: The Resounding Relevance of John Dewey's Tacit Tradition." *JAC: A Journal of Composition Theory* 16.1 (1996): 81–102.

Julier, Laura. "Community Service Pedagogy." *Composition Pedagogies: A Bibliographic Guide.* Ed. Gary Tate, Amy Rupiper, and Kurt Schick. Oxford: Oxford UP, in press.

Kendall, Jane C. *Combining Service and Learning: A Resource Book for Community and Public Service.* 3 Vols. Raleigh: National Society for Internships and Experiential Education, 1990.

Kendrick, Richard J., Jr. "Outcomes of Service-Learning in an Introduction to Sociology Course." *Michigan Journal of Community Service Learning* 3 (fall 1996): 72–81.

Kerr, Clark. *Higher Education Cannot Escape History: Issues for the Twenty-First Century.* Albany: State U of New York P, 1994.

Kintgen, Eugene R., Barry M. Kroll, and Mike Rose, eds. *Perspectives on Literacy.* Carbondale: Southern Illinois UP, 1988.

Kloppenberg, James T. "Pragmatism: An Old Name for Some New Ways of Thinking?" *The Revival of Pragmatism: New Essays on Social Thought, Law and Culture.* Ed. Morris Dickstein. Durham: Duke UP, 1998. 83–127.

Knoblauch, C. H. "Literacy and the Politics of Education." *The Right to Literacy.* Ed. Andrea A. Lunsford, Helene Moglen, and James F. Slevin. New York: MLA, 1990. 74–80.

Knoblauch, C. H., and Lil Brannon. *Critical Teaching and the Idea of Literacy.* Portsmouth, NH: Boynton, 1993.

Kolb, David A. *Experiential Learning: Experience as the Source of Learning and Development.* Englewood Cliffs, NJ: Prentice, 1984.

Kozol, Jonathan. *Savage Inequalities: Children in America's Schools.* New York: HarperPerennial, 1992.

Kraft, Richard J., and Marc Swadener, eds. *Building Community: Service Learning in the Academic Disciplines.* Denver: Colorado Campus Compact, 1994.

Kroll, Barry M. "Writing for Readers: Three Perspectives on Audience." *College Composition and Communication* 35 (1984): 172–85.

Lankshear, Colin. "Functional Literacy from a Freirean Point of View." *Paulo Freire: A Critical Encounter.* Ed. Peter McLaren and Peter Leonard. New York: Routledge, 1993: 90–118.

Leder, Drew, and Ilona McGuiness. "Making the Paradigm Shift: Service Learning in Higher Education." *Metropolitan Universities: An International Forum* 7 (1996): 47–56.

Lempert, David H. *Escape from the Ivory Tower: Student Adventures in Democratic Experiential Education.* San Francisco: Jossey, 1996.

Lindemann, Erika. "Three Views of English 101." *College English* 57 (1995): 287–302.

Lipson, Carol. "Teaching Students to 'Read' Culture in the Workplace: Reply to Gerald Parsons." *Technical Writing Teacher* 14.2 (1987): 267–70.

———. "Technical Communications: The Cultural Context." *Technical Writing Teacher* 13.3 (1986): 318–23.

Lisman, C. David. *Toward a Civil Society: Civic Literacy and Service Learning.* Westport, CT: Bergin, 1998.

Long, Elenore. Personal interview. 14 November 1996.

———. "The Rhetoric of Literate Social Action: Mentors Negotiating Intercultural Images of Literacy." Diss. Carnegie Mellon U, 1994.

Lovitt, Carl R., and Art Young. "Rethinking Genre in the First-Year Composition Course: Helping Student Writers Get Things Done." *Profession 1997.* Ed. Phyllis Franklin. New York: MLA, 1997. 113–25.

Lutz, Jean A., and C. Gilbert Storms, eds. *The Practice of Technical and Scientific Communication: Writing in Professional Contexts.* ATTW Contemporary Studies in Technical Communication Series. Stamford, CT: Ablex, 1998.

Mabry, J. Beth. "Pedagogical Variations in Service-Learning and Student Outcomes: How Time, Contact, and Reflection Matter." *Michigan Journal of Community Service Learning* 5 (fall 1998): 32–47.

Mahala, Daniel. "Writing Utopias: Writing across the Curriculum and the Promise of Reform." *College English* 53 (1991): 773–89.

Mahala, Daniel, and Jody Swilky. "Remapping the Geography of Service in English." *College English* 59 (1997): 625–46.

Mansfield, Margaret A. "Real World Writing and the English Curriculum." *College Composition and Communication* 44 (1993): 69–83.

Markus, Gregory B., J. Howard, and D. King. "Integrating Community Service and Classroom Instruction Enhances Learning: Results from an Experiment." *Educational Evaluation and Policy Analysis* 15 (1993): 410–19.

Matelene, Carolyn B., ed. *Worlds of Writing: Teaching and Learning in Discourse Communities of Work.* New York: Random, 1989.

Matthews, Catherine, and Beverly B. Zimmerman. "Integrating Service Learning and Technical Communication: Benefits and Challenges." *Technical Communication Quarterly* 8.4 (1999): 383–404.

Mattson, Kevin. "Can Service-Learning Transform the Modern University? A Lesson from History." *Michigan Journal of Community Service Learning* 5 (fall 1998): 108–13.

Mattson, K., and M. Shea. "The Selling of Service-Learning to the Modern University: How Much Will it Cost?" *Expanding Boundaries: Building Civic Responsibility Within Higher Education* 2 (Feb. 1997): 12–19.

McEwen, Marylu K. "Enhancing Student Learning and Development Through Service-Learning." *Service-Learning in Higher Education: Concepts and Practices.* Ed. Barbara Jacoby. San Francisco: Jossey, 1996. 53–91.

McGuiness, Ilona. "Educating for Participation and Democracy: Service-Learning in the Writing Classroom." *The Scholarship of Teaching* 1.2 (1995): 3–12.

McKnight, John. *The Careless Society: Community and Its Counterfeits.* New York: Basic, 1995.

———. "Professionalized Service and Disabling Help." *Disabling Professions.* Ed. Ivan Illich. New York: M. Boyers, 1977. 69–91. Rpt. in *Service-Learning Reader: Reflections and Perspectives on Service.* Ed. Gail Albert. Raleigh: National Society for Experiential Education, 1994. 233–42.

McLaren, Peter, and Tomaz Tadeu da Silva. "Decentering Pedagogy: Critical Literacy, Resistance, and the Politics of Memory." *Paulo Freire: A Critical Encounter.* Ed. Peter McLaren and Peter Leonard. New York: Routledge, 1993. 47–89.

McLeod, Susan H. *Strengthening Programs for Writing Across the Curriculum.* San Francisco: Jossey, 1988.

———. "Writing Across the Curriculum: The Second Stage and Beyond." *College Composition and Communication* 40 (1989): 337–43.

———. "WAC at Century's End: Haunted by the Ghost of Fred Newton Scott." *WPA: Writing Program Administration* 21.1 (1997): 67–75.

Miller, Jerry. "The Impact of Service-Learning Experiences on Students' Sense of Power." *Michigan Journal of Community Service Learning* 4 (fall 1997): 16–21.

Minter, Deborah Williams, Anne Ruggles Gere, and Deborah Keller-Cohen. "Learning Literacies." *College English* 57 (1995): 669–87.

Mintz, Suzanne D., and Gary W. Hesser. "Principles of Good Practice in Service-Learning." *Service-Learning in Higher Education: Concepts and Practices.* Ed. Barbara Jacoby. San Francisco: Jossey, 1996. 26–51.

Moffett, James. *Teaching the Universe of Discourse.* Boston: Houghton, 1968.

Mortensen, Peter. "Going Public." *College Composition and Communication* 50 (1998): 182–205.

Morton, Keith. "Issues Related to Integrating Service-Learning into the Curriculum." *Service-Learning in Higher Education: Concepts and Practices.* Ed. Barbara Jacoby. San Francisco: Jossey, 1996. 276–96.

———. "The Irony of Service: Charity, Project and Social Change in Service-Learning." *Michigan Journal of Community Service Learning* 2 (fall 1995): 19–32.

Morton, Keith, and John Saltmarsh. "Addams, Day, and Dewey: The Emergence of Community Service in American Culture." *Michigan Journal of Community Service Learning* 4 (fall 1997): 137–49.

National Community Service Trust Act of 1993. Pub. L. 103–83. 21 Sept. 1993. Stat. 107. 785–923.

Nemiroff, Greta. *Reconstructing Education: Toward a Pedagogy of Critical Humanism.* New York: Bergin, 1992.

Novak, Cynthia Cornell, and Lorie J. Goodman. "Safe/r Contact Zones: The Call of Service Learning." *The Writing Instructor* 16.2 (1997): 65–77.

Novek, Eleanor M. "Service-Learning Is a Feminist Issue: Transforming Communication Pedagogy." *Women's Studies in Communication* 22 (fall 1999): 230+.

Odell, Lee, and Dixie Goswami, eds. *Writing in Nonacademic Settings.* New York: Guilford, 1985.

Ogburn, Floyd, and Barbara Wallace. "Freshman Composition, the Internet, and Service-Learning." *Michigan Journal of Community Service Learning* (fall 1998): 68–74.

Ong, Walter, S.J. "The Writer's Audience is Always a Fiction." *PMLA* 90 (Jan 1975): 9–21.

Orrill, Robert, ed. *Education and Democracy: Re-Imagining Liberal Learning in America.* New York: College Entrance Examination Board, 1997.

Osborne, Randall E., Sharon Hammerich, and Chanin Hensley. "Student Effects of Service-Learning: Tracking Change Across a Semester." *Michigan Journal of Community Service Learning* 5 (fall 1998): 5–13.

Ostrow, Jim. Personal Interview. 2 December 1996.

Park, Douglas B. "The Meanings of 'Audience'." *College English* 44 (1982): 247–57. Rpt. in *The Writing Teacher's Sourcebook.* 2nd Edition. Ed. Gary Tate and Edward P. J. Corbett. New York: Oxford UP, 1988. 158–68.

Parks, Steve, and Eli Goldblatt. "Writing Beyond the Curriculum: Fostering New Collaborations in Literacy." *College English* 62.5 (2000): 584–606.

Parsons, Michael H., and C. David Lisman, eds. *Promoting Community Renewal through Civic Literacy and Service-Learning.* San Francisco: Jossey, 1996.

Peck, Wayne Campbell. "Community Advocacy: Composing for Action." Diss. Carnegie Mellon U, 1991.

Peck, Wayne Campbell, Linda Flower, and Lorraine Higgins. "Community Literacy." *College Composition and Communication* 46 (1995): 199–222.

Peters, R. S., ed. *John Dewey Reconsidered.* London: Routledge, 1977.

Petraglia, Joseph. "Spinning Like a Kite: A Closer Look at the Pseudotransactional Function of Writing." *JAC: A Journal of Composition Theory* 15.1 (1995): 19–33.

Purpel, David E. *The Moral and Spiritual Crisis in Education: A Curriculum for Justice and Compassion in Education.* South Hadley, MA: Bergin, 1989.

Putnam, Hilary. "A Reconsideration of Deweyan Democracy." *Renewing Philosophy.* Cambridge: Harvard UP, 1992. 180–200.

Reeb, Roger N., Ronald M. Katsuyama, Julie A. Sammon, and David S. Yoder. "The Community Service Self-Efficacy Scale: Evidence of Reliability, Construct Validity, and Pragmatic Utility." *Michigan Journal of Community Service Learning* 5 (fall 1998): 48–57.

Rehling, Louise. "Doing Good while Doing Well: Service Learning Internships." *Business Communications Quarterly* 63 (Mar. 2000): 77–89.

Reither, James A. "Bridging the Gap: Scenic Motives for Collaborative Writing in Workplace and School." *Writing in the Workplace: New Research Perspectives.* Ed. Rachel Spilka. Carbondale: Southern Illinois UP, 1993. 195–206.

Rhoads, Robert A. *Community Service and Higher Learning: Explorations of the Caring Self.* Albany: State U of New York P, 1997.

Rhoads, Robert A., and Jeffrey P. F. Howard, eds. *Academic Service Learning: A Pedagogy of Action and Reflection.* New Directions for Teaching and Learning 73. San Francisco: Jossey, 1998.

Robertson, E. "Is Dewey's Educational Vision Still Viable?" *Review of Educational Research* 18 (1992): 335–81.

Robinson, Jay. "Literacy and Lived Lives: Reflections on the Responsibilities of Teachers." *Literacy and Democracy: Teacher Research and Composition Studies in Pursuit of Habitable Spaces: Further Conversations from the Students of Jay Robinson.* Ed. Cathy Fleischer and David Schaafsma. Urbana, IL: NCTE, 1998. 1–27.

Rorty, Richard. *Achieving Our Country: Leftist Thought in Twentieth-Century America.* Cambridge: Harvard UP, 1998.

Rose, Mike. *Lives on the Boundary: The Struggles and Achievements of America's Underprepared.* New York: Free Press, 1989.

Roskelly, Hephzibah, and Kate Ronald. *Reason to Believe: Romanticism, Pragmatism and the Teaching of Writing.* Albany: State U of New York P, 1998.

Rubin, Sharon. "Institutionalizing Service-Learning." *Service-Learning in Higher Education: Concepts and Practices.* Ed. Barbara Jacoby. San Francisco: Jossey, 1996. 297–316.

Russell, David. "Activity Theory and Its Implications for Writing Instruction." *Reconceiving Writing: Rethinking Writing Instruction.* Ed. Joseph Petraglia. Mahwah: Erlbaum, 1995. 51–77.

———. *Writing in the Academic Disciplines, 1870–1990: A Curricular History.* Carbondale: Southern Illinois UP, 1991.

Ryan, Alan. *John Dewey and the High Tide of American Liberalism.* New York: Norton, 1995.

Saltmarsh, John. "Education for Critical Citizenship: John Dewey's Contribution to the Pedagogy of Community Service Learning." *Michigan Journal of Community Service Learning* 3 (fall 1996): 13–21.

Sax, Linda J., and Alexander W. Astin. "The Benefits of Service: Evidence from Undergraduates." *Educational Record* 78.3/4 (1997): 25–32.

Sax, Linda J., Alexander W. Astin, and Helen S. Astin. "What Were LSAHE Impacts on Student Volunteers?" *Evaluation of Learn and Serve America, Higher Education: First Year Report.* Ed. Maryann Jacobi Gray. Santa Monica: RAND Corp, 1996.

Schine, Joan G., ed. *Service Learning: The Ninety-Sixth Yearbook of the National Society for the Study of Education.* Chicago: U of Chicago P (distributor), 1997.

Schutz, Aaron, and Anne Ruggles Gere. "Service Learning and English Studies: Rethinking 'Public' Service." *College English* 60 (1998): 129–49.

Shor, Ira. *Critical Teaching and Everyday Life.* Chicago: U of Chicago P, 1987.

———. "Education Is Politics: Paulo Freire's Critical Pedagogy." *Paulo Freire: A Critical Encounter.* Ed. Peter McLaren and Peter Leonard. New York: Routledge, 1993. 25–35.

————. *Empowering Education: Critical Teaching for Social Change.* Chicago: U of Chicago P, 1992.

Shor, Ira, and Paulo Freire. *A Pedagogy for Liberation: Dialogues on Transforming Education.* South Hadley, MA: Bergin, 1987.

Silva, Tomaz Tadeu da, and Peter McLaren. "Knowledge Under Siege: The Brazilian Debate." *Paulo Freire: A Critical Encounter.* Ed. Peter McLaren and Peter Leonard. New York: Routledge, 1993. 36–46.

Spilka, Rachel, ed. *Writing in the Workplace: New Research Perspectives.* Carbondale: Southern Illinois UP, 1993.

Stanton, Timothy K., Dwight E. Giles, Jr., and Nadinne I. Cruz. *Service-Learning: A Movement's Pioneers Reflect on Its Origins, Practice, and Future.* San Francisco: Jossey, 1999.

Staples, Katherine, and Cezar Ornatowski, eds. *Foundations for Teaching Technical Communication: Theory, Practice, and Program Design.* ATTW Contemporary Studies in Technical Communication Series, Vol. 1. Greenwich, CT: Ablex, 1997.

Stock, Patricia, and Janet Swenson. "The Write for Your Life Project: Learning to Serve and Serving to Learn." *Writing the Community: Concepts and Models for Service-Learning in Composition.* Ed. Linda Adler-Kassner, Robert Crooks, and Ann Watters. Washington: American Association for Higher Education and NCTE, 1997. 153–66.

Stotsky, Sandra. "Participatory Writing: Literacy for Civic Purposes." *Nonacademic Writing: Social Theory and Technology.* Ed. Ann Hill Duin and Craig J. Hansen. Mahwah, NJ: Erlbaum, 1996. 227–56.

Sullivan, Patricia. "Taking Control of the Page: Electronic Writing and Word Publishing." *Evolving Perspectives on Computers and Composition Studies: Questions for the 1990s.* Ed. Gail E. Hawisher and Cynthia L. Self. Urbana, IL: NCTE, 1991. 43–64.

Talarico, Ross. *Spreading the Word: Poetry and the Survival of Community in America.* Durham: Duke UP, 1995.

Thaiss, Christopher. "The Future of Writing Across the Curriculum." *Strengthening Programs for Writing Across the Curriculum.* Ed. Susan H. McLeod. San Francisco: Jossey, 1988. 91–102.

Torres, Carlos Alberto. "From *The Pedagogy of the Oppressed* to *A Luta Continua.*" *Paulo Freire: A Critical Encounter.* Ed. Peter McLaren and Peter Leonard. New York: Routledge, 1993. 119–45.

———. *The Politics of Nonformal Education in Latin America*. New York: Praeger, 1990.

Turnbull, Lisa Meeder. "Writing for Government and Nonprofit Social Service Agencies." *The Practice of Technical and Scientific Communication: Writing in Professional Contexts*. Ed. Jean A. Lutz and C. Gilbert Storms. ATTW Contemporary Studies in Technical Communication Series. Stamford, CT: Ablex, 1998. 211–37.

Villanueva, Victor, Jr. "Considerations for American Freireistas." *Cross-Talk in Comp Theory: A Reader*. Ed. Victor Villanueva, Jr. Urbana, IL: NCTE, 1997. 621–37.

Vygotsky, Lev. *Thinking and Speech*. Ed. and trans. N. Minick. New York: Plenum, 1987.

Walvoord, Barbara E. "The Future of WAC." *College English* 58 (1996): 58–79.

Waterman, Alan S. "The Role of Student Characteristics in Service-Learning." *Service-Learning: Applications from the Research*. Ed. Alan S. Waterman. Hillsdale, NJ: Erlbaum, 1997. 95–105.

———, ed. *Service-Learning: Applications from the Research*. Hillsdale, NJ: Erlbaum, 1997.

Watters, Ann, and Marjorie Ford. *Writing for Change: A Community Reader*. New York: McGraw, 1995.

———. *A Guide for Change: Resources for Implementing Community Service Writing*. New York: McGraw, 1995.

West, Cornel. *Prophetic Reflections: Notes on Race and Power in America*. Monroe, ME: Common Courage, 1993.

———. *Keeping Faith: Philosophy and Race in America*. New York: Routledge, 1993.

———. *The American Evasion of Philosophy: A Genealogy of Pragmatism*. Madison: U of Wisconsin P, 1989.

Westbrook, Robert B. *John Dewey and American Democracy*. Ithaca: Cornell UP, 1991.

Wickliff, Gregory A. "Assessing the Value of Client-Based Group Projects in an Introductory Technical Communication Course." *Journal of Business and Technical Communication* 11.2 (1997): 170–91.

Zlotkowski, Edward. "Linking Service-Learning and the Academy: A New Voice at the Table?" *Change* 28.1 (1996): 20–27.

———. Personal Interview. 2 December 1996.

———. *Successful Service-Learning Programs: New Models of Excellence in Higher Education.* Bolton, MA: Anker, 1998.

INDEX

Academic development, 4
Academic Exchange Quarterly,
    248
Action-reflection
    Dewey and, 30–33, 115
    Freire and, 41–45
    student, 77–81, 104, 132
Activity theory, 249n. 1
Adler-Kassner, Linda, 35, 107
Agency, individual, 5, 50, 119,
    120, 121, 123, 250n. 8,
    253–54n. 2
Agency profile, 156–57, 183–84,
    204–6
Alzheimer's Disease, 107
American Association for Higher
    Education, The, 12, 245
American Association of
    Community Colleges,
    12–13, 246
Anson, Chris M., 57, 58
Arca, Rosemary, 106
Aristotle, 10, 68
Arizona State University, 93, 219
Aronowitz, Stanley, 39
Assessment, 17, 83
Attention Deficit Disorder (ADD),
    95–96
Audience, 9, 59, 67–75, 181
    definition, 72
    as motivation, 69–71
    multiple, 71, 252n. 8
    target, 73
Augsburg College, 220
Azusa Pacific University, 220–21

Bacon, Nora, 44, 60, 70, 74,
    250n. 7
Barber, Benjamin, 105
Bartholomae, David, 121
Baskins, Joyce, 116, 132
Bazerman, Charles, 63
Belmont University, 221
Bentley College, 13, 85–109, 167,
    221
Berlin, James, 25, 119, 121
Bernstein, Richard J., 36
Berthoff, Ann, 91
Binarism, 74, 250n. 6
Bizzell, Patricia, 121
Blyler, Nancy, 63
Bok, Derek, 7
Booth, Wayne, 60
Bouldin, Tyler, 63–64
Boundary crossing, 9
Boyer, Ernest, 7, 142
Brannon, Lil, 88
Braxton, John, 2–3
Britton, James, 14, 16, 68, 168
Brown University, 221–22
Burke, Kenneth, 59

California, University of
    (Berkeley), 222
California, University of (Los
    Angeles), 3–4, 249n. 2
Campbell, JoAnn, 23
Campus Compact, 12, 245, 247
Carnegie Mellon University,
    110–41, 163, 222

AUTHOR

Photo by Bruce Hutchinson

Thomas Deans is assistant professor of English at Kansas State University, where he teaches courses in writing, literature, and professional communication, as well as mentors graduate students in the teaching of writing. Much of his scholarship explores the relationship of the academy to the larger community, especially with respect to literacy. Other interests include pragmatism, writing across the curriculum, writing program administration, Shakespeare, and connections between composition studies and literary studies. He has served in administrative and teaching posts at Georgetown University and the University of Massachusetts Amherst, and he currently lives in Manhattan, Kansas, with his wife, Jill, and son, Griffin.

This book was typeset in Adobe Sabon by Electronic Imaging.
Typefaces used on the cover were Garamond and Eras.
The book was printed on 50-lb. Lynx Opaque
by IPC Communication Services.